SharonÉzoliRona

Spiritual Nutrition
and
The Rainbow Diet

Gabriel Cousens, M.D.

D1016144

Cassandra Press
P.O. Box 2044
Boulder, Co. 80306

Copyright © by Gabriel Cousens, M.D., 1986.
All rights reserved. No part of this book may be reproduced in any manner whatsoever without the written permission of the publisher.

Printed in the United States of America
First printing 1986
ISBN 0-96158752-0
Library of Congress Catalogue Card No.: 86-072339

Front cover art by Rowena Pattee and copyright © Gabriel Cousens, M.D., 1986.
Cover design by Jane English.
Illustrations and charts by Nan Love and copyright © by Gabriel Cousens, M.D., 1986.

Acknowledgements to the following for granting permisssion for quotes and reproductions from:

•*Autobiography of a Yogi* by Paramahansa Yogananda,
Self-Realization Fellowship, Publisher.
•*Tao Te Ching,* by Lao Tsu, translated and copyrighted by
Gia-fu Feng and Jane English, and published by
Alfred A. Knopf, Inc.
•*How to Get Well Health, Are You Confused, Hypoglycemia,
A Better Approach, How to Keep Slim, Healthy, and Young
with Juice Fasting* by Paavo Airola, Health Plus Publishers.
•*The Realms of Healing* authored and copyrighted by Stanley
Krippner-Alberto Villoldo, Celestial Arts publisher.
•*Live Food Longevity Recipies* by Viktoras Kulvinskas
Ayurveda, The Science of Self Healing by Dr. Vasant Lad,
Lotus Press
•*Kundalini, The Secret of Life* by Swami Muktananda,
published by the SYDA Foundation.

Dedication

To Swami Muktananda Paramahansa, without whose transmission of Grace and guidance in my spiritual unfoldment this book would not have been able to be written.

To Paavo Airola, Ph.D. and N.D. who introduced me to and personally inspired me in the field of nutrition.

To my family.

And to the One I Love: You.

Please Note

   Nothing in this book is intended to constitute medical advice or treatment. For development of an individualized diet or use of fasting cycles, it is advised that any person first consult his or her wholistic physcian. It is advised that he or she should remain under the doctor's supervision throughout any major shift in their diet or while fasting.

                              ---Gabriel Cousens, M.D.

Table of Contents

Preface

I have in the past made several attempts to meet Dr. Gabriel Cousens during my trips in California, but had to wait till we both shared the same flight to and from Yugoslovia, for the World Vegetarian Congress. Our first meeting was in total silence; I felt his special presence on the plane, without introductions. The return home was quite different. High above the clouds of confused earthly thinking, we shared experiences along the spiritual path that we had both traveled from slightly different directions. We touched upon Kundalini, kinetic mechanics of love, God and consciousness. I was just as excited as he was, that he was creating a book on spiritual nutrition. Six months later, I was delighted to have the book in my possession. The table of contents, gave me an exciting menu of delicacies, on which my mind was eager to feast and digest. This book is definitely not a fast food folly or the standard vegetarian verborrhea. This brother is not only Divinely inspired, but has been transformed by God in his very entrails. He tastes God, as well as, is one with, and dines with, yes... God.

During the last 20 years, I have witnessed an onslaught of books in nutrition which prove to be useful within a certain clinical range of individuals, but which in general, create further confusion and disagreement. Finally, we have a book, *Spiritual Nutrition and The Rainbow Diet* **which removes all contradiction. It will become a standard for ages to come against which all other books will be measured and put into perspective of relative importance. It is truly a book on wholism that redefines the human organism on the premolecular level, and as having a relationship with all of existance.**

This is not a book that any normal mortal can be expected to read in a day, but many will be enticed to go through it in a single sitting. Fasting, while reading the book, will help to keep the mind clear enough to understand the quantum leaps of consciousness from traditional wholistic to Divine nutrition. **Reading** *Spiritual Nutrition and The Rainbow Diet* **feels like having a conversation with God over a glass of wheatgrass juice.** Patiently, in the precise, yet poetic language of science, spirituality and love, he explains the One, how we can get to know that One, and how the subtle as well as the gross universe exist and interact. We are treated to a symphony of ideas, using eternal truths, well tested theories, hypothesis, historic personalities and spiritual phenomena as notes. Dr. Cousens plays for us a concert of timeless, eternal wholism which oscillates our chakras with new found happiness and outlines a natural map for activating their powers. We are shown how to bathe in an interlude of infinite love.

The material is subtle and abstract. With Divine kindness Dr. Cousens, to keep us from going into potential mental overload, shares anecdotal stories for illustrating a point or personal poetry that crystalizes a moment. In each chapter, he introduces us to the intellectual terrain, then dives into the adventure of their expression and play, and finally ends up summarizing, restating, unifying chapter ideas, and giving an overview from still another perspective. I never felt left behind or lost in the forest of words. Like any good teacher, he holds our hand and reassures us, for which I feel the readers, as I was, will be grateful.

His model of Subtle Organizing Energy Fields (SOEFs) for organizing energies as they manifest in more dense forms, helps to explain, the many, seemingly exclusive phenomena: nutrition, breatharianism, resurrection, longevity, chakras, consciousness, biological transmutation. We are presented with an unified theory, not only of nutrition, but of existence. This theory lends itself to exploration beyond the limited precepts of nutrition into the realms of divinity. He describes an energy continuum, with a spectrum of laws that apply within the specific frequency range of our material plane.

Dr. Cousens designs a nuclear theory of nutrition. It is of controlled fission and fusion within enzymatic cyclotrons which create new elements. These enzymatic cyclotrons control the micronuclear atomic bombs that energize our essence within the full spectrum potential of existence. We are seduced into the experience of at-onement with the source of all, our own God presence. His poetry is divinely inspired by love of the Divine Self and dedication to express it by love of all. His naked personal revelation of the spiritual transformation process within the context of SOEF will leave the readers eternally grateful and inspired to dedicate themselves to the inner world of adventure.

My first reading will certainly not be the last. The book is spiritual history, scientific, and humanistic phenomena in a nutshell. Great thinkers have been supported and have stood on the shoulders of other great thinkers in order to see further and deeper. Dr. Cousens has built an intellectual pyramid of ideas, creating a unified field of thought.

This book is much more inclusive than the title implies. Its concepts, when applied in everyday life, ashrams, and monastaries will lead to the highest manifestation, of what some folks might call, 'saintly people'. It is a blueprint for creating the critical mass of conscious people necessary for the planetary transformation into a peaceful, loving, humanistic world. This book is for all God's children. For many, it will take years to read, for others, it will be understood without reading. For this book is one whose time has come to reveal the truths to all.

Spiritual Nutrition and The Rainbow Diet has helped me a great deal to better understand my path and put more energy into correcting spots of weakness. It is a view that is taken into my everyday existence, and the SOEF help me to understand more fully the daily phenomena of life. What I find especially exciting, is that it helps to clarify the live food concept and how the processing of food affects consciousness, energy and spiritual aspiration. The book further led me to a deeper understanding of my experiences with Kundalini energy: a reawakening which took place after a period of 7 months of live food and many years of celibacy, revealing itself through physical actions in the spine; the delicacies of taste, smell of ecstatic fragrances, sounds of creation, and light of crystalline evolution as well as gifts of healing, parapsychology phenomena of ESP, astral travel, and above all else, the meltdown of ego mass and the surrender to love of all and desire to serve all and experience the presence of God through every manifestastion. It explained my childhood communions. My experience in a seven w k coma has helped me, in retrospect, to reconfirm the experience and ฺ .   the reality of the SOEF as well as the holograms and vortexe   utiful architecture as is described by Brother Gabriel.

   As the   appreciation, I want to highlight the excellent pragmatic
     roach of the   k. It presents an approach and information for designing
            persona.   piritual nutrition program. It helps to clarify spiritual
nu   ๋e or even one who is old as the hills. We are inspired
with unฺ   otal rejunvenation and filled with enthusiasm to use
the given tools   red for participating in the adventure of our total
fulfillment.

Yours in Service Through Love,

Brother Viktoras
Kulvinskas, M.S.
Survival Foundation Inc.
P.O. Box 255
Wethersfield, CT 06109

Author's Introduction

The Essence

When we eat in a healthy, harmonious way, our ability to attune and commune with the Divine is enhanced. With this perspective, I suggest that rather than "living to eat," or "eating to live," **We Eat to Intensify Our Communion with the Divine**. Our hunger for the Divine then becomes the overwhelming appetite. In this way, it is okay to become a glutton... for the Divine.

A New Paradigm of Nutrition

Writing this book has been an adventure. To explore fully the relationship of nutrition to spiritual life, I had to evolve beyond the present materialistic-mechanistic paradigm of nutrition to an expanded definition of nutrition that included subtle energetic principles. The word nutrient is discussed in terms of its material, emotional, energetic, and spiritual qualities. The pillars of the materialistic-mechanistic paradigm of the last 200 years are shaken, but not discarded. The new paradigm that is evolved more completely answers the questions: What is the purpose of nutrition? What is it we call nutrition? What is assimilated? What is assimilating? What is the relationship between the moment assimilated and spiritual unfolding?

A new conceptual dimension of the meaning of nutrient assimilation according to these subtle energy principles is formulated. To do this adequately, a more refined model of the key energy assimilating systems of the body is shared. This includes a detailed discussion of the body as a "human crystal", and as such, how it functions to absorb plant material and energy into our energetic and biomolecular structures.

The Rainbow Diet

The Rainbow Diet is the key to a practical, comprehensive approach to spiritual nutrition. It is a diet system that is based on the relationship of the color of the foods eaten to the corresponding rainbow colors of the human chakra system. As part of the Rainbow Diet approach, I discuss some of the major nutritional questions that are important in empowering individuals to develop their own individualized diets which are appropriate to their unfolding lifestyle and spiritual practices. This includes a discussion of raw versus cooked foods, high versus low protein, alkaline-acid balance, attitude about food, and spiritual fasting. These issues are discussed from the points of view of the new spiritual nutrition paradigm, current scientific-materialist research findings, and a comparison of Essene and Biblical context. I also discuss the relationship of food to the mind. After all these considerations are discussed, I make a summary recommendation for creating a diet which completely supports the spiritual life of any person within any religious or spiritual path. I also describe a path which involves intense meditation and fasting as major components of developing spiritually. It is in the discussion of diet that these new conceptual tools are of immediate and practical use because they provide a simple and consistent framework for developing an individualized diet.

Nutrition, Meditation as Nutrition,
And Kundalini Unfolding

The Kundalini energy is the physio-psycho-spiritual energy latent in the body, which when awakened, becomes an active, spiritually transforming force. It is an extremely important energy to understand in spiritual development. I present a clear description of the process of Kundalini unfolding and the relationship of nutrition to the spiritualizing process of Kundalini. Inspired by my own inner experiences, I also elaborate a new subtle energy vortex model correlating the chakra system, the Kundalini energy, and the transcendent potential of the human organism.

About the Author and How This Book Came About

My initial focus on investigating the role of nutrition in spiritual life was for my own personal development. Also, many of my clients would often ask for advice in this area. Over a period of time, it became obvious that there is a great need for a comprehensive understanding of the relationship between nutrition and spiritual life.

This book represents over 14 years of clinical experience, research, and contemplation on these issues. Because of the complexity of the subject material and the diversity of my own background, I am writing as a generalist, rather than through the narrow vision of a specialist. At different times in the book I will be writing from the following perspectives:

1. As a medical doctor, trained at Columbia Medical School, who has taken care of people in North America and Asia, many of whom came for nutritional consultation and were interested in optimum health and spiritual development.

2. As a biochemist, nutritionist, medical researcher, psychiatrist, family therapist, homeopath, and wholistic health physician.

3. As a former co-director of the first Kundalini crisis clinic in the United States. This was a clinic designed inform the public, physicians, and psychologists that people were having such things as Kundalini awakenings in our society, to supply general information about the meaning and characteristics of the awakening, and to help people who were totally unfamiliar or having difficulty with such an awakening.

4. As a certified meditation teacher since 1976 who has spent many years teaching meditation throughout the the United States, India, and Europe.

5. As I AM.

This book is semi-autobiographical because it is based primarily on my intuitive and direct clinical experience. Its theoretical base is further supported by various scientific findings, historical and cultural evidence, and anecdotal suggestive evidence. Although there is much traditional scientific information shared, the real "proof" is an intuitive sense of direct knowingness. It has evolved from my years of living the various diets discussed, including the Rainbow Diet, and my experience with a variety of fasting approaches, including a 40-day fast. This writing has been influenced by my personal and clinical observations of the interplay between nutrition, meditation, and spiritual life. I also share certain unfolding spiritual experiences and Kundalini activity that sheds some light on the evolution of spiritual life .

In reading this book, I encourage the reader to become like Einstein's description of a parachute... "that which functions best when open." The book stretches the mind to the limit with new concepts of nutrition, assimilation, the Rainbow Diet, Kundalini, the subtle anatomies of the body, meditation, and spiritual life in general. Let the proof be your experience through your practice with these new tools and concepts.

This book also represents a merging of Eastern and Western traditions. It is greatly influenced by the Torah, the mystical Essene fellowships in which Jesus was allegedly raised, and the direct teachings of Jesus. It also reveals some of my direct experiences and training in a yoga tradition, which has given me a much deeper appreciation of my own Judeo-Christian tradition. For me, each tradition is based in the same One God as Love, and so superficial differences merge into a Oneness under God as source.

Writing Style and Approach

I will raise some issues about writing style and approach that need clarification. Philip Callahan, Ph.D., a professor of Entomology at the University of Florida and a brilliant scientist and author, has pointed out that since World War II, there has been a trend for scientists not to admit their innermost thoughts and to avoid the use of the word "I". Personal reference implies that a mere human is at work.[1] This avoidance of the word "I" creates the illusion that there is such a thing as an objective observation and that there is a sort of research infallibility that goes beyond any subjectivity. One might ask, "Is this possible, a medical doctor and nutritionist with a biochemistry background admitting fallibility and subjectivity ?" Yes! Indeed it is! However, it is my contention that this may be the most honest scientific approach. Since the emergence of quantum mechanics, the illusion of objective exactness has been exposed. Physicist Fritjof Capra in his foreword to Larry Dossey's book, *Space, Time, and Medicine* , states it nicely, "In 20th-century physics, the universe is no longer perceived as a machine, made up of a multitude of separate objects, but appears as a harmonious indivisible whole; a web of dynamic relationships that include the human observer and his or her conscious in an essential way."[2] Paavo Airola, Ph.D., a world-respected nutritionist who produced a very popular book, *Are You Confused ?*, humorously makes the point with his title about the degree of subjectivity in the area of nutrition.

The other so-called scientific assumption that this book does not accept is that all proof is based exclusively on the five senses and the technological extension of them with our sophisticated measuring instruments. We need only to remember the validity of Joseph's interpretation of the Egyptian Pharaoh's dream, or how most of us are able to sense the energy in a room as we walk into it, or how dogs sense bad intentions in some people. These are all experiences that indicate information taken in by subjective means is an everyday assumption for us. It was said that Einstein got valuable information for his theory of relativity by examining his subjective experience of what it would be like to ride on a light beam. It is not uncommon for scientific discoveries to be based on an image that first appeared in a dream. In practical reality, there will be no acceptable proof of this material to a mind that assumes there is exclusively an objective world, knowable only to the five senses. For this reason, I ask my readers to challenge those assumptions in their own lives while reading this book.

Perspective

For those of you who are reading this book in search of the perfect diet that will be the spiritual practice which will lead to self-realization, please reconsider your perspective. A perfect diet is not synonymous with spirituality. Without the proper context of meditation, right life, right fellowship, wisdom, and love, the focus on diet falls into a dry, conceptual, empty worship of the body-mind ego, contracted in self-righteous concepts of purity. Such a perfectionistic and materialistic focus, which is not at all uncommon, can create quite an unbalanced ego. Jesus in Matthew 15:11 is quoted as saying it is "not what enters his mouth that defiles a man, but it is what proceeds out of his mouth." What in my reality is perfect is that which also exists beyond the physical body and mind. The realization of that which transcends the imperfection of body and mind is the only real perfection.

Diet in the right context, however, is one of the important practices that supports and aids our total body-mind-spirit transformation and transcendence. Sri Ramana Maharishi, one of the great saints of India, taught that a regulated diet of pure foods, taken in moderate quantities, is the best of all rules of conduct and the most conducive to the development of pure qualities of the mind.[3] This is the answer to those spiritual purists who denigrate any concern with the bodily and nutritional concerns as evidence of lower states of awareness. It is okay to be healthy. It is okay and appropriate to eat healthy and spiritually uplifting foods. Not only is the body the temple for the spirit, but proper care of it creates a   clear, conductive channel for the Kundalini energy to flow through and to transform the body spiritually. When we eat in a healthy, harmonious way, our ability to attune and commune with the Divine is enhanced. The total effect of nutrition brings about health for the body, peace for the mind, and harmony with the spirit. It is an experience of total alignment.

In this book we share an exciting new paradigm of the meaning of nutrition and assimilation. It is supported by its intuitive correctness and some interesting scientific data. It may take years to prove this paradigm completely according to rigorous academic standards, but that is not the point of this work. Its purpose is to suggest new concepts for the reader to use as tools, not as facts. It asks readers to make a paradigm shift in their basic framework for understanding nutrition and to examine who it is that is assimilating. The conceptual tools given are of immediate practical use because they provide a simple and consistent framework for developing an individualized diet. An understanding of this new paradigm for nutrition and assimilation establishes an obvious and profound connection between nutrition and spiritual life. As we incorporate these new conceptual tools into our nutritional and spiritual lives our positive experiences begin to establish this new paradigm and the Rainbow Diet as a viable approach. And finally, among all the exciting information and concepts, I pray that the reader not lose sight of the right spiritual perspective for applying these concepts. Proper nutrition is only a support for spiritual evolution. This book is a blueprint of how to prepare our bodies to handle the increased energy released in the quantum evolutionary leap in consciousness the world is taking.

For proper nutrition to be of maximum benefit, as I have mentioned earlier, it needs to be integrated into a harmonious balance of right life, good fellowship, wisdom, meditation, prayer, and love. Please remember the information and concepts shared in this book are given to inspire and empower the reader. Let these be as guidelines and tools, and not rules. It is my prayer that all who read this book are benefited, and that there be an increase of peace in the world as a result of the inner peace and harmony with nature gained from applying the understanding of spiritual nutrition to our lives.

Acknowledgements
Many people have put their love and input into the creation of this book. I want to thank my dear brother Kevin Ryerson whose love and support has encouraged me in the writing of this book. Kevin is an expert intuitive who possesses the ability to obtain highly refined bodies of information. Some of the elements of the theory in this book arose out of the seeds of the dynamic interaction of our mutual intuitive processes. Kevin and his work have also been helpful in helping me develop an understanding of the Essene way of life.

My love and grateful appreciation also go to: Ken Cousens who freely spent hours as a copy and general editor. Kurt A. Krueger, founder of the Institute of Sports Psychology, and Richard Page, Director of

Conference Coodinating Company, who with much love gave hours of their time refining the manuscript. Jane English, Ph.D. in physics and published author and photographer, who served as my science editor, book format designer, and general guide for putting the book together. Karen Rose, who helped edit and computer format this book. Nan Love, who provided illustrations and back cover design. Eunice Combs, copy editor. Marcel Vogel, who has a background 29 years as an IBM scientist and is a world famous crystal expert, for the advice on crystals and structured water. Viktoras Kulvinskas, M.S. a world expert in raw food nutrition with a rare understanding of diet and fasting as a spiritual path, who graciously wrote the preface. Victoras, himself, and his work have been an inspiration.

I also want to specifically give my loving thanks to: Lisa Lissant in whose kitchen the concept of the subtle organizing energy fields took final shape. Adam Trombley, an astro-physicist, who helped me understand some of the concepts of zero point physics; Norm Mikesell, M.S. an expert in structured water, who shared his work and who reviewed the sections on it. Stephen Levine, author of *Antioxidant Adaption: Its Role in Free Radical Pathlogy* and avant-garde Ph.D. in biochemistry who shared his anoxia hypothesis and reviewed the book for its biochemical accuracy. Lee Sannella, M.D. author of *Kundalini: Psychosis or Transcendence?* who reviewed my chapters on Kundalini. Father Dunstan Morissey, a 40 year Bendictine monk with whom I enjoyed discussing biblical issues. Bruce Lipton, Ph.D. and professor of anatomy at St. George's University School of Medicine who checked chapters 10 and 11 for accuracy. Dio Neff, methaphysical writer, whose initial comments on the begining chapters greatly aided my writing style. Dick Stehr, a quiet yogi, who helped with the three simple breathing exercises.

I am grateful for the patience and loving support of my wife Nora, who has shared, supported, and given valuable feedback at every step of the birthing of this book. I also appreciate her and our two teenagers, Raf and Heather for creating a positive space for me to write this book.

I give my thanks and love to all who have helped. I am grateful for God's grace which has allowed me to serve through the offering of this book. It has been inspiring to be part of this collective process.

In Service to the One

Gabriel Cousens, M.D.

1

The Need for a New Nutritional Paradigm

To enter into our discussion of the relationship between nutrition and spiritual life, it is necessary to develop an expanded concept of the human organism as having subtle energetic and spiritual qualities. We must develop a new paradigm, or concept, of nutrition that is able to answer certain basic questions and account for unusual observations that the present materialistic-mechanistic concept of nutrition cannot answer adequately. In the next four chapters we will focus on developing a new paradigm of nutrition that more fully answers these basic questions.

1. What is the purpose of nutrition?
2. What is nutrition?
3. What do we assimilate?
4. Who is assimilating?
5. How does the understanding of the subtle energy fields that surround and run through the body fit into an understanding of nutrition for spiritual life?
6. What is the relationship between the nutrient that is taken in and the living system taking it in?
7. What is the relationship of the nutrient absorbed to the spiritual unfolding of the person absorbing it?
8. What is the meaning of assimilation?
9. What is the explanation for people who are reported to live on air alone, or air and water alone (inedia or breatharians)?
10. What is the explanation for biological transmutation (a process in which one element within a living system is transformed into another element)?
11. What is the explanation for documented cases of the physical body not decomposing after death?

To answer these questions in depth, we must develop a wholistic paradigm of nutrition that includes the material, mental, energetic, and spiritual aspects of the human organism. This wholistic paradigm does not throw away the present materialistic-mechanistic paradigm, but rather includes it as part of the whole.

Confusion of the Conventional Paradigm

The conventional paradigm has developed from the materialistic-mechanistic view of life in which living organisms are regarded as physio-chemical machines. All the phenomena of life, including nutrition, are thought to be explained solely in terms of physio-chemistry. Although the materialistic paradigm has led to a certain amount of success in understanding the molecular structure of our food and bodies, the tremendous diversity of opinions in the nutritional world today suggests that we have not developed a comprehensive understanding of the basics of nutrition. The great 20th-century mystic, Ramana Maharishi, once said that the most important thing in spiritual life, in addition to meditation, is to eat correctly. This sounds simple, but if we look in our bookstores, there are so many different books on nutrition that this simple act of eating seems quite perplexing. In my medical practice I have had people come to me who have become so confused about deciding what is right to eat, based on all the different theories, that they have anxiety attacks at meal time.

There are only three gross substances that we consciously take in to support our life process: food, air, and water. In the past, breathing and drinking water did not take much thought. Before the days of air and water pollution, it was fairly automatic. Food, on the other hand, consumes a lot of our time. We forage in the supermarket or health food store for our food, then we have to gather it, prepare it, bless it, eat it, and digest it. We must also grow it or earn money to buy it. By the time this process is completed, we ought to have a unique understanding of and relationship to our food. Yet in the last 200 years, for most of us, this relationship has remained a mystery. It is especially mysterious when we think about nutrition for the enhancement of our spiritual life. Why is it that we have lost touch? Why is it that we are stumbling around in the forest of nutrition, bumping into the trees of this new diet or of that new recommendation for a supernutrient that will solve all our health problems? Presently, if we are concerned at all, perhaps it ought to be with the loss of our basic instinctual connection with the quality of our food and mother earth. With the overload of so many new discoveries in the "science of nutrition," there are so many diverse factual details that we cannot fully keep up with what and how to eat. Our basic conceptual frameworks, our perceptions of the meaning of nutrition, and our own natural instincts have become muddled. We can't see the forest through the trees.

Basics of the Conventional
Materialistic-Mechanistic Paradigm

Where did we start to limit our understanding? A major cause of this confusion about the purpose and function of nutrition is the present exclusive materialistic-mechanistic view point that in essence developed in the late 1780s when the great chemist, Lavoisier, established the doctrine that life is a chemical function and foods are the combustibles. Food is the vehicle for the intake of calories. The materialistic view, which is still predominant today, was very simple then. The complete process of nutrition was considered a combustion process in which foods were seen as carriers of caloric energy which, in conjunction with oxygen, released energy in the digestive process. One needed simply to count the calories needed and select nutrients which had the matching number of calories.

Since the 1780s, we have discovered that nutrition is more complex than simply calories. Food has additional factors such as proteins, carbohydrates, fats, vitamins, minerals, micronutrients, enzymes, subtle hormone factors, alkaloids, auxones, pacifarins (natural antibiotic substances), and whatever new microfactors that have been or will be discovered. But these new discoveries have only reinforced our materialistic-mechanistic conceptions of food and the human system. Many people are still holding tightly to the caloric approach of Lavoisier. Calorie counters are still in vogue today.

Lavoisier, who is considered by many to be the father of modern chemistry, also contributed another of the major principles of the presently accepted nutritional paradigm. It is called the law of conservation of matter and energy. This law states that nothing is lost, nothing is created; everything is transformed. The atom was considered the smallest particle of matter and a constant in nature. From this law it was assumed that no element could be created and no atom could disappear in nature. Today, except for the later observation that this doesn't hold true for radioactive materials, we are still trying to comprehend nutrition from the exclusively materialistic-mechanistic point of view. The result of this conceptual approach is an excessive and unbalanced focus on individual nutrients and their interactions. This nutrient-supernutrient focus has served to lock us into materialistic conceptions about food, the human system, and the interrelationship between the two.

The next major step in the development of nutritional materialism took place in 1847, when four great scientists, Helmholz, Dubois-Reymond, Brucke, and Ludwig, met in Berlin in order to put physiology into a physio-chemical foundation. They proposed that the laws of chemistry could completely describe the process of human physiological function. Since this historical turning point, the law of conservation of matter and energy has been the foundation of physiology, metabolism, and nutrition. It has led to the establishment of quantitative research methods and to the implicit acceptance of the laws of thermodynamics as a description of the functioning of the living organism. From this sort of thinking came the popularly accepted statement, made by Ludwig Feuerbach, that "Man is what he eats." It is also the basis for the consumerism in nutrition we see today. People tend to consume excessive vitamins, minerals, and amino acids in the hope of making their bodies live longer, perform faster, endure more, and be healthier. The implied motto is ... "more is better." It is the underlying assumption behind calorie counting, nutritional computer printouts, and fad dieting.

The focus on gathering nutritional capital is based on the inaccurate belief that nutrition is additive: to be safe, extras of everything should be taken. This is not to say that, at the beginning of a health program, my client may not need extra nutrients to replenish deficiencies and to rebalance metabolism. But after a few months, as my client's health improves, he or she needs fewer nutrients to sustain good health. I am not against the judicious use of vitamins and minerals in the appropriate stages of a person's health.

It is important to note that not everyone followed this limited materialistic approach. Paavo Airola, Ph.D., my nutritional mentor and a man whom many considered a nutritional genius, stressed a personal and historical approach in his consulting rather than a materialistic, computerized focus. Nutritional groups such as the raw foods movement, sproutarians, the natural hygiene movement, and now the wholistic health movement, have all, at least indirectly, refuted the narrow materialistic conceptualization of nutrition. In these health movements there is an implicit assumption that we need to look at the subtle energy qualities of food and the human body. This awareness is shared by many healing systems around the world. In the ancient Indian science of yoga and Ayurvedic medicine, for example, subtle body and food energy is termed "prana." In Chinese medicine it is called Chi. It's known as Ki in Japan; Mana in Hawaii; Tumo in Tibet; Odic force by Reichenbach; and orgone energy by Reich.

The new paradigm is what this book is about. It states that food can no longer be seen as calories or proteins, fat or carbohydrates, or any material form only. **Food is a dynamic force which interacts with humans on the physical body level, the mind-emotional level, and also the energetic and spiritual level. The study of nutrition is the study of the interaction with and assimilation of the dynamic forces of food by the dynamic forces of our total being.** Before we develop this new paradigm, it is important to clearly understand the fundamentals of the old materialistic paradigm.

Shaking the Pillars of the Conventional Paradigm

The materialistic paradigm is based on three principles. The first is Lavoisier's principle that nothing is lost, nothing is gained, and everything is transformed. This, together with the "law" of energy conservation postulated by Mayer and Helmholz, has been refined as the law of conservation of matter and energy. The second principle is called the second law of thermodynamics. It states that, in the course of nature, all things are breaking down to their most basic and stable forms, and the total energy in a system moves from more organized to less organized forms or states. This process is called entropy. There is a third implied belief that there is no essential difference between the interactions of substances inside the human body or outside the human body.

In the West, all three of these ideas have been challenged in the last 100 years. One group that attacked it is the anthroposophical movement under the leadership of Rudolph Steiner. Steiner was a well-known turn-of-the-century European philosopher, educator, and scientist who stated that the greatest obstruction to understanding the effect of food on the the human organism is what people have accepted as the "law" of preservation of matter and energy. He felt it contradicted the process of human functioning and development. In his lectures in the early 1920s, he insisted that the second law of thermodynamics (the law of entropy) and the law of the preservation of matter and energy were not valid for what happens inside the human organism. This position is supported by scientists such as the physicist Louis de Broglie, who is considered to be the father of wave mechanics. Louis de Broglie has stated that "It is premature to suppose that we can reduce vital processes to the inadequate conceptions of physio-chemistry of the 19th or even the 20th century."[1]

A significant work recently challenged the concept that the law of conservation of matter and energy applies within the living system in vivo, or "inside the skin." This work was done by a brilliant Frenchman, Louis Kervan, director of Industrial Hygiene Services, Vocational Diseases, and Industrial Medicine in Paris since 1946. Kervan has been a member of the New York Academy of Science since 1963, and has been on the UNESCO advisory council for scientific research. Since 1935 he has thoroughly documented the phenomenon of biological transmutation. **Biological transmutation is the natural "alchemical" process which happens, to a greater or lesser extent, when one element in the body is transmuted into another element. This directly contradicts the law of conservation of mass and energy.**

To better understand this very significant process, and to appreciate its historical and practical perspective, it seems best to look at some of the research that has led up to proof of the existence of biological transmutations. Modern research on the subject dates back to 1799, when the French chemist Vanquelin measured lime in the oats he was feeding hens and found the hens excreted five times more lime than they took in. Vanquelin could only conclude that the lime had been created, but he could not determine the cause. Interestingly, this was only twenty years after Lavosier's work became public. In 1831, another Frenchman, named Choubard, measured watercress seeds for their minerals and measured them again after they had germinated in an insoluble dish (so that they could not have possibly gotten minerals from any other source). He found that the germinated seeds contained minerals that the seeds did not originally have. In 1875 von Herzeele carried the research with germinated seeds one step further by using a controlled nutrient medium. He concluded that a transmutation of elements had occurred. This work was updated by Baranger, chief of the laboratory of organic chemistry at the Ecole Polytechnique in Paris, who published results concerning the variations of phosphorous and calcium in germinated seeds. He also concluded that a transmutation of elements had occurred but was unable to understand how it had happened.

Biological Transmutations

In 1962 Kervan published his book *Biological Transmutations,* which explains transmutation as a phenomenon completely different from that of atomic fission or fusion in physics. He considers biological transmutation to be a phenomenon that has not been revealed in the era of modern science, a property which does not take place in the realm of either chemistry or physics. He strongly states that many of the biochemical and physiological processes of life are produced by chemical reactions. However, he refutes the beliefs that chemical reactions are the only processes that take place within the human body and that every observation must be explained in terms of a chemical reaction.[2] Kervan does not reject the laws of chemistry. He does reject the attitude that the laws of chemistry must apply to every domain.[3]

To appreciate fully the meaning of his work and to adjust our minds to these new concepts, I would like to share some of his research. His observations started as a child on his parents' farm in Brittany, France. He noticed that the chickens who had no limestone in their diets ate a great deal of mica, a component of silica. When the chickens were killed, one could never find the mica, but inside was lots of sand. Somehow, from all of the mica, they were able to make calcium shells. Later experiments showed that when the mica was taken away, the egg shells became devoid of calcium, and the chickens stopped producing eggs. When the mica was added back into the diet, they began to produce eggs again. The implication is that the mica contains some silicate of potassium which is converted to calcium by biological transmutation.

In his research in the Sahara Desert, Kervan discovered that the workers ate an excess of salt and excreted far more potassium than they took in. This he observed to be a result of an endothermic reaction (a reaction which uses up heat in the body and therefore is cooling) of sodium plus oxygen becoming potassium ($Na_{23} + O_{16} :=: K_{39}$). (The symbol $:=:$ means 'transmutes to'). This then was another example of transmutation - - sodium into potassium.

In another observation of biological transmutation, Kervan had noticed a continual production of saltpeter by the limestone walls in his own home. Researching this more closely, he discovered that calcium in the limestone was being converted to potassium (saltpeter) by subtracting a hydrogen through the enzymatic processes of the bacteria on the walls. In the hens, he had deduced that potassium from the mica was converted to calcium by the addition of a hydrogen $K_{39} + H_1 :=: Ca_{40}$. With the limestone (Ca) to saltpeter (K), he was observing a reverse reaction.

Kervan also researched the black formations on the cave walls and the temples of Banteay Srei in Cambodia. He discovered that the black layer was 5 percent manganese and the temple rocks were 15 percent iron.

This laid the foundation for the later proof in a controlled experimental setting that iron minus hydrogen converts to manganese. Kervan has therefore found several different ways that calcium is created, through transmutation, by the combining of different atoms to make a larger calcium atom. A summary of these reactions is:

1. potassium and hydrogen --- $K_{39} + H_1 +$ specific enzyme $:=:$ calcium Ca_{40}
2. magnesium and oxygen --- $Mg_{24} + O_{16}$ + specific enzyme $:=: Ca_{40}$
3. silicon and carbon--- $Si_{28} + C_{12}$ + specific enzyme $:=: Ca_{40}$
4. sodium and hydrogen--- $Na_{11} + H_1$ + specific enzyme $:=: Mg_{24}$ magnesium and then repeat (2) to get calcium
5. sodium and oxygen --- $Na_{11} + O_{16} +$ specific enzyme $:=: K_{39}$ potassium and then repeat (1) to get calcium

This leads to some of the potential clinical applications of his work. Kervan himself has done some research on the use of horsetail grass, which is high in silica (reaction 3), to speed up the calcification of broken bones. His research, using rats and some people, suggests that bone recalcification with silica seems to happen more efficiently than with a direct calcium supplement. In some people, bone decalcification may be caused by a deficiency of the enzyme which transmutes sodium to magnesium (reaction 4). If there is a deficiency in the enzyme which converts magnesium to calcium, then it might be advisable to strengthen the bones with potassium (reaction 1) and organic silica. We may also need to consider that decalcification may occur in some people when salt-free diets (reaction 5) are prescribed, since the sodium may be needed to transmute into calcium. Another implication of the transmutation work is that mothers who do not absorb calcium well might want to try supplementing their diet with horsetail silica, which might be more easily transmuted to calcium.

People who are having trouble raising their blood iron with iron supplements might want to take manganese, as some people in France are doing, which transmutes to iron by a separate metabolic pathway. Kervan may be establishing the existence of a variety of secondary pathways, which the body can utilize via transmutation of elements when it is missing the enzymes or nutrients needed for the main pathways.

Kervan's basic explanation of biological transmutation is that, through the action of enzyme conversion within the living system, particles from one nucleus either combine with those of another nucleus to form a new element, or one nucleus of an element divides into two new elements.[4]

The scientific finding of biological transmutation is a phenomenon which is completely contrary to the law of conservation of matter and energy. It involves a process completely different from the process of chemistry, which deals with the displacement of electrons in the shell around the atomic nucleus. It is also different from the process of physics, which deals with fission and fusion and follows the law of conservation of energy and matter. Biological

transmutation is the science that deals with the exchanges that occur between the nuclei of the different atoms in living organisms and results in the creation of new elements.[5] Kervan also points out that through the activity of biological enzyme systems, the process of biological transmutation consumes only one millionth the energy of the same reactions when duplicated by nuclear physics in vitro (outside a living system).[6]

Nobel Prize laureate Szent-Gyorgyi has commented that biology is the science of the improbable, and physics is the science of probabilities.[7] We are also forced to consider the scientific position of Claude Bernard, who felt that when one is confronted with a fact which is in opposition to a prevalent theory, one must accept this fact and abandon the theory.[8]

I have raised the issue of transmutation because a comprehensive theory of nutrition and its role in spirituality must include and be able to explain all aberrant observations. The current materialistic-mechanistic view cannot account for the observation of biological transmutation. The possible existence of biological transmutation directly challenges the law of conservation of mass and energy on which the materialistic paradigm is based.

The ramifications of the existence of biological transmutation are very great. Kervan felt that the light of biological transmutation may be a new guide to geologists, biologists, philosophers, and metaphysicians, helping them understand the creation and evolution of our planet.

For our purposes we don't have to consider the whole evolution of our planet. It is enough to apply these concepts to the development of our new nutritional paradigm. It is significant that the concept of biological transmutation gives an added depth to understanding Roger Williams' work on nutrition, *Biochemical Individuality* , published in 1963. The point he makes is that everyone has different biochemical needs and, therefore, unique nutritional needs.[9] We can connect biological transmutation with Roger Williams' work by seeing that these nutritional needs are determined by the amount of enzymes available for biological transmutations. Williams' work suggests that the functioning of everyone's cells is a very individualized pattern. In my medical practice it has been my consistent experience that the healthier a person becomes, the less supplementation he or she needs. The implication is that the stronger the vital force (health energy), the more energy and ability a person has to transmute. It also suggests that the individualized pattern of transmutation and nutritional needs can change.

If this principle of biochemical individuality is taken to its extreme, it is conceivable that there are some people throughout the world who no longer need to eat food. Later in this book there is some evidence which implies that this could indeed be true. The observations on biological transmutation provide one explanation for the observed phenomenon of breatharianism. Actually, we are all breatharians because we all breathe air. The more accurate word for living only on air is inedia. Before we come back to inedia in detail, however, we still must examine the second law of thermodynamics, entropy, in terms of its applicability to human systems.

Challenging the Role of Entropy in Living Systems

The concept of entropy as applied to the human system implies that it is the natural order of things for the body to break down or age. Because of the degenerate lifestyles many people on this planet live, this is indeed the case. However, it is not the natural order of things. What may be more accurate is that what seems natural is unnatural, and what seems miraculous is natural. Kervan conceptualized the issue of entropy in biological systems as essentially a struggle of the life forces against the degradation of matter.[10] Rudolph Steiner makes the point that one of the main purposes of a nutrient is to activate the dynamic forces in us that directly counter the process of entropy. The implication is that if we maintain our body's life force or body energy at a high level, entropy is indeed overcome, and we do not age. In our society, with all its pollution, we have created a world lifestyle that allows us, with few exceptions, to reverse only partially this entropy or aging process. Nevertheless, on a more rudimentary level, we can see that individuals who deplete their body energy with degenerate lifestyles tend to age more quickly. I have noticed with my clients that those who pick lifestyles and diets that increase their life force often seem to become younger and more vital in their appearance and functioning.

Further support for a system's ability to reverse entropy comes from the recent research by Richard Brewer and Erwin Hahn reported in *Scientific American*.[11] They demonstrate that atomic systems that have decayed or undergone entropy from some ordered states can be induced to recover their initial order. This means a reversal of entropy has occurred. This is accomplished by reversing the motions of some of the particles in the disordered system in such a way that they can remember their original condition or pattern. This is called atomic memory phenomena. Brewer and Hahn's research supports the belief that entropy can be reversed, in certain circumstances, both outside of living systems and within living systems.

The main fallacy, however, in applying the second law of thermodynamics to a living system, is that it only holds in a closed system (a system in which energy and matter are neither moving in nor moving out), or in a system formed of elements which are independent of each other. In general, not only can we say that the human system is not a closed system, but through the understanding of modern quantum physics (Bell's theorem) we can say that there is nothing in the universe which does not affect everything else. With this awareness we must conclude that everything is an open system. It can therefore be said that the application of the second law of thermodynamics, or the process of entropy, does not apply with complete accuracy to human systems. Kervan writes that it is not difficult to see that life itself works in complete opposition to the law of entropy.[12] He asks key questions which lead us to developing some elements of our understanding of nutrition for spiritual evolution. Why is life in complete opposition to the force of entropy? What is the secret? How are human systems able to reverse entropy naturally and therefore not be slaves to the process of entropy?

Summary   Chapter 1

1. The conventional materialistic-mechanistic paradigm of nutrition is focused on the component, additive, and interactive effects of material properties such as calories, vitamins, proteins, and minerals. It is based on three shaky pillars: (1) the applicability of the law of conservation of matter and energy to living systems; (2) the applicability of the second law of thermodynamics to living systems; (3) and the belief that there is no essential difference in the interactions of substances inside or outside of the human body.

2. Contemporary scientific findings such as the discovery of biological transmutations, the inability of this conventional paradigm to account for "aberrant phenomemon" and our own intuitive awareness directly challenge this materialistic-mechanistic concept of nutrition as the sole way to understand nutrition.

3. The new nutritional paradigm does not throw away the physio-chemical paradigm, but instead interfaces with it at the level of the material body. The materialist view regains validity as part of an emerging dynamic system.

4. A new paradigm is evolving which describes nutrients as a dynamic force which interacts with humans on the physical body level, the mind-emotional level, the energetic level, and the spiritual level.

5. The study of nutrition is the study of the interaction with and the assimilation of the dynamic forces of a nutrient by the dynamic forces of our total being.

6. The new paradigm is crucial to understanding the relationship between nutrition and spiritual life.

2

Creation of a New Paradigm of Nutrition

Subtle Organizing Energy Fields, a New Concept

A key in understanding the wholistic paradigm of nutrition lies in the concept of what I call **Subtle Organizing Energy Fields (SOEFs).** The concept of SOEFs is a synthesis which is intuitively derived yet rooted in historical, cultural, spiritual, and scientific evidence. It incorporates an integration of nutrition with spiritual life and accounts for all the aberrant observations that remain unexplained by the materialistic-mechanistic paradigm. It is important to be aware that energy is not a thing but a concept that is useful for organizing and communicating phenomena and experience.

Historically and culturally, the idea that the human system is organized around an energy pattern that determines its functioning has been with us for thousands of years. The Chinese science of acupuncture is based on the subtle energy fields called meridians and the subtle energy called Chi. In India, both the sciences of yoga and Ayurvedic medicine use the word prana to describe the subtle energy of bodies and the life force in other living fields . In the book *The Secret Life of Plants,* the concept that plants have a specific energy field and a specific energy pattern has already been popularized.

The further understanding that living systems are surrounded by subtle energy fields was greatly advanced by the discovery and use of Kirilian photography, a type of photography that demonstrates the form of these SOEFs. What is critical to our understanding about these SOEFs is that they exist prior to the existence of the physical form. They are not emanated from the physical form like the magnetic field lines of a bar magnet. In this hypothesis, **SOEFs are a template for physical biological forms and structures.** The picture in Figure 1 shows an energy pattern in the shape of a complete leaf surrounding a half-missing leaf. This wouldn't happen if the field were actually emanating from the molecular structure of the physical leaf. More recent supportive evidence for the existence of SOEFs has been supplied by Marcel Vogel from his laboratory. In his experiments with the crystallization of cholesterol esters, Vogel was able to photograph with a polarizing light microscope using an Ehringhouse compensator a complete blue energy form that revealed itself a fraction of a second before the unstructured liquid cholesterol melt entered the structured cyrstalline phase.[1]

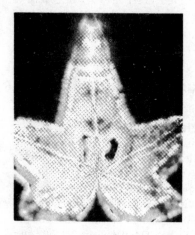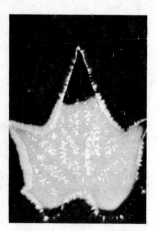

Figure 1

By accepting the concept of the pre-existence of SOEFs in both plant and human systems, we can take an expanded view of food, which has body, life force, and Subtle Organizing Energy Fields similar to the human system. **It is the dynamic interaction of these human and plant SOEFs that is important in understanding the new paradigm of wholistic nutrition.** The next question we might ask is, what is the source of these SOEFs?

Zero-Point Physics and SOEFs

There is a theory, created by such greats as Einstein and the relatively unknown physicist Nikola Tesla, of how material existence comes into being. More and more, the theory is included in the "new" physics, and in quantum mechanics field theory thinking. It is that our bodies exist as a precipitation out of an invisible, unbounded totality of perfect order. The theory has been called by several names: aether, virtual energy, anergy, or vacuum state. Gradually, some scientists are beginning to believe that matter is simply the condensation of a vibrating universal subtle energy substratum, or that it is a virtual state or a vacuum in a matrix of time and space, made of particular forms and densities of energy. In other words, matter is the manifest structure of all of nature and the laws governing all physical phenomena. In spiritual terminology, pure consciousness, cosmic energy, and universal prana are terms analogous to this perfectly orderly unmanifest state. SOEFs are an attempt to describe how this precipitation from subtle energy to material form takes place and how it is ordered.

What is this aether in terms of physics? Beardon says that at the level of the aether, there is a separation of charge and mass. He calls it anergy, insisting it is not energy, but a more fundamental component of energy that exists as vacuum, virtual state, or aether. The aether, or virtual state, however, has no mass, and is not filled with this massless charge, but is charge.[2] It seems to be an almost limitless charge.

The potential energy which fills the cosmos is called zero point energy -- that energy which exists prior to the materialization of an object. Adam Trombley, an astrophysicist and expert in zero-point technology, told me in an interview that the materialization of an object in space represents one quadrillionth of the energy available in that volume of space.[3] It is from this state of zero-point, or virtual energy, that we, as a precipitation of this energy, come into existence in a physical form. The zero-point energy in one cubic centimeter of space is said to equal the energy available in a million, million tons of uranium. This is virtually limitless energy. The U.S. Department of Defense acknowleged the existence and potential importance of zero point technology when it sent out a program solicitation in 1986 which included an interest in esoteric energy sources for propulsion, including zero-point quantum dynamic energy of vacuum space.[4]

Researchers have theorized that the first stepping down of this virtual energy is into a tachyon field space.   Tachyon fields were first theorized by the outstanding German researcher Hans Niebhor. A tachyon can be thought of as a slightly contracted form of anergy, or of the virtual state trying to become a particle. A tachyon field, sort of a quasi-state of matter, is thought to be made of quasi-particles. It exists at the interface of energy and matter.   Philip Callahan, the entomologist who developed the first experimental evidence of tachyons by hooking a weeping fig plant up to a special electromagnetic sensing device, defines a tachyon as a particle moving faster than the speed of light.[5]   He theorizes that the tachyon field energy is next stepped down as vortical forms of energy which precipitate near the speed of light as a particle of matter called a photon. The photon continues to be stepped down and patterned into material forms, and it also interacts in various energetic ways with material forms.

This interplay of research and theory provides the matrix for my **hypothesis of Subtle Organizing Energy Fields. These are fields which both create and energize the template form of living systems.** Emerging out of the virtual state, they are capable of organizing on any level of the human body, from tachyon to cellular structure to organ systems. These SOEFs resonate with the unlimited virtual state energy, transferring it through various step-down systems that eventually transduce it into the energy fields of the human body. The SOEFs thus resonate with and energize the body-mind complex. Virtual energy is omnipresent, thus we are always resonating to some extent with this cosmic energy.   Most of the time we have only indirect or brief experiences of this, but at certain stages of spiritual evolution it is possible to experience this resonance in direct attunement, consistently and consciously. For many, this sort of experience first happens in meditation. As we become more aware of and resonant with this virtual energy state, our minds merge and identify with this awareness as the unchanging truth and the reality of our existence. The resonance becomes part of our conscious awareness in our everyday activities. Eventually, it becomes a continual awareness and attunement with the cosmic energy. This is known as cosmic consciousness.

There is another important ramification of zero-point energy physics which is relevant to our new nutritional paradigm. Developed by Beardon, it is called the law of conservation of anergy. Beardon's law states that the total equivalency of mass, energy, and massless charge is conserved.[6] If this law eventually proves to be correct, it explains how entropy can be reversed and biological transmutation can take place in the human system without breaking any fundamental laws. It is ultimately the conversion of the essentially unlimited virtual energy into SOEFs, and the transduction of this energy into the human body that reverses entropy and therefore aging. This explains how the body can, in effect, become a "free energy" machine., since we are linked to the unlimited virtual energy as our ultimate source of energy. If this energy is free flowing, then we have an endless source of energy to rebuild our SOEFs, and we continually reverse entropy. As a result, the body-mind complex becomes more clear and balanced in spiritual evolution, and it becomes an increasingly better transducer and conductor of anergy to energy. As this happens, the body is able to store and transmit greater and greater amounts of this higher energy. It is this process which can account for some of the many miracles said to occur in the presence of spiritual masters. For example, spontaneous healing occurred when people simply touched the robe of Jesus. We now understand that there was a flow of this pure cosmic or God energy into people, which reorganized and reenergized their SOEFs, allowing the disease processes to be reversed. People's faith allowed them to draw and be receptive to the healing energy.

Characteristics of SOEFs: Form and Energy

SOEFs have form. They can hold, gain, lose, resonate with, transduce, and transmit energy. Because of this, they are different from Rupert Sheldrake's hypothesis of morphogenic fields, described in *A New Science of Life* . His morphogenic fields are concerned only with form; they are neither a type of matter nor a type of energy.[7] Sheldrake's description of the morphogenic fields and his brilliant hypothesis of formative causation describe the form of SOEFs beautifully. According to Sheldrake, morphogenic fields play a causal role in the development and maintenance of the forms of systems at all levels. Sheldrake uses the term morphic unit as a way to describe the subunits in a system, i.e., a morphic unit for protons, another for atoms, water molecules, and muscle cells, and another for organs like kidneys. The higher morphic fields coordinate the interplay, organization, and pattern of the smaller morphic units. Like the SOEFs, these morphogenic fields correspond to the potential state of a developing system and are present before it materializes into its final form.

Once the body is present, it becomes a focal point for the SOEFs in time and space as they emerge in their purest form from the virtual state. These more highly purified SOEFs resonate with the less refined SOEFs that are immersed in the biogravitational fields of the human body and thus reenergize and increase their degree of organization. This is contrary to the materialist paradigm in which the physical life form is seen as the creator of the energy fields around it. Bob Toben in *Space, Time, and Beyond* points out that Einstein repeatedly stresses the view in his unified field theory that the **energy field creates the form**. The emerging particle is simply a space-time concentration of the nonlinear master field (analogous to the SOEFs).[8] To put it succinctly, these fields generate matter. The body, in this wholistic paradigm, is a form stabilized by the SOEFs.

If the energy of a SOEF is dispersed, the organizing field is disrupted, and the living system operates in a less organized way. This is one important aspect in which the form of SOEFs specifically differs from Sheldrake's theory of morphogenic fields. This dissipation, which drives the system toward disorganization, can be termed entropy. In concrete terms, the dissipation of the SOEF means imperfect cell replication, poorer enzymatic function, decreased capacity for biochemical transmutation, and increased tendency toward chronic disease. This translates as aging. When the SOEFs are significantly depleted, to assimilate our food completely we must reenergize incoming food directly from our own life force, depleting the energy of our SOEFs. An example of this eating highly refined white bread. The chromium that is necessary to aid its assimilation into the system has been depleted in the processing and must be supplied by the body. Eventually, the body becomes depleted of chromium. Analogously, when the SOEFs in food are disrupted by food processing procedures, especially with radiating our foods with over 100,000 rads (chest X-ray is 1/4 to 1/2 a rad), the energetic value of the food, in terms of its ability to increase our total SOEF energy, is diminished. When we eat high energy food, the result is just the opposite; the energy of the SOEFs is enhanced.

When SOEFs are energized, they develop a more structured and defined organization that better maintains the form and function of the human system. This energizing reverses entropy. It is this property of the SOEFs that reverses the aging process. A nice physical model for this is shown in Figure 2. Brown sugar is added to water. At first, it has no defined form. It lies in a disorganized pile on the bottom. When we add vortexual energy to the system by stirring with a spoon, the pile of brown sugar is pulled upward into a more defined form. When we stop the spoon and hold it in the water, it disrupts the vortexual pattern, the energy in the system is diminished, the brown sugar particles begin to lose their well-defined form, and entropy takes place. In the same way, the vortexual energy patterns of the different SOEFs create different patterns of matter. As the vortexual energy of the SOEFs moves into the realm of time and space, they begin to organize into a physical pattern. The more energy

Figure 2

they have, the better defined and organized are the physical structures they are organizing. The intertwined vortex structure of RNA and DNA are archetypical physical manifestations of vortex forms. They, of course, represent the key to cellular organization. From this vortex analogy and the SOEF concept, we can begin to see the connection between living an energizing, harmonious lifestyle and eating foods that are raw, organic, and living. These energized lifestyles and live foods, whose natural high energy is not dissipated by processing, can help to slow down and even reverse the aging process. Much of this book is about how an energized and organized human body supports health and spiritual evolution.

Structured Water in Biological Systems

Structured water is an excellent example of how increasing the energy in a biological system makes it more organized and healthier. It will help our understanding if we now take a detailed look at structured water. In structured water, both the angle of the water molecule bond and the surface tension of the water change. Structured molecules form more stable water hydration shells, and actually give more order and structure to the water.[9]

When water is exposed to sunlight, crystal energy, or a pyramid (these are all generators, transmitters, and/or magnifiers of subtle energy), the actual molecular configuration of the water changes. This moving from less structure to more structure represents a specific reversal of the system's entropy. Clegg reports that in a normal cell the structured water tends to gather around the surfaces of the inner and outer cell membranes and the cytoplasmic matrix of the cell.[10] It is established that the polar qualities (electromagnetic fields) of macromolecules in general and specifically of enzymes, a class of macromolecules, attract shells of structured water. Each macromolecule has a unique pattern of structured water in its shell. Biologists are shifting their view of the cell as no more than a membranous bag containing liquid water with enzymes, other macromolecules, and ions in a free solution. Cells are now regarded as containing a structured water matrix which holds enzyme systems and other macromolecules, complexed with sodium and potassium ions, in a polarized water structure.[11]

In fact, the water appears to be structured in three levels of intensity.[12] The increased intracellular structured water in these intracellular membrane locations is thought to increase the concentrations of intracellular enzymes as the structured water of the enzymes gains more affinity for the structured water in intracellular membrane sites.[13] This network of structured water, generated by the intracellular membranes and macromolecular surfaces, creates a matrix in which most intracellular metabolism takes place.[14] An increase in intracellular structured water, resulting from increased order and enzyme concentrations, is thought to improve the quality of enzymatic reactions.[15] On a practical nutritional level, there is a structuring of water around co-enzymes (vitamins) which makes it easier for them to penetrate the structured water barriers of the extracellular fluids and the intracellular system. Therefore, vitamins arrive more efficiently at the correct enzyme reaction site. The structured water around the enzymes also stabilizes the energy state of the enzyme, improving enzyme reactions.[16] An important conclusion from this research is that the more structured water there is in a system, the better the enzyme systems function, the more easily the vitamins are assimilated into the cells, and the better the enzymes metabolize.

This research is of particular significance because it correlates with the SOEF theory that the more energy in a system, the more structured it is, and the healthier and the better it functions. Nuclear magnetic resonance studies have shown that the intracellular water of cancer cells has significantly less structure than normal cells.[17] Mikesell demonstrates that when there is a decrease in structured water, there is a shift from the healthly intracellular sodium/potassium ratio.[18] This upset seems to be associated with a lower quality of health in general.[19]

Another generally accepted property of structured water is that it has a higher solubility for minerals than unstructured water. Like vitamins, minerals also become surrounded by a structured water cell because of their polarity, and are absorbed more readily for similar reasons. The implication is that people with higher SOEF energy have more structured water in their systems and are therefore better able to absorb needed minerals.

Summary of Structured Water

Structured water research is of significance to us because it correlates with the SOEF theory that the more energy in a system, the more structured it is, the less entropy it experiences, and the better it functions.

As an example, when there is more structured intracellular water in a system, there are more concentrated and balanced intracellular ions such as calcium, potassium, and sodium. From this new perspective we can can see a positive relationship between an increased energy of our SOEFs, increased intracellular and structured water, and   increased general health.

In general, there is more structured water in biological systems than in plain water. Fruits, as a biological system, have the highest percentage of water, approximately 80 to 90 percent. Their aboveground growing position exposes them to more sunlight, an established structurer of water. They are the most important source of structured water for our systems. The structured water of fruit can be said to best help cleanse the system and carry enzymes, minerals, and other nutrients most easily into the cells.

But since the focus of this book is not intracellular physiology, I'd like to shift back to the simple statement that increased subtle energy in a living system results in more structured water in that system and therefore generally better health.   Interesting findings have been supplied by Orie Bachechi's eight-year study using Kiva lights, a balanced form of full spectrum light. Bachechi claims that by exposing food and water to Kiva lights, the amount of structured water they contain increases.[20] He reports that many diseases, such as atherosclerotic cardiovascular disease, high blood pressure, dry skin, kidney and gallbladder stones, ulcers, candida albicans infections, allergies, and arthritis, are ameliorated.[21] He has also found that bread made with nutrients exposed to Kiva lights contains 15 percent more protein, a result, he feels, of improved nutrient and enzyme function in the bread. It is not my interest to make health claims for Kiva lights. It would also be nice if his results of eight years of clinical research were confirmed by controlled studies by independent investigators. But his results confirm that increasing the subtle energy and therefore structured water in a system improves body function and health.

Summary Chapter 2
1. Subtle Organizing Energy Fields (SOEFs) are a template for the multiple levels of organization of living systems.
2. SOEFs have both form and energy properties.
3. SOEFs resonate with the unlimited virtual or cosmic energy, and through resonance, transfer this energy to us through a series of step-down systems. As our body-mind complex becomes more spiritually transformed, it is easier for this energy to be directly transferred to us and for us to experience a direct resonance with the cosmic energy.
4. All nutrient elements have their own individual SOEFs.
5. When SOEFs are energized, they maintain and strengthen both their organization and that of the physical body. This property allows us to resist and reverse the aging process we call entropy.
6. When the energy level of SOEFs is depleted by eating low-energy foods and living energy-depleting lifestyles, the SOEFs become less organized, resulting in increased entropy and aging.

3

Aberrant Phenomena
And the New Paradigm

For any theory of nutrition and the working of our human bio-psycho-spiritual system to be valid, it must explain such possible "aberrant" phenomena as people who claim to have lived for many hundreds of years, biological transmutations, and inedia.

Longevity: Approaching Physical Immortality

Let us start with evidence suggesting extended longevity that approaches physical immortality. There are yogis presently alive in India who claim they have mastered the secret of how to live for hundreds of years. The great seer Sri Nisargatta Maharaj met such a man, who offered to teach him the secret of how he could live to 1000 years. Sri Nisargatta, incidentally, rejected the offer because to him, living 1000 years was not the point of being on this planet.[1]   There are reports of a Trailanga Swami who, at the time Swami Yogananda wrote of him in 1946, was already reported to be 300 years old. Hotema reports that Numas De Cugna of India died in 1565 at the age of 370 years.[2] There are also reports of an ageless master called simply Babaji, who claims to have given initiation to the great saint Shankaracharya, born in 788 A.D., and to Kabir, the great Sufi saint born around 1440. In *Autobiography of a Yogi* , Swami Yogananda, a well-respected spiritual master who lived in the United States for the last 30 years of his life, described Babaji from his interviews of those who actually spent time with him. His body was said to look like that of a 25 year old. It was said that he did not need to eat. Yogananda's assessment of the meaning of Babaji's extraordinary physical state of maintaining his physical body for centuries is that it is to provide an example and guidance for our own fantastic possibilities.[3] I am not asserting these anecdotes are true. I have added them to stimulate our imagination. As the saying goes, "Where there is smoke there may be fire."

In Taoist teachings, immortality is described as being part of the highest stage of union with the Tao.[4] Mantak Chia, a Taoist teacher, claims that in some Taoist literature, the names of individuals who reached this stage can be found. He feels the Taoist teachings talk about immortality in a concrete way rather than metaphorically.[5]   The best documented Chinese man of longevity is Professor Li Chung Yun, who is reputed to have lived 256 years, from 1677 to 1933.[6] Proving his age, it is documented that at the age of 100 he was awarded a special Honor Citation for extraordinary service to his country,[7] and that he gave a series of 28 lectures at the University of Sinkiang at the age of 200.

Another piece of what might be considered by some as anecdotal or symbolic evidence (and by others as hard-core proof of near immortality) are Biblical references to one person in each of the the first ten generations following Adam who lived many hundreds of years. In the Old Testament, Adam is reported to have lived for 930 years, Seth for 912 years, Enoch for 905 years, Methuselah for 969 years and Noah for 950 years.

Some modern examples of longevity are cited by Hotema: Flora Thompson of North Carolina, who died in 1808 at the age of 152; Jose Calverto of Mexico who died in 1921 at the age of 186; Thomas Garn of England who died in 1795 at the age of 207. There is also Dando the Illyrian who is said to have lived over 500 years.[8] In the book *Maharaj,* a biography of the great holy man Shriman Tapasviji Maharaj, who himself lived from 1770 to 1955 to the age of 185, Maharaj describes meeting two people, aged between 2000 and 3000 years, who were alive at the time of Krishna.[9] One man's name was Ashvatthaman; he was one of the commanders-in-chief of the Kauravas army as described in the *Mahabarata,* an epic book. He had received the boon of longevity from Drona, his father. The other man was an eight-foot tall man who, in the course of his solitary aesthetic life in the Himalayas, discovered a bush with a special herb that conveys longevity. It could be the much sought after soma plant. These are fantastic anecdotes which boggle the mind with the possibility of incredible longevity.

These anecdotal, Biblical, and historically documented examples of longevity cannot be said to prove our potential absolutely, but there are enough of them to convince us to consider it a possibility. After all, a wild hog in its native state is said to live 300 years, and an eagle 500 years. Who is to say that, if we were to live according to the laws of nature, we couldn't live as long as a wild hog? My reason for bringing up these examples is not only to show what must be explained by any complete theory of nutrition, but also to expand our awareness to the awesome possibilities that are ours.

The Phenomenon of the Divine Body

A complete theory must also include the phenomenon of the Divine Body -- the finding that the bodies of certain holy people do not decompose after the spirit has left the physical shell. Examples of this discovery include the following:

A. Jnaneshwar Maharaj, who had himself buried alive at the age of 21 in a cave. Three hundred years later, he was found by the great 16th-century saint Eknath Maharaj to have a perfectly glowing and lifelike body. Eknath Maharaj was drawn to the burial place because he was receiving messages in meditation about a tree limb that had wrapped around Jnaneshwar's neck. When he was granted permission to enter the cave, there indeed was a tree limb around the holy man's neck. He removed it and thus completed his mission.

B. When the Nazis dug up the body of the Bal Shem Tov, the spiritual founder of Hasidim, not only was his body totally intact after 200 years, but a great light streamed forth from his eyes and scared them away.

C. In *A Treasury of Chassidic Tales* [10] by Rabbi Shlomo Zevin, it is written that when the Nazis attempted to desecrate the grave of the great rabbi Elimelech in Lyzhansk, they found a perfectly preserved, radiant body and were thrown into a panic. Rabbi Zevin reports the same amazing discovery when the Jewish community dug up the body of Rabbi Avraham of Chechanov to protect it from Nazi desecration. They found the holy body of the tzaddik intact and whole, as though he had just been buried, though he had been buried for 68 years.[11]

D. When Paramahansa Yogananda left his physical body, his body was kept out for 20 days so disciples from all over the world could come to pay their last respects. Although it is normal for a body to begin to decay within one to two days, the director of the mortuary, in a certified letter, wrote, "The absence of any visual signs of decay in the dead body of Parmahansa Yogananda offers the most extraordinary case in our experience. No physical disintegration was visible in his body even 20 days after death. No indication of mold was visible on his skin, and no visible dessication took place in the bodily tissues. This state of perfect preservation of a body is, so far as we know, unparalleled. Yogananda's body was apparently in a phenomenal state of immutability."[12]

E. It is reported that in 1859, when St. John of the Cross was exhumed 268 years after he died, his body was perfectly preserved.[13]

Resurrection

A complete theory of nutrition must account for the possible phenomenon of resurrection. The most well known, of course, is that of Jesus the Christ. As is pointed out in Corinthians 15:54-55, "Death is swallowed up in victory. O death, where is thy sting? O grave, where is thy victory?"

A. Another example of a resurrected master was Yogananda's report of the resurrection of his spiritual master Sri Yukteswar, who spent two hours with him in a Bombay hotel in 1936, four months after Yukteswar died.[14] Responding to Yogananda's amazed questions about the form Yogananda was physically hugging, Yukteswar said, "O yes, my new body is a perfect copy of the old one. I materialize or dematerialize this form any time at will, much more frequently than I did while on earth."[15]

B. Yogananda also reports the phenomenon of resurrection in connection with Sri Yukteswar's guru, a householder named Lahiri Mahasaya. Just before he died he said to his devotees, "Be comforted; I shall rise again."[16] Yogananda writes that Lahiri Mahasaya resurrected himself after his physical body was cremated. He said to one devotee: " It is I. From the disintegrated atoms of my cremated body, I have resurrected a remodeled form."[17]   In order to confirm the event of resurrection, Yogananda cites the testimony of three of Lahiri Mahasaya's greatest disciples that their Guru appeared before them on the day after his cremation, each in a different location. One disciple claimed to have been invited to touch his physical body as proof of the physical resurrection.

Inedia

Evidence of breatharians (inedia) actually exists in many traditions. It is unfortunate that there are occasional frauds who claim to be breatharians, but these three examples seem to be authenticated. One such person is Therese Neuman, a devoted Catholic woman of Konnersreuth, Germany. She abstained from food and drink, except for the ritual swallowing of one paper-thin sacramental wafer at specific times during the week and one teaspoon of water per day.[18] By ecclesiastical permission, Therese was allowed to be under scientific investigation for this phenomenon of inedia. The most famous investigation was by Dr. Friz Gerlick, editor of a Protestant German newspaper who supposedly went to expose the "Catholic fraud." Instead, he wrote her biography.

Another example of inedia is that of an 83-year old Buddhist priest who has lived for 47 years in a cave in the Himalayan mountains. Dr. Krishnan Lal, head of a medical team of four experts who studied the monk for 43 months, reported that he seemed to live only on sips of water.

In the Taoist tradition, according to Mantak Chia, the sixth stage of spiritual evolution is marked by inedia. He claims his own teacher reached this stage in which he lived in the mountains and was able to subsist on the subtle energies of mother nature.[19]

There is documentation by Parmahansa Yogananda of a woman by the name of Giri Bala who stopped taking food and drink at the age of 12. At the time of his interview with her, she had not taken food or water in 56 years.[20] She affirmed that her nourishment was derived from the finer energies of the air and sunlight and also from the cosmic power that recharges the body through its higher energy centers. These centers, called chakras, will be discussed in later chapters.

Longevity and the New Paradigm of Nutrition

These aberrant phenomena and the existence of biological transmutation are simply not able to fit into the materialistic-mechanistic theory of nutrition. But when we explain them with our new nutritional paradigm, they support the wholistic concept of nutrition, which is that it is the natural course of things to have the potential for nearly immortal physical bodies and spirits. It is natural, rather than unusual, to increase the life force and degree of organization in our human system. The reason it isn't experientially obvious is that our personal and world lifestyles tend to break down our system's natural organizational and energy. Aging equates with the decrease in energy and organization of the pattern of the SOEFs that organize our body function. If we eat irradiated foods in which the SOEFs have been destroyed, if we eat processed, antibiotic and pesticide filled foods, if we smoke, drink, take drugs, and in general lead a disharmonious, disorganized work, family, and personal life, we increase our entropy and decrease our SOEFs. By not following the universal laws of nature, we specifically decrease life span.

For the rationalist, who has no other framework than that of the law of entropy, these Yogic, Torah, Hasidic, and Christian stories may seem to be fantasy. But for those who understand how entropy does not completely apply to living systems as the sole governing force, the implication and explanation of these examples must be examined more closely. For example, Rabbi Moshe Maimonides, a 12th-century physician and one of the great Jewish sages in history, explained that one reason the great leaders of the first ten generations (starting with Adam) lived so long was that they were very careful of their diets.[21] It is said that they did not eat meat or any animal products, nor did they ever drink wine or any other intoxicating beverage. Their entire diet consisted only of carefully measured amounts of natural, vegetarian foods, and their only beverage was pure water. They were said to have practiced extreme moderation in sexual activity.[22] These sources referred to in the *Torah Anthology* also point out that longevity decreased after the time of Noah because there was a change in atmospheric vitality and because meat was added to our diet.[23] I do not know the original sources of this information; some seems to have come from ancient texts and some from oral tradition or revelation. However, it is completely concordant with living a SOEF life-affirming approach, an approach in harmony with the universal laws of nature.

A life approaching relative immortality is a possibility; a life of healthful longevity is a practical reality. The Essenes studied and lived in harmony with nature's laws, and they too are reported to regularly live over 120 years.[24] The science of Ayurveda teaches that a state of immortality can be achieved if we are completely attuned to the universal laws of nature.

A recent book called *Maharaj* describes how the Mahatma Shriman Tapaviji Maharaj lived to from 1770 to 1955 using a process called kaya-kalpa.[25]   In essence, this process is an intense adherence to and amplification of natural laws, including a total re-energizing and reorganizing of the SOEFs. He did this rejuvenation process three times: once for 90 days, then 365 days at age 150 years, and the last time for 40 days.[26] A personal witness, the book's biographer, testifies to the regrowth of new teeth, hair, and a robust young body on the last kaya-kalpa rejuvenation treatment. At the age of 185, instead of repeating it, he felt his work on earth was complete and it was time for him to leave his body. The potentials we humans have are indeed very interesting. The essence of this treatment will be discussed in later chapters.

Today we experience imbalanced living conditions on our planet.

Our **world lifestyle** of radiation, pesticides, smog, strife, and other forms of pollution, hatred, violence, and war between nations makes attaining such ages of the physical body rare. However, studies of the cultures which do enjoy health and longevity show a pattern conserving and enhancing SOEFs. In studies of cultures such as the Hunzakuts in Pakistan and the Vilcabamba people of Ecuador, researchers have found it is normal for people to live active lives for more than 100 years. Paavo Airola sums up the basic factors : a low calorie, low fat, low protein, simple diet consisting of mostly vegetarian foods, accompanied by systematic undereating; exercise and fresh air in the context of a contented, relaxed and loving atmosphere, and a positive state of mind.[27]   Li Chung Yun, the Chinese man documented to be 256 years old, calls it "inward calm."[28] This factor of inward calm is an important point which will be discussed in detail in Chapter 21. Inner calm enhances SOEFs, while stress disrupts SOEFs and depletes the vital force. The Transcendental Meditation researchers at the annual meeting of the American Geriatrics Society in 1979 reported a study which showed that long term Transcendental Meditators (TM) were, on the average, 12 years younger physiologically than they were chronologically.[29]

Although longevity is not the goal of nutrition for spiritual life, it is a common result in a human system with highly energized and well-organized SOEFs. Longevity is not necessarily a sign of spirituality. It is a common assumption among the wholistic health and human potential movement that we are completely independent and free to create our own reality. The direct meditation experience of continual merging into universal consciousness and the findings of the physics of quantum mechanics over the last half century both offer a different understanding: we are not separate and independent from the totality of the universe. As part of the whole, we are affected by the whole. I believe we have choice and because of this some responsibility, but our overall destiny is a result of our total universe. Translating this into everyday terms, just how long we live is not entirely up to us and our ability to follow nature's laws. **To be in harmony with the universal laws of nature maximizes the quality of our existence, but not the quantity.**

Divine Body, Physical Immortality, and Superconductivity and the New Paradigm of Nutrition

The key thing to understand about the health of the physical body in relationship with its SOEFs is that as the energy of the system increases the SOEF, which is the matrix of the physical body, becomes stronger. The more perfectly the SOEF is aligned with the virtual energy state, the better it functions. If we damage the functioning of our system as an accumulator and a superconductor of cosmic energy by destructive diet and lifestyle, the free flow of cosmic energy cannot occur. The system disorganizes, and cell replication and cellular and enzyme functions are disrupted. The results are aging and disease. The other end of the spectrum, which is our highest natural evolutionary function, is the establishment of our SOEFs to such a degree of strength, conductivity, and perfection that even on the molecular level the physical body continues to act as a stabilized SOEF superconductor after the soul has left the body. In essence, a divine or immortal body becomes a stabilized superconductor of cosmic energy.

The traditional use of the term superconductor refers to certain metals which, below a transition temperature near absolute zero, enter a state in which a stream of electrons can flow without encountering any resistance in the form of friction. Since friction is the cause of failure in all mechanical perpetual motion machines, when there is no friction to impede the flow of electrical energy, the initial current is able to persist indefinitely without any further input of energy. This is a critical exception to the traditional doctrine of the impossibility of perpetual motion, or in our case, a divine or living immortal body.

The question of stability is important. A superconductor is also thought to be unperturbable. In what is called the Meissner effect, in a superconducting substance, the electron flow spontaneously rejects any external magnetic influence and thus maintains its unperturbable superconducting state. Little, in his article *Superconductivity at Room Temperature,* published in *Scientific American,* speculates that if nature wanted to protect the information contained in the genetic code of a species against all environmental influences, establishing superconducting biological systems would do it.[30] He points out that a superconductor requires a high degree of internal organization, and theorizes a superconducting molecule could exist at room temperature. Frank Barr, M.D., in his work on the melanin hypothesis, suggests that melanin could be such a room temperature superconductor.[31] Melanin is a biomolecular structure found in the brain and throughout the body which may contain the information memory necessary for directing the flow of brain chemistry molecules.

Another theoretical discussion is added by McClare who, in his article on *Resonance in Bioenergetics,* states that the classic second law of thermodynamics does not exactly apply to biological systems. He feels that the energy released via resonance is exchanged so rapidly that it is not thermally available, rather remaining in a form of stored energy.[32] The implication is that the perfectly organized SOEF can resonantly transfer energy from the level of purely cosmic to the biological level without a loss of energy. He also points out that the second law of thermodynamics does not state that entropy has to be created in every conceivable process, so superconductivity does not necessarily contradict the second law of thermodynamics.

The existence of the physical body is then maintained, and we observe what we have called the divine body. This explains this human potential as evidenced by the stories of St. John of the Cross, Bal Shem Tov, Rabbi Elimech, Reb Avraham, Jnaneswar Maharaj, and Parmahansa

Yogananda. Their bodies were so perfect that their SOEFs and physical bodies continued as stabilized accumulators after their souls departed.

Resurrection and the New Nutritional Paradigm

The process of resurrection as evidenced by Christ, Sri Yukteswar, and Lahiri Mahasaya also fits into the wholistic paradigm. The following intuitive explanation should serve as food for thought. These men had reached such a high level of spiritual perfection and their cosmic energy was so great that, by the profound awareness of their oneness with the source of all creation, they could actually use their divinely attuned minds to materialize tangible physical forms from their perfected SOEFs. This will be more thoroughly discussed in the last chapter.

Biological Transmutation and the New Nutritional Paradigm

The knowledge of the properties of SOEFs also allows an intuitive understanding of the phenomenon of biological transmutation. In the transmutation process, the pattern for the new atoms needed is contained in the SOEF pattern, which draws component atoms into the correct relationship. Let us recall the step-down transduction of energy from virtual energy to the subtlest SOEF, then the tachyon field particles moving faster than the speed of light and finally vortexing into a particle of mass. There is a continual dynamic relationship between SOEF vortexes and physical atomic structure. As the energy from these field vortexes energizes a component atom, the axis of the atom's nucleus begins to rotate closer to the speed of light or the alchemical transmutation point. As it rotates faster, the size, but not the mass of the nucleus, appears to expand. As it expands, it interacts with the nucleus of another component atom at the same energized alchemical point within the vortexual field. These two nuclei, and the enzymes involved, are all energized by the intensified energy vortexes, and the two nuclei merge to form a new atom. The enzymes Kervan talks about in this process become transmitters and carriers of high levels of energy, transferring this energy at the critical alchemical point to allow the binding energy of the resulting nucleus to overcome the opposing binding energies of the two individual atoms. The enzymes, like the merging atoms, are drawn into the time and space framework of the biochemical pattern by the specific SOEF governing the interaction. A helpful way to think about this is to picture iron filings being synchronized into the pattern of a magnetic field. The filings are the atoms and the enzymes, and the magnet symbolizes the SOEF which draws them into the appropriate pattern. The availability of the specific enzymes for the transmutation process is variable. If a person is unhealthy, energy is used to fight disease and to strengthen weakened SOEFs instead of being used for enzymatic processes. As we build our health, SOEFs have more energy available for enzyme activation and transmutation.

Divine Light: The Ultimate Spiritual Nutrition

The more we transmute biologically, the less material food we need take into our systems. This process explains the phenomenon of "breatharianism," in which the nutrients we need can be completely transmuted from the molecules in air and water. Inedia, like longevity, is not the goal of spiritual nutrition. But it shows the extraordinary human potential that can be explained by our paradigm of nutrition.

There is another level to the meaning of inedia. It is illustrated by the more complete story of Giri Bala. At the age of 12, Giri prayed to God to send her a guru to teach her how to live without food. Much to her surprise, a guru appeared and taught her a yoga technique, telling her: "From today you shall live by the astral light; your bodily atoms shall be recharged by the infinite current."[33] When asked why she had been singled out to live without eating, she replied, "To prove that man is Spirit. To demonstrate that by divine advancement he can gradually learn to live by the Eternal Light and not by food."[34]

For me, this is part of the more subtle meaning of the Torah when it said that on Mt. Sinai "Moses remained there with God for 40 days and 40 nights. He did not eat bread, nor did he drink water. As Moses descended from the mountain he did not realize that the skin of his face had become radiant..." (Exodus 34:30) The implication is that he drew his nourishment directly from the radiance of the Divine. Another example of subsisting on divine radiance is that of Enoch who was said to have ascended alive, seen the many heavens, and then been instructed by God to return for 30 days to the earth to share heaven's teachings with his children before he ascended again. When offered food by his children, he refused it, explaining that from the time the Lord annointed him with the ointment of his glory he had taken no food.[35] These examples are a profound expression of the deeper meaning of nutrition for spiritual life. The direct energy of God's light is the ultimate spiritual nutrition. We do not have to become breatharians, but it happens any time our awareness merges with the Divine.

Summary Chapter 3

1. Examples of longevity-immortality, divine body, resurrection, and inedia have been given.
2. The SOEF theory has been used to show how these phenomena and biological transmutation are possible.
3. The divine light of God is the ultimate spiritual nutrition.

General Conclusion to Chapters 1, 2, and 3

To develop fully an understanding of nutrition for spiritual life, it is obvious that we must also develop an overall new paradigm of nutrition that includes the material, mental-emotional, energetic, and spiritual qualities of our being. In these three chapters we have strongly questioned the underlying assumptions of the materialistic paradigm of nutrition. We have shown that the three basic assumptions on which the materialistic-mechanistic paradigm stands; the second law of thermodynamics, the law of conservation of mass and energy, and the idea that what goes on inside the body is the same as what happens outside the body, are not fully valid for the dynamics of human nutrition. Findings such as biological transmutation, the existence of the divine body phenomenon, unusual longevity, and inedia have been presented which cannot be adequately explained by the materialistic paradigm. In chapters 2 and 3, we have developed the SOEF concept within the wholistic paradigm of body, mind, energy, and spirit. This concept includes and accounts for these "aberrant" phenomena. The wholistic paradigm does not exclude the materialistic paradigm, but rather includes it as part of an overall totality. Much anecdotal, historical, and scientific research, along with my own empirical findings and intuitive insights, support this new nutritional paradigm.

There has been a subjective awareness of the energy principles and qualities in nutrition for thousands of years in traditions such as the Vedic teachings of India and spiritually advanced societies such as the Essenes of the Dead Sea scrolls. There are Biblical references to these ideas, and there are great spiritual leaders such as Enoch, Moses, and Jesus whose lives radiated these principles. Although the merging of science and spiritual knowledge has progressed to a certain level of development, it has not reached the level of refinement that will convince the minds of conservative scientists. As I have pointed out before, there can be no "acceptable proof" of this material to a mind that assumes there is exclusively an objective world knowable only to the five senses. Sir Arthur Eddington, who offered the first proof of Einstein's relativity theory and who also made important contributions to the theoretical physics of the motion, evolution, and internal constitution of stellar systems, offers the following eloquent statement of the impasse:

"Verily, it is easier for a camel to pass through the eye of
a needle than for a scientific man to pass through a door.
And whether the door be barn door or church door it might be
wiser that he should consent to be an ordinary man and walk
in rather than wait till all the difficulties involved in a
really scientific ingress are resolved."

The evidence is growing in support of these findings. But I must remind you that what I am sharing is an understanding and a theory of SOEFs. This theory describes completely the dynamics of human nutrition, transmutation, and certain "aberrant" phenomena that do not fit into any other theory of nutrition and human life. By using the framework of this wholistic paradigm, we can develop a penetrating understanding and practical application of a system of nutrition for spiritual development. I invite you to consider these new concepts as tools for understanding and not necessarily as dogmatic facts. When this understanding is applied to a

4

The Question of Assimilation

There are questions from Chapter 1 which still must be answered.
What is the purpose of nutrition?
What is nutrition?
What is the relationship between the nutrient taken in and the living system taking it in?
What do we assimilate?
Who is assimilating?
What is the meaning of assimilation?
What is the process of assimilation?
And a new question,
How does our understanding of SOEFs fit into our understanding of nutrition?

To answer these questions, it is important that our theory of assimilation incorporate the subtle energetic aspect of food. We can see that the relationship of food to the human system is more than just adding up calories, vitamins, and minerals to be materialistically accumulated as building blocks in our bodies. Food, as do we, has an energy essence and SOEFs. It is the relationship between the energy fields of the human system and of the substance being ingested that is important to assimilation. Rudolf Steiner alluded to this in 1924 when he said we should not concern ourselves with the quantity of food in metabolism, but rather with whether we can assimilate the vitality from food in the most effective way.[1] On one level, assimilation is overcoming the foreign nature or individualized SOEFs of our food. It is through the process of assimilation that we enter into a very intimate relationship with our food. Food is a major interface between ourselves and our physical environment. Food is a way of extracting energy from the environment.

Not only are we affected by the environment in which food is grown, we are also affected by the consciousness of the people who prepare our food. In Muktananda's ashrams, food was always prepared with love so the people eating the food would receive that love. Marcel Vogel has shown that water infused with the thought form of love has a different taste and a subtle vibration.[2] We are interacting with food on subtle energy levels as well as on the material level of assimilation. Gerhard Schmidt, M.D., author of *The Dynamics of Nutrition* points out that nutrition is concerned with the assimilation of different levels of energy, which increase in quality the closer they are to sun or light energy.[3]

Eating allows the forces of food to penetrate us, and without proper assimilation and digestion, these foreign forces can make us ill. For example, most foods injected directly into our physical bodies will cause an inflammation, but if we take them in orally they will not because they undergo a normal assimilation process. There is an old Arab proverb that "one eats oneself sick and digests oneself back to health" that illustrates this point. Digestion involves overcoming and assimilating the energetic forces in our foods, stimulating our own inner forces, and strengthening us in the overcoming of entropy. If this sounds like too much work, just think of it this way: if we are not walking around strengthening ourselves by overcoming the force of gravity, our muscles and bones begin to weaken and deteriorate, just as astronauts, in a gravity-free environment, begin to lose bone mass. To further elucidate this point, a study in Europe was done in an effort to find easier ways to feed mentally disadvantaged institutionalized children.[4] They were fed a synthetic mixture of vitamins, minerals, calories, and proteins that was the calculated equivalent of what they had been getting on the material level from their three meals a day. After a period of time on this liquid, synthetic diet, researchers were amazed to find that the organs of taste and digestion in the children began to atrophy. One implication of this is that without the stimulating forces of the raw foods, the organs of assimilation are not energized or exercised, and therefore begin to atrophy just like bone mass in a gravity-free environment. These experiments may make us think about the long-term results caused by the high consumption of high potency synthetic vitamins, minerals, amino acids, and proteins currently practiced. This is not a statement against the use of nutritional supplements. I suggest that synthetic supplements should be used with the awareness that assimilation involves the interaction of dynamic forces between us and the food and not just the mechanical absorption of nutrients, and that the indiscriminate use of synthetic supplements is something to be aware of.

Wholistic digestion, then, involves an intimate relationship with the nutrients we take in. It involves the liberation of the cosmic forces that are at the core of the material food. On a more subtle level, Sri Nirsargatta, the late seer from Bombay, has pointed out that it is consciousness which is the very essence of the food that has been assimilated.[5] Our model for nutrition and assimilation must also account for the truth of this concept.

Summary Chapter 4

1. Understanding nutrition involves the study of the interaction of the dynamic forces of food and the dynamic forces of our total being.
2. This dynamic interaction strengthens our own organism.
3. It is through the process of assimilation that we enter into an intimate relationship with our food and therefore with our environment.
4. Consciousness is the essence of food.

5

The Chakra System

To understand how energy is assimilated, we have to be aware of the subtle energy systems that assimilate it. As a first step in defining the meanings of nutrition and assimilation, we will explore the first of three main subtle energy systems of the human organism. This lays the foundation for understanding the relationship of nutrition to spiritual development.

The chakra system is a subtle energy system that has been described for thousands of years in spiritual traditions. In Sanskrit, the word chakra means wheel. It has come into common usage in the west through yoga teachings that have diffused into our culture. The Tibetans refer to these energy centers as khor-lo, which also means wheel. In the Sufi tradition, some call them latifas, or subtle ones. In the Bible, John refers to these centers as the "seven seals on the back of the Book of Life." In early Christianity they were often referred to as the "seven churches". The Kabbalists refer to these centers as "the seven centers in the soul of man." There is obviously a historical cross-cultural tradition among many of the major religions that validates the existence of these subtle energy centers. For our purposes, I would like to use the commonly accepted term chakra for this system of subtle energy centers.

The chakra system has been described by western clairvoyants and eastern yogis over the centuries. More recently, medical doctors and other researchers have begun to explore its existence and function. In the late 1960s and early 70s, Dr. Hiroshi Motoyama, Director of the Institute for Religion and Psychology, a yoga expert, and a scientist who is considered by many to be one of the leading researchers in the area of chakras, has done some important work documenting the physical reality of chakras.[1] He constructed a light-proof room that was shielded from outside electrical emissions. In this room he placed what he calls his Chakra Instrument, designed to detect minute emissions of physical energy from the human body in the form of light, electrical, or electro-magnetic energy. In his experiments, he put the detectors 12 to 20 centimeters in front of the particular chakra area that the subject was trying to activate. The Chakra Instrument was able to detect a quantifiable difference when subjects concentrated directly on a particular chakra, but only when a chakra was chosen on which the subject had previously practiced mental activation. When a chakra was tested on which the subject had not previously practiced, no change was noted before or during the test. These results suggest the existence of a scientifically measurable chakra location.

In 1973 the physician W. Brugh Joy discovered these energy centers spontaneously. He found that when he held his hands over certain areas of a patient's body, there were areas of increased heat energy. Mapping these areas, he realized that they were approximately the same as the yoga descriptions of the chakra locations.[2] Another physician, Laurence Bagley, M.D., in the 1984 issue of the *American Journal of Acupuncture,*[3] describes how by using the Nogier pulse, an auricular acupuncture pulse system developed by Paul Nogier, M.D., he was able to determine the location, size, shape, and rotational direction of the chakra system. My own experience with detecting the physical existence of the chakra system began in 1976 when I was exploring the possible relationship between a person's mental state and the chakra system. I found that when I let a crystal pendulum rotate over the chakra areas, it circled either clockwise or counterclockwise. One day when it rotated counterclockwise over a patient's head, his headache got worse and he felt energy-depleted. When I purposefully rotated the crystal in a clockwise direction over his head, the headache disappeared and he felt more energized. It became clear in further experiments that subtle energies, such as those generated by a crystal, could be used in a way that would be healing and energizing to people.

Chakra Location

As Dio Neff pointed out in her article on chakras in the *Yoga Journal,* [4] there is no absolute agreement on the number of major chakras, their location, and function. There does seem to be a general consensus, however, that there are seven main body chakras and an eighth transpersonal chakra above the head. Most agree that these chakras start at the base of the spine and ascend to the top of the head in a line approximately midway through the body. The first chakra is at the base of the spine in the perineal area. The second chakra is located between the pubic bone and the umbilicus. The third is located between the umbilicus and the solar plexus region. The fourth is in the midline at the heart level. The fifth is at the thyroid level. The sixth is between the eyes at the brow. The seventh is like a skull cap on the vertex of the skull.

Some western groups locate the second chakra over the spleen rather than in the midline area. It is my feeling that some of the variances in locations are due to cultural differences in where the spiritual traditions focus their energy. For example, the Chinese and Japanese tend to focus on the hara, located at the umbilicus or slightly below -- between the second and third chakra locations. Theosophists tend to de-emphasize the second, or sexual, chakra and focus on the spleen region for the location of the second chakra. This differs from the yoga tradition. Besides the various cultural differences, the location and size of the different chakras may also vary with an individual's spiritual evolution. Motoyama, for example, has found that the measurable chakra and associated meridian energies vary depending on which chakra a person tends to use the most. It may be that the yoga traditions describe the chakra system of more evolved spiritual aspirants, in whom the spleen center is less important than it is in westerners. In my own work with western spiritual aspirants, I find a more predominant midline second chakra; the spleen chakra seems to be a secondary center. What matters, beyond these details, is that from many perspectives, researchers and spiritual practitioners agree that chakras exist as an important system of subtle energy in the body.

It also seems to be generally agreed that each chakra has a specific energetic nature that relates to color, sound, and geometric shape. Each chakra is associated with certain mental states and with a specific spiritual awareness. Each chakra also seems to be associated with the physiology of a specific glandular system, organ system, and nerve plexus. (See Figure 3.) Dr. Motoyama validated the relationship of chakras to organs, glands, and nerve plexus by developing an instrument he calls the AMI, or Apparatus for Measuring the Functional Conditions of Meridians and their Corresponding Internal Organs.[5] He found that in people who were judged by a panel of experts to have a particular chakra activated, there was a change in meridian energy related to the specific organs associated with that activated chakra.

Essential Function of the Chakras

There is general consensus on the essential function of the chakras. Differences exist, however, on the details. David Tansley, an English radionics practitioner and author of many books on subtle energies, feels the chakra system picks up energies originating from every level of the cosmos. This includes our physical, emotional, and mental selves, as well as the collective unconscious of our nation and our planet. Brugh Joy, M.D., is completely certain that the chakra system exists, but that no one completely understands all its functions. In his book, he tentatively takes the position that the chakra system is an inter-dimensional transducing system.[6] He feels it is affected by thought and capable of converting matter into various levels of more subtle energy, transmitting them into the physical system. Its functioning transcends the limitations of time and space.

One of the first westerners to describe the chakra system was the Reverend C.W. Leadbeater, a Theosophical leader and extremely well-known clairvoyant who had worked as a vice-rector of the Church of England, was well-practiced in yoga. In his book *The Chakras,* written in 1927, he describes chakras as centers of conduction in which energy flows from one subtle body of man or women to another level of subtle body. These subtle bodies will be described in detail in the next chapter; they are the subtle layers of energy and consciousness that surround the physical body, forming its aura. Leadbeater describes these chakras as perpetually rotating; the primary force from the higher world is always flowing into their open vortex. He saw the force as sevenfold, all its forms operating in each of these centers, but one of them predominating over the others. He feels that without the absorption of this higher energy into the chakras, the physical body cannot exist. Dr. Motoyama also feels the chakras function as intermediaries for energy transfer and conversion between two neighboring subtle bodies. In Motoyama's system there are two subtle bodies: astral, and causal. He feels the chakras convert energy from one body to another in either direction; they can convert physical energy into psychological energy.

It is generally agreed that these chakras rotate in a vortex that extends out from a point in the midline of the body, a sort of funnel for bringing the energy into the physical body. Lawrence Bagley, M.D., in his book, *Chakra Chrome* describes how these chakra vortexes can be measured using the Nogier pulse technique. The direction in which the vortexes rotate when they are healthy and balanced is not universally agreed upon, but the majority consensus, with which my research agrees, is that a clockwise rotation suggests a healthier chakra function.

Energy Flow in the Chakras

Our chakras, to a greater or lesser extent, are always active. It is common to describe chakras as either "open" or "closed," giving the impression that a chakra may somehow be blocked and energy not able to flow through it. But chakras are neither open nor closed. The difference, from my perspective, is that some chakras have less energy flowing through them. I call them less activated, meaning the energy charging through them is disrupted in its transduction through the subtle bodies.

There is also the implication that an "open" chakra, through which much energy is flowing, is better. This is not necessarily the case. For example, it has been my intuitive experience in working with people suffering from manic psychosis that their crown chakra is wide "open," or activated. It is so activated, in fact, that these patients' lives become imbalanced. A person experiencing a manic psychosis often describes a rush of energy flowing through them from the top of their heads. This sort of description correlates with what people experience with an activated chakra. In some clients in a hypomanic state, by specifically working to slow down the flow of energy through the crown chakra, it has been possible to lessen the excessive activation, rebalance their chakras, and thus decrease their hypomania.

Discarding the language "open" or "closed" does not negate a difference in the energy levels of the different chakras. Dr. Brugh Joy describes feeling these energy differences with his hands. This is relatively easy to do and I suggest the reader experiment with this to get a feeling for chakra energy and location. Lawrence Bagley, M.D., describes mapping out the difference in energy fields around the various chakras. Dr. Motoyama, with his Chakra Instrument and AMI device, has begun to quantify these differences. He has established that a chakra with more energy flowing through it has a wider range of dynamic balance between the sympathetic and parasympathetic nervous system. He also discovered that in these more activated chakras, the associated organ systems have more energy running through them. Some of his preliminary research suggests that people with more activated chakras have more disease susceptibility in the organs related to that activated chakra.[7] My clinical impression, on the basis of observing many hundreds of people with activated chakras, is that this disease susceptibility may be just a temporary phenomenon related to the time it takes to incorporate an increased input of energy into the system harmoniously. Disease susceptibility may also be connected to the mental overstimulation of one chakra in a way that knocks it out of harmony with the rest of the chakra system. Another explanation is that when one chakra is overstimulated by the mind, the organs associated with it have too much energy moving through them. Perhaps, in a way, it is analogous to a wire burning out when too much electricity passes through it and there is no protective fuse. The fuse in this case is common sense. This example represents the danger in trying to activate specific chakras by mind-will power, rather than letting them awaken spontaneously and naturally through meditation and the development of higher awareness.

A highly activated chakra has more energy flowing into it through the transducing system of the subtle bodies. Therefore, more energy is flowing into the body in general, and specifically into the organs connected with that chakra. The first question I ask in evaluating the meaning of an activated chakra is whether the individual is able to integrate this increased energy into his or her overall functioning. My second consideration is whether the total chakra system is in balance. As has already been pointed out, the chakras in an average person are not at exactly equal levels of activation. Depending on a person's life situation and how that person consciously or unconsciously uses the different chakras, they will vary in strength and activity over time. In my clinical experience, being aware of the energetic balance of the total chakra system, rather than just focusing on a single unbalanced chakra, has given me some additional clues about the energetic functioning of the chakra system. I began to notice that when one chakra became balanced through the crystal work and I retested the remaining unbalanced chakras, they became spontaneously balanced. It became clear to me that chakras have an energy entrainment system. This is especially true of the linkage of the first, second, and third chakras as a unit and also seems to be often the case with the fifth, sixth, and seventh chakras. These two units seem to form a linkage at the fourth, or heart, chakra. It is like an infinity sign with the heart at the center.

An additional point in appreciating chakras as a total interconnected system is that there seems to exist a polarity within each chakra area. For the base chakra, polarity seems to exist between the feet or ground and the base of the spine. The second chakra polarizes between the two testicles or ovaries. The third is between the solar plexus and the spleen. The fourth is between the heart and the thymus (ancient heart). The fifth is between the thyroid and parathyroid. The polarity for the sixth and seventh chakras is between the pineal gland (associated with the seventh) and pituitary gland (associated with the brow chakra). There also seems to be some degree of polarity between the different chakras on a vertical basis, such as first and sixth and seventh, second and fifth, and third and fourth. Because of this, whenever I am working at the chakra level with a patient, I will finish with an overall spiral balancing of the main chakras. One of the most common situations in which the chakras become disorganized in relationship to each other is severe emotional trauma. Doing a crystal spiral balancing alone is very helpful to someone in such a crisis.

Awakened Chakras

Chakras are either awake or asleep. This is not the same as the activity level of a chakra, which is primarily associated with keeping our organism supplied with vital life force for our general functioning. The awakening aspect of the chakras is primarily associated with the development of more evolved spiritual awareness. Dr. Brugh Joy has noted that an awakened chakra functions on a different level and that it feels and looks different to clairvoyants.[8] When a chakra is awakened, it is part of a spiritually evolving process in which the mind merges with the higher awareness stored in that chakra. In some cases, certain psychic abilities associated with the chakra are also activated. Psychic ability, however, is not necessarily a sign of spiritual evolvement or of a chakra's awakening, and it is not the same as spiritual awareness. It is misleading to associate it with the spiritual awareness that is stored in each chakra and released to the consciousness of the awakened mind.

There is general agreement that each chakra has a spiritual awareness associated with it, but no simplified system for understanding this awareness is either found or agreed upon. There is a variety of esoteric teachings and descriptions of powers that may be associated with the awakening of the different chakras, but these will not be part of our discussion. With the awakening of each chakra, there occurs a key transition from mundane consciousness to a more complete spiritual awareness. Just as the general energies of the chakras are linked, the awakened chakras function as combined units of awareness. The first through the third chakras are linked as one unit, with the heart chakra the pivotal integrator. The fifth through the seventh chakras comprise the second unit, and its relationship to the heart is also important.

The first three chakras are life force energies primarily concerned with issues of survival on the physical and emotional planes. The spiritual awareness associated with their awakening manifests in mastery of all the issues of living in the world. Their awakening is essential for integrating the knowledge of how to live in the world with a spiritually transformed consciousness. Without it, the more intense energies released by the spiritual awakenings of the upper chakras can throw us out of balance in our everyday lives. It is difficult to be stabilized in the higher awareness without integrating the awakened first three chakras into our daily lives.

The fourth through the seventh chakras are primarily concerned with spiritual life. Their awakening activates spiritual energies and the transmutation of mundane consciousness into higher consciousness. It is important to understand that development of higher awareness in the chakras is not necessarily linear; rather it seems to be both simultaneous and spiral, yet neither. It is wholistic. Awareness of the different chakras seems to fuse at nodal points and depend on each other for a spiral, integrated, individualized, simultaneous awakening at different levels of intensity. Once the Kundalini is awakened (see Chapter 7), there is an ongoing awakening of all the chakras simultaneously, but at different levels of intensity in each chakra at various times. An individual, for example, may be in the primary process of first and second chakra awakening but may also be reveling in the bliss of the divine communion of the seventh chakra. We often notice a new awareness or awakening when this awareness reaches a point of stabilization and integration in our conscious awareness. This is when our mind has fully merged with the total awareness of that chakra.

One need not have the awakening of the Kundalini to experience divine communion. It may occur with the setting of the sun, when the mind becomes completely still and all time stops and one is right there in that oneness. One of my first divine experiences came in the middle of a college football game. It was the last game of the season, a tie game with two minutes left to play. I went into a state of bliss in which I experienced all on the field as one. I played perfect football for those two minutes as we marched 80 yards to win the game in the last ten seconds. In a book titled the *Psychic Side of Sports* ,[9] experiences like this are cited as common. The mind becomes so focused that we move into a meditative state.

We have the total truth inside of us all the time. Spiritual practices and the awakening of the Kundalini help us maintain contact with the awareness of our inner selves, rather than waiting for perfect experiences to arise spontaneously from our interaction with our environment.

The first chakra is often known as the survival chakra. In its unawakened state, it is governed by the misconception that we are separate from nature and and need to conquer nature in order to be safe and to survive. Its drive is to master the forces of matter. As a result, this limited awareness and lack of understanding allows us to become immersed in the material plane, fearing, doubting, and distrusting the environment. In this state, it is difficult to believe that there is a God. One's own ego is one's God. The awakening of the Kundalini energy which is stored in its potential state in the first chakra often helps to shake us out of this limited awareness by giving us a taste of communion with God. We learn that we are more than just physical bodies and that there is a higher purpose to life than simply making money and surviving on the material plane. This is the link between the first and sixth-seventh chakras, in which we become completely in tune with our higher vision and purpose. From fear, doubt, and nonbelief, there is a shift to faith, trust, and belief in a higher force, or God. From disharmony with nature we move into a desire to be harmonious. We begin to understand the elements of nature. Our sense of separation begins to diminish, and we seek to live in unity with nature and the natural laws rather than to subjugate them. Trust in the illusion of one's ego power shifts to a trust in God. Primary fear and survival is transmuted to the awareness that there exists a unity with a higher force.

The second chakra is characterized by the drive to procreate. When awakened, a shift in consciousness allows us to overcome the control of our lives by obsessive instinctual sexual desires. This does not mean we deny sex. It means we experience it on a higher level of communion, love, harmony, and creativity. Physical sexual activity becomes a choice. Life becomes a creative communion. The primordial energies of procreation are transformed into more refined creative aesthetic and artistic energies. In the awakened state, the raw procreative energies of the second chakra transmute into more refined spiritual energies. Creativity without understanding can create havoc because it can degenerate into a lustful desire to pursue personal creativity at the expense of others. Understanding in the first chakra is necessary to give a grounding energy to the creativity of the second chakra.

The third chakra is marked by an innate awarenesss of what is happening on all planes of consciousness, both in the environment and within the person on a physical, emotional, mental, and spiritual level. It is a sensitive and perceptive ear to all forces. With the awakening, we transcend instinctual reactions to the emotional-psychic states of others. We become conscious of our reactive use of raw psychic-emotional power to attract, repel, project, magnify and control others. We begin to operate in a balanced emotional state of reflection, discrimination, and sensitivity. We begin to develop a quality of sensitive perception of our inner and outer lives, to balance the raw forces of the first and second chakras and become interactors rather than reactors.

In the process of a full awakening, the solar plexus chakra becomes harmonically linked with the heart chakra. This linkage allows the information input of the solar plexus chakra to be interpreted through the love of the heart chakra. The awakening leads to the fusion of the balanced emotion and power of the third chakra with the universal love of the heart, or fourth chakra. The fusion of the emotions with the love-harmony of the fourth chakra gives us joy within, and we unite with one another in the unity of a moment of mutual sensitivity. It leads to a cooperative service between people. Ann Ree Colton metaphorically describes this fusion occurring when the lion initiate master of the solar plexus chakra lies down with the lamb initiate master of the heart.[10] This fusion marks a full awakening. It may be what Jeremiah describes in 31:33: "I will put my law in their inward parts and write it in their hearts; and will be their God, and they shall be my people." This speaks to an attunement with an inner conscience or morality which is released into consciousness when the third chakra is awakened. As this awareness merges with the mind, judgment of self and others merges into an awareness of the spirit of the universal law. When the third chakra is harmonized with the heart, the awareness of the upper chakra manifests more easily as spirituality in everyday life. Another aspect of this awakening is the transmutation of the primordial desire-will power of the third chakra into attunement with the will of God. It manifests as the awareness that whatever God does is for the best. It allows us to change the self-service of the first chakra to selfless service. It is another step in developing a trust in God. This awakened awareness helps us move from desire and attachment toward more sensitivity and less attachment to our desires. The awakened third chakra allows the life force of the first three chakras to be used as a strong healing power, the same power that the shamans and bruhus use in their healing and magical work. I believe a developed hara, which is the centering and grounding energy center focused on the martial arts and in some Chinese and Japanese religions, reflects the combined and integrated energy of the first three chakras.

The fourth, or heart chakra awakens us to the experience of love in any form in our lives. Eventually it awakens us to the experience of universal love. Its awakening helps us transform attached forms of love associated with such emotions as lust, greed, pride, envy, infatuation, and even hate into a more peaceful universal love. The raw instincts of self-preservation and survival are transmuted into full heart unity with all of humanity. It motivates us toward working for peace without oppression in the world. It is the love that extends beyond the love of our nuclear family to the one world family. An awakened heart acts as a balancing and integrating point for all the chakras. The conscience and virtue we develop from the awakening of the other chakras need love as the energy to reach their full quality and power. It is with the awakening of this fourth chakra that we begin to experience ourselves and God as Love. Many people feel the Divine Self of all creation is centered in the heart. As the awareness of my heart chakra matured, I regularly saw and experienced a blue flame of consciousness within my own heart. This occurred both during meditation and in my everyday activities. The opening of the heart is very special.

The awakening of the fifth, or throat chakra has to do with expression and communication of the more sublime meanings of existence. It has to do with the ability to translate all thoughts in the mind into form and shape. It involves all forms of communication such as aesthetics, art, language, music, and dance. Salespeople, lawyers, advertisers, and artists often have well-developed throat chakras. The awakening reflects a shift from using the power of communication for our own selfish purposes to the communication of true inner feelings, spiritual teaching, and truths. Through our own forms of expression, we become mediators and manifesters of the Truth. Our being disperses peace and good tidings.

The awakening of the sixth, or brow chakra brings us into a higher state of vision of the Truth. The mind becomes spiritualized. Intuition and attunement reach a spiritualized and integrated state of development. This chakra is sometimes called the entry into the Christ mind. It is the "eye of the needle"; when fully awakened, it opens to the crown chakra. In the awakening of this sixth and seventh chakra, we become fully connected with the "inner guru" or teacher. The full awakening of the sixth chakra seems to be associated with a state of self-realization in which we experience the Truth of the Universal Self within. It is at this stage that we directly know ourselves as this awesome Truth. It is the stabilization of the "I Am" awareness, becoming our primary identity. We are no longer deluded by the multiple material gods of ego, power, sex, or form. We enter into a state of beingness rather than doingness as our primary identity. We feel at one with the will of God. All concepts and ego blocks have been sufficiently purified out of the system, and we are free to follow the will of God.

The awakening of the crown chakra is very much interconnected with awareness of the sixth. As this awakening matures, we go beyond self-realization into a merging with the Godhead. It is a sense of total oneness with all of creation. Dualistic thinking fades, and we rest in the beingness of non-dual awareness. We become more and more stabilized into the awareness of all as God. There is no separation. We become the purpose of life that we vaguely feel with the awakening of the first chakra. It is with this awareness that the merging of the heart and the sixth-seventh chakra complex becomes clearer. The debate between whether universal consciousness is centered in the heart or in the sixth-seventh chakra no longer has any meaning, because these chakras are linked on the planes of spiritual awareness. We spontaneously feel great, unrelenting love with all. It is the spontaneous fulfillment of Christ's message of... "turn the other cheek." We never stop loving, because there is no one not to love. Separation ends, and only love exists. This is not so much an opening of the heart chakra as the experience of the Self as Love, of the World as God. It is another spiral of the meaning and experience of love. It exists as our totality of experience.

The awakening of the crown chakra also intensifies the link with higher levels of cosmic energy. We begin to experience directly the flow, or cosmic pulse of energy into the system. We seem filled with this more refined cosmic energy, as though a barrier between ourselves and the cosmos has been lifted. The awakening of the sixth and seventh chakras goes beyond our linear time space limitations and our words. It is a simple, yet totally other awareness.

Summary Chapter 5

1. A subtle energy system which is commonly known as the chakra system exists. One function is transducing subtle cosmic energy into the body.
2. Each of the seven main chakras has a specific energetic nature that corresponds to a specific color, sound, and mental and spiritual awareness.
3. Each chakra is energetically associated with the physiology of a single or small group of locally associated nerve plexes, endocrine glands, and organs.
4. Chakras are never closed; they fluctuate between more and less activation.
5. Chakra health is related to the overall synchronistic balance of the main chakras, as well as to the function of a particular chakra.
6. An awakened chakra is one in which the individual's consciousness merges with the higher awareness stored in that particular chakra.

6

Subtle Anatomies

The Subtle Body System

The subtle anatomies are another energy system which needs to be explored for our understanding of spiritual nutrition. As with the chakras, there is general agreement among spiritual authorities, Essene tradition, yoga teachings, Vedantic scriptures, and Western researchers that several layers of subtle energy bodies exist. In some Western systems, two to seven subtle anatomies are reported. In most of these subtle anatomy systems, the same basic functions and levels of consciousness are generally included. In the Vedantic, and in most yoga traditions, four bodies are reported: physical, subtle, causal, and supercausal. With each subtle anatomy level there is an associated "mind" of functioning and awareness.

By name, the seven subtle anatomies are: etheric, emotional, mental, astral, spiritual, causal, and soul bodies. As the refined energy condenses from its cosmic or virtual state, it is stepped down via the seven subtle anatomies, which personalize it and densify it to a level at which our bodies can incorporate it. It is my feeling that these subtle anatomies work in conjunction with the chakra system in this transduction process. Each subtle anatomy has a subtle chakra system that regulates the flow of energy within it. The chakra systems also regulate the flow of energy between the different subtle anatomies. It is my clinical experience that the energy does not just flow in one direction from the cosmos into the body; it can also flow in the opposite direction. For example, when someone's physical energy increases, I often see a corresponding increase in psychological energy. By implication, some of the increased physical energy has been converted to psychological energy. In general, however, the flow is from the state of virtual energy to a more condensed form that we eventually perceive as electromagnetic fields (EMFs). This stepped-down energy is absorbed through the vortexes of the measurable chakra system and then transduced as EMFs into our brains, central and autonomic nervous systems, organs, endocrine systems, and skeletal structures. The chakras that are measurable with our current, limited, scientific instrumentation are those that interface between the subtle body system and the physical body. It is this level that is most commonly thought of as the chakra system.

EMFs are the final links between the etheric and physical bodies. Recent work by Jose Delgado, an internationally known Spanish neuroscientist, gives indirect evidence of the effect EMFs can have on our

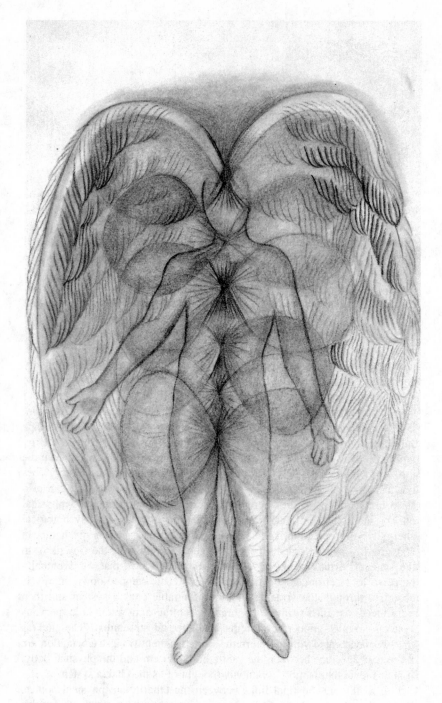

Figure 3

biological systems. Delgado uses EMFs that are one-fiftieth the strength of the earth's own magnetic field. These fields, which I feel are of the same nature as those transduced by the chakra system into the body, have been shown to alter the mental functioning of a variety of vertebrate nervous systems and other body system activities. For example, by exposing monkeys to different types of EMFs, Delgado could make some go to sleep and others become irritable. Researchers have also detected EMFs in the brain and around the denser area of the nervous system.

Functions of the Seven Subtle Anatomies

These seven subtle anatomies comprise what is also known as the human aura. They act in a way that is analogous to a prism in that they break cosmic energy into seven rays. Each ray tends to be the predominant energizing ray for one of the seven chakras. In different yoga systems, and in the direct experience of clairvoyants, the chakras are said to have spokes, like a wheel. These spokes, called nadis, radiate out of the chakra. They are essentially a subtle nervous system of the physical body. It is said that there are 72,000 nadis in the body. It is my feeling that these nadis intersect with what are called the the meridian lines of the Chinese acupuncture system; where the nadis and meridian lines intersect lie the acupuncture points. Though there is not enough research to clarify this point, I feel the meridians and nadis are not the same. It is enough, however, to say that the nadis carry energy from chakras into the brain, the nervous, endocrine, and organ systems, the skeletal structure, and finally to the cell level.

The chakra system interpenetrates the seven subtle bodies and interfaces among their different levels as part of the energy transduction system. Depending on the alignment of the subtle bodies, the energy flows through with more or less resistance to the measurable chakra level. These interdimensional chakras can be thought of, metaphorically, as tubes between the subtle bodies. When all subtle bodies are aligned, then all seven interdimensional chakra "tubes" become synchronized, and cosmic energy flows through the body with the least resistance. In Figure 3 we see the author's visualization of how the subtle bodies are an extension of the vortex energy spin of the chakras. As the vortex energy of the chakras increase, the centrifugal spin expands the subtle body. As the cosmic energy increases, our angelic wings are unfolded. Perhaps these subtle bodies are the angelic wings that are sometimes seen by human folk. Perhaps we are even those angels.

When the left and right hemispheres of the brain are balanced, as is commonly experienced during meditation, the subtle anatomies and chakra "tubes" are in alignment and cosmic energy flows through smoothly. Conversely, during times of mental agitation or anxiety, the subtle anatomy-chakra system becomes misaligned resulting in more resistance and less energy flowing through. It is times like these when a person might describe this chakra or chakras as "closed." This decreased energy flow into the system seems to correlate to a state of constricted awareness and a feeling of disharmony.

Recent research by Brother Charles of MSH Associates in Virginia seems to support the point that increased right and left brain synchronization correlates with an increased flow of spiritualizing energy into the system. MSH has developed an audio tape program called *Synchronicity, the Recognitions Experience,*™ as an aid to spiritual development. In this program the brain hemispheres are progressively synchronized through sound phasing. In reviewing reports from nearly one thousand participants, the preliminary findings are that, with increased right and left brain synchronization, participants experience a more consistent, deeper meditation.[1] In post-meditation journals, participants reported an increased sense of overall harmony with themselves and their world.

The etheric, emotional, and mental bodies comprise what we would normally associate with the conscious mind. The seven subtle bodies as a whole comprise what can be called the larger mind. This larger mind is the interface between the physical body, or unconscious level of awareness, and the virtual energy level, or cosmic consciousness. It mediates between the body and the cosmic energy level. We can think of the seven subtle bodies as the larger mind. It acts as a transducing system that personalizes the energy flow from the cosmic level of virtual energy to a denser energy which our bodies can incorporate on the physical level.

Summary Chapter 6

1. The subtle anatomy system consists of seven subtle energy levels. It comprises what is known as the aura, or larger mind.

2. This seven-layer subtle body system mediates as a step-down transducer to conduct the flow of energy from the highly purified virtual, or cosmic, energy state to a condensed, personalized state which our bodies use as life force.

3. When all seven subtle bodies are aligned, cosmic energy flows through more intensely and with less resistance to energize and spiritualize the body-mind-spirit complex.

7

Kundalini

The inner force that opens us to the ecstasy, love, and God awareness inherent in the transpersonal awakening is often referred to as the Kundalini. This is the most important subtle energy system in terms of the spiritual evolution of the human species. Carl Jung in *Psychological Commentary on Kundalini* said that, "When you succeed in awakening the Kundalini, so that it starts to move out of its mere potentiality, you necessarily start a world which is totally different from our world. It is the world of eternity."[1] Gopi Krishna, inspired by his own experience of Kundalini awakening, has written much to describe its meaning. He says of Kundalini, "A new center presently dormant in the average man and woman has to be activated and a more powerful stream of psychic energy must rise into the head from the base of the spine to enable human consciousness to transcend the normal limits. This is the final phase of the present evolutionary impulse in man....Here reason yields to intuition and revelation appears to guide the steps of humankind...This mechanism, known as Kundalini, is the real cause of all genuine spiritual and psychic phenomena, the biological basis of evolution and development of personality, the secret origin of all esoteric and occult doctrines, the master key to the unsolved mystery of creation..."[2] Ramakrishna, considered by many to be one of the greatest Indian saints of the last century, taught that an individual's spiritual consciousness is not awakened unless their Kundalini is aroused. Swami Muktananda, a recent spiritual master in the yoga of Kundalini who has awakened the Kundalini energy in thousands of spiritual hopefuls, said, "It is only when the Kundalini is awakened that we become aware of our true nature, of our greatness."[3] He points out that "as long as the inner Kundalini is sleeping, it doesn't matter how many austerities we follow, how much yoga we practice...we will never realize our identity with our inner Self... The awakening of the inner Kundalini is the true beginning of the spiritual journey."[4]

Although the various yoga traditions have been the main source of our detailed knowledge of Kundalini in the West, a spiritualizing energy which seems to be the same as Kundalini is acknowleged in many cultures. Katz, in the *Journal of Transpersonal Psychology,* describes how the Kung people of the Kalahari Desert in Northwest Botswanna, Africa, danced for hours to awaken the n/um (Kundalini) to attain the ! kia state. He feels that the n/um is analogous to the Kundalini and the ! kia is a state of transcendence.[5] He describes how about one half of the Kung people are able to heat up the n/um. In the Chinese Taoist tradition, Luk, in his book *Secrets of Chinese Meditation*, describes an awakening process that is directly parallel to Kundalini awakening.[6] In the Christian tradition, Saint Terese of Lisieux, when she enrolled in a Carmelite convent at the age of ten, was reported to have had several months of spontaneous spells with a "strange melange of hallucination, comas, and convulsions."[7] Sometimes she had spontaneous movements like springing from her knees and standing on her head without using her hands. Her history is compatible with descriptions of classical Kundalini awakenings and also with those reported by Lee Sannella, M.D., in *Kundalini--Psychosis or Transcendence?*[8]

Kundalini, a Scientifically Acknowledged Force

In Dr. Sannella's book and the Kundalini crisis clinic, of which I was an original co-director with Dr. Sannella, we have become aware of the growing numbers of documented Kundalini awakenings occurring in our own Western society. A model called the physio-Kundalini cycle, initially coined by Izak Bentov, a physicist and meditator, has begun to evolve from observing and recording these ever-increasing American awakenings. This cycle is a beginning scientific effort to describe the initial Kundalini awakening process from a physiological and clinical basis. The details of this process are described in Dr. Sannella's book.[9] They present a plausible physiological explanation for the initial awakening process. This model seems basically compatible with the initial stages of the classical yoga description, except for some variance in the exact path of the energy flow after it reaches the crown chakra. The exact path is of minor significance compared with the overall shift in awareness that comes from the full awakening. As with the details of the other subtle systems, it is hard to achieve full agreement among all researchers. It is more important that this physio-Kundalini cycle obtains scientific validity and becomes a guide for helping clinicians understand that this process might be going on.

In his book, Dr. Sannella describes the physio-Kundalini process as a "dynamic, self-directed, self-limited process of mental and physiological purification, leading to a healthier and more developed state than what we usually consider normal." [10] The physio-Kundalini model is limited, however, in its lack of description of the subtle transformation and awakening of the human consciousness that occurs over time. Dr. Sannella alludes to this unresolved issue when he says "all the characteristic elements of the physio-Kundalini complex are included in the classic description. And yet we find quite 'ordinary' people who complete the physio-Kundalini cycle in a matter of months, whereas yogic scriptures assign a minimum of three years for the culmination of full Kundalini awakening even in the most advanced initiates. Here we have the suggestion that full Kundalini awakening includes a larger complex, of which the physio-Kundalini process is only a part." [11] In my personal and clinical experience, the physio-Kundalini process is primarily a description of the initial Kundalini awakening step, which may take place almost immediately or over several months to two or more years. There are many people who have experienced a Kundalini awakening, but because of lack of effort, discipline, interest, or awareness of the great potential, or even because of their fear of the unfolding, do not undergo a permanent transformation. They might experience profound moments of awareness in the beginning of the physio-Kundalini cycle, but without the continued and spiritually disciplined effort to nurture the unfolding power of this spiritualizing energy, profound moments of awareness become memories. The process seems to fade out.

Poetry and Power of Kundalini

The unfolding of Kundalini is the most important process in our spiritual evolution. To describe it within the limited confines of scientific terminology deprives the reader of its poetry and significance. This book, as the reader is no doubt by now aware, represents the merging of traditional left-brained scientific with right-brained intuitive and direct, experiential input. At this point it seems appropriate to switch from a technical dialogue to a poetic style to communicate more multidimensionally.

Kundalini is the power of consciousness. As Muktananda poetically describes it, "She is the supreme creative power of the Absolute Being... Dwelling in the center of the universe, she holds it together and maintains it. Similarly...she dwells at the center of the human body, in the muladhara chakra (first chakra) and controls and maintains our whole physiological system through its network of 72,000 nadis...she makes everything work in our bodies...our mind, senses, power of motion..."[12]

Another term for Kundalini energy is prana. In Yoga, the term prana is used to describe three different manifestations of the same basic universal energy. One is the prana, called that which is intelligent, aware of itself, and which permeates all creation as the supreme creative power of the Absolute Being. This is known as cosmic prana, or all-pervading or universal prana. The yogic scriptures teach that universal consciousness evolves into prana and that the entire universe arises from prana. A scientific term we have been using, analogous to universal prana, is the virtual energy state. As explained in Chapter 1, it is the all-pervading energy state from which energy condenses -- at a rate faster than the speed of light -- to tachyon field-particles, and ultimately condenses to particles of matter moving at the speed of light. Another way the term prana is used is as the life force within the body, called mundane Kundalini. It is the form that Muktananda referred to as maintaining and controlling our whole physiological system. It is on this level, as the energizer of the human body, that the Kundalini is considered already awake. Although the vital force prana of the body is only one, there are five active forms of it at work in the body: apana, which expels waste; samana, which distributes nourishment in the body; uyana, which pervades the power of movement; udana, which brings the energy upward in the body; and prana, which is breath. Prana as breath is the most common association people have with the word prana, though it is the third use of the word.

The aspect of Kundalini we refer to when we use the term Kundalini awakening is called the Kundalini Shakti. This spiritual potential energy is said to be stored in the etheric body in the base chakra. When it becomes sufficiently energized, it emerges out of its potential state and begins to move throughout the subtle nervous system, which consists of 72,000 nadis. It moves upward through the chitrini nadi, located inside the central nadi, or sushumna. Once activated, it begins a process of cleansing.

Experience of Kundalini Awakening

From my direct experience witnessing Kundalini awakening, I have begun to think fondly of the Kundalini as the power of God which leads us to God. It is such an incredible occurrence, such a profound ecstatic spiritual birth that the best way I can communicate it is to share the joy and mystery of my own awakening. It took place during my second meeting with Swami Muktananda at a two-day meditation retreat designed to awaken the Kundalini. Muktananda did this through a spiritual transmission called shaktipat, a process by which someone with an already awakened Kundalini sends awakened energy into the spiritual aspirant. This powerful energy activates the "sleeping" Kundalini energy, which is stored in the first chakra. This is not the only way that Kundalini can be awakened, but it is powerful, effective, and considered by many to be the most direct method. It is also a historically traditional way. Kundalini is referred to in the Old Testament in Deuteronomy 34:9 in the passage, "And Joshua the son of Nun was full of the spirit of wisdom, for Moses had laid his hand upon him." In the New Testament, Kundalini is referred to in John 20:22, which says that Jesus "blew upon them and said to them: 'Receive Holy Spirit.'" In the Yogic traditions, shaktipat is a well recognized approach for awakening the Kundalini.

My awakening started in the first meditation of the two-day meditation retreat. Muktananda gave me shaktipat by hitting me with his peacock feather wand. He followed this by putting his hand over my mouth in a funnel and blowing directly into my mouth. After this he squeezed me at the bridge of the nose and pushed my head back. After what seemed a few minutes I went into a deep meditation. In the midst of this, my mouth spontaneously opened and my tongue stuck out as far as it could go. These sorts of unusual physical movements are known as kriyas, and they may occur on an emotional, mental, physical, and spiritual level. They may be gentle pulsation or swirling feelings over a chakra area, very vigorous physical movements, sudden changes in emotional states, spontaneous crying, rapid thought production, or spiritual visions. They are evidence of the purifying movement of the Kundalini as it travels through the nadis spontaneously working through blocked areas of energy. Often the Kundalini puts the body into a particular physical posture to remove a specific energy block. I later found out that the pose with my tongue sticking out is a yoga position called the lion pose. While the lion pose was happening, I experienced a peaceful wavy bliss. At some point after this, I began to have a vision of Muktananda in which he guided me into a fusion and awareness of my Inner Divine Self. Following this, the experience of oneness between my inner world and the universe began to emerge into my awareness.

A little later in the meditation, I had the inner vision of my third, fourth, and fifth chakras in their anatomical locations all bathed in a full, golden light. As the energy moved upward in my body, my eyes turned upward to the brow chakra to see Nityananda (Muktananda's guru) sitting in a lotus posture looking down at me. As my inner vision continued to turn upward, I experienced and saw the crown chakra blazing in what looked like thousands of lights. Sometime during this meditation, I began to experience intense pains in the sacral and lumbar areas. This back pain, in many people, is associated with the awakening of the Kundalini.

Following this awakening, my meditation experience at home became very intense. Certain emotional issues seemed to come up intensely and then quickly pass. I continued to have more physical kriyas, including spontaneous forms of rapid and slow breathing - sequences which I later found out were called pranyama, a yogic breathing exercise often used to activate the Kundalini energy. About ten days after this awakening, a red rash developed on my back, starting in my lower back, curving back and forth across my spine twice before it veered off to my left shoulder. It disappeared after about a week. Dr. Sannella and I thought it might be a stigmata representing the spiral path of the Kundalini up the spine. I also began to hear high-pitched sounds during meditation, which I later learned are called nada. These sounds represent the opening of higher centers.

A few weeks after the first intense session, I took another meditation retreat with Muktananda, feeling it would enhance the energy of the newly awakened Kundalini. During the retreat, Muktananda again directly channeled his activating Kundalini energy into me. The result of this was an even more intense movement of the Kundalini energy in my body and up the spine. Hot-cold shooting pains occurred in my upper back and neck, and there were burning pains in the thyroid area and throat region. My head and neck spontaneously went through many different movements. Although this all seemed strange, throughout it all I experienced a background of deep peace and a feeling of love. As the retreat proceeded, I began to see colors and flashes of light around people, especially Muktananda. My brow chakra began to spin and pulsate. So many things seemed to be happening, that it all became rather humorous. In the final meditation of the retreat, the energy began to move up my spine with great heat and culminated in a great explosion of white light in my head. It seemed I was exploding with energy. With inner vision, I could see my crown chakra as a golden light, sometimes like an inverted saucer of gold and other times like thousands of golden lights. Following this explosion, I moved into an experience of deep inner peace and knowledge. In the brow chakra region, I directly experienced a golden, brilliantly shining two-petaled lotus flower. It gave off a pure and beautiful light. Pure ecstasy and love became my total being. While this was happening, a deep feeling of belonging and total freedom pervaded my awareness. It came with a sense of knowing that whatever the situation in my life, I could merge in this awareness and be forever content. My body pulsed in total ecstasy. I am free! It was at this point I realized that death did not exist...for the Self. The physical body might die, but the Truth, the I Am of my existence, was immortal.

I've included this experiential report to share my feeling for the power and awesomeness of the awakened Kundalini. It has irrevocably altered my life. This awakening was reported in Dr. Sannella's book as a case example. It covers much of what may occur in a Kundalini awakening and also much of what Dr. Sannella and I feel is included in the physio-Kundalini circuit and the Taoist idea of the microcosmic orbit. For me, it represented only the first step of the unfolding. A little later in this initial unfolding, some of the phenomena associated with the activated Kundalini appeared to move over the top of the head and down to the stomach area. This fits more closely to the circuit described in the physio-Kundalini model. My feeling, however, is that this probably represents the activation of the central meridian circuit. It seemed quite secondary compared to the focus of energy toward the crown chakra.

Feeding the Kundalini,
A Central Theme of Spiritual Nutrition

Because this awakening was so profound for me, it has been a powerful motivation for discovering all means possible for increasing the flow of spiritualizing energy in my body. The second meditation retreat strongly reinforced for me how the transforming power of Kundalini was intensified by cultivating the optimum situation for increasing the spiritualizing energy available to the body-mind-spirit complex. It has supplied the basic theme of nutrition for spiritual life: **How do we eat in a way that will stimulate the awakening of, nurture, and intensify the spiritualizing energy flow of the Kundalini ?**

This awakened Kundalini literally transforms the body and makes it able to withstand and conduct the more intense and subtler energies involved in spiritual practice. Muktananda points out that it is only after the body has been purified that the Kundalini spiritualizing energy can act with full force. He says that "the basis of all disease and pain is the impurities which block the flow of prana in the nadis. These blockages are caused by imbalances and disorders in the three bodily humors...due to undisciplined habits of eating and immoderate living."[13] The main point of quoting this yogic and Ayurvedic medical system language is not to describe the cause of all disease, but to make an important connection between nutrition for spiritual life and the unfolding, purifying, and transforming action of Kundalini. With an appropriate diet, the transforming and purifying action of the Kundalini takes place faster and more easily. In the following chapters this will be discussed in more detail.

When the subtle energy channels are cleaned, the mind also becomes purified of negative thought patterns. Then, a subtle process of transformation of consciousness occurs. The first stage of purification seems to correlate most closely with Dr. Sannella's physio-Kundalini process. In my observation of hundreds of people, after the Kundalini is awakened it usually takes from one to two years for this physio-Kundalini process to unfold. This applies to an aspirant who follows a regular spiritual discipline of meditation, devotion to God, keeping good company, living a balanced and harmonious life, and of course, following a diet supportive of the Kundalini. The second stage of permanently transforming consciousness and reaching the highest awareness seems to require not only the grace of having the Kundalini awakened but a more heroic and dedicated effort. This is why Dr. Sannella reports that so many people are able to experience the physio-Kundalini cycle and yet none were reported to have completed the full classical cycle.

During the process of the full Kundalini spiritual transformation of consciousness, the Kundalini works to purify and awaken each chakra so that our mind merges with the highest awareness. The Kundalini energy continues to work as a spiritualizing force in the physical anatomy and in all the subtle anatomies, until it merges with the consciousness of the aspirant in the Divine oneness and awareness of the crown chakra. At this grand time, the spiritualizing process of the Kundalini is completed. One of the main purposes of nutrition for spiritual life is to eat in a way that will enhance this Kundalini unfolding.

Summary Chapter 7

1. The inner force that takes us to the ecstasy, love, and cosmic awareness inherent in the transpersonal awakening is called the Kundalini. The same force is described in some of the different cultures and spiritual paths of the world. It is the most important subtle energy system in terms of the spiritual evolution of the human species.

2. The awakening of the Kundalini is considered by many to be a necessary step toward reaching higher levels of spiritual evolution.

3. Once the Kundalini is awakened, it moves through the subtle nervous system, or nadis, removing all blocks. When the nadis are purified, the Kundalini spiritualizing energy can act with full force.

4. With proper nutrition, the transforming and purifying action of the Kundalini occurs more easily.

5. Appropriate nutrition for spiritual life enhances the body's capacity to withstand and conduct the fuller and more intense spiritualizing force of the Kundalini.

6. Unimpeded Kundalini moves through the physical and subtle bodies, spiritualizing the consciousness of the aspirant until the Kundalini and the aspirant merge in divine oneness in the crown chakra.

7. A major purpose of nutrition for spiritual life is to eat in a way that enhances the spiritualizing force of the Kundalini.

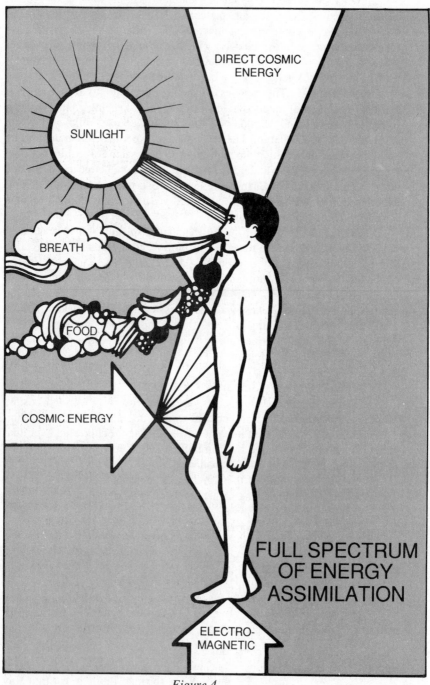

Figure 4

8

Nutrients: The Many and the One

A New Definition of the Word Nutrient

"In the beginning was the word, and the word was with God, and the word was God." (John 1:1) This familiar quotation from the Gospel of John is a key to comprehending nutrition for spiritual life. One of its meanings is that all comes from God and is nourished by the God, or cosmic, force. This is the ultimate source of all nutrition. This cosmic force, or prana, in various levels of density, is the basic nutrient for our bodies and in this context all levels of energy available to us are considered nutrients. This includes sunlight and all kingdoms - mineral, vegetable, and animal. Once we understand that various densities of prana are the essential nutrients to all life function, we are able to expand our definitions of nutrition and assimilation. It allows us now to appreciate a paradigm of nutrition which sees material food as just one level of energy density in the context of a larger spectrum of nutrients important for aiding our spiritual development. It is through this knowledge that we can now understand Sri Nisargatta's teaching that consciousness is the essence of food that has been digested. In the Judeo-Christian heritage there are several indications of some who were able to live on the less dense energies. In *The Forgotten Books of Eden,* in the section on the "Secrets of Enoch," Enoch, after returning from his visit to heaven, is quoted as saying, "Hear, child, from the time when the Lord anointed me with the ointment of his glory, there has been no food in me, and my soul remembers not earthly enjoyment, neither do I want anything earthly."[1] In Exodus 35:27, it is said of Moses, "And he was there with the Lord forty days and forty nights; he did neither eat bread, nor drink water." Jesus, in John 4:31, when his disciples said "Rabbi eat," said to them, "I have food to eat which you do not know...My food is do the will of him who sent me...." Recent documented cases of inedia include several examples of people who, aside from water, were able to maintain their bodies on the less dense, nonmaterial energies alone.

A foundation of the wholistic paradigm is: **nutrition is what we absorb into our overall body-mind-spirit from the different density levels that have precipitated from the cosmic force.** It is this principle which allows us to explain how the system is not completely subject to both the law of conservation of mass and energy and the second law of thermodynamics, or entropy. These two pillars of the old paradigm apply primarily for a system of energy absorption based on the assimilation of solid food as the only source of nutrition. In Kervan's work on biological transmutation we found that these laws do not hold. This does not mean that we should discard the materialistic-mechanistic paradigm, because it explains many things on the strictly material level. Rather, it should be included as a limited part of our wholistic paradigm.

The Nutrient of Pure Cosmic Energy

There are many major avenues through which different levels of energy are assimilated into the system. At the top of the head is the crown chakra. It is the only place in the whole system which can directly take in pure, unprecipitated cosmic energy. Initially this point of assimilation plays only a small role in the total energizing of the body, but at more progressed levels of the spiritualizing process it becomes an increasingly important source of energy. After the merging of the Kundalini in the crown chakra, it reaches its maximum importance. Muktananda refers to this as sushumna breathing, saying this is where he did his "real breathing" from. This pure prana moves down through the crown chakra, initially energizing the brain, the central nervous system, and the pineal and pituitary glands. It is interesting to note that researchers have found that sunlight penetrates the skulls of chickens and directly stimulates their pineal glands. Dr. Richard Wurtman in a *Scientific American* article on the "Effects of Light on the Human Body" states that light is able to penetrate inside the brain of living sheep.[2] If sunlight can do this, is feasible that the purer cosmic prana can also penetrate and influence our core brain structures. From there it moves down the spinal cord and sushumna. It has both a direct spiritualizing effect on the body-mind-spirit complex and an energizing effect on the chakras and their associated nerve plexus, endocrine glands, and organs. This downward spiritualizing energy is called spiritual Kundalini. As the system becomes a clear conductor of this energy, it is better able to energize the system and gain the potential to awaken the Kundalini stored in an inactive state at the base of the spine.

Stepped-Down Cosmic Energy as a Nutrient

The other portals of entry are avenues for stepped-down cosmic energy. This energy is the primary life force energy for activating and regulating the life functions of the body. One important way this life force enters the system is through the chakra systems after it is stepped down through the seven subtle bodies. The more synchronized these subtle bodies are, the more easily the cosmic force can pass through the subtle bodies and energize the system. The larger mind, or total ego, is the sum of the function of the seven subtle bodies. When it becomes harmonious, as during meditation, more cosmic energy is assimilated into the system. In this indirect way, we can say that meditation is the key digestive process through which the life force is taken into the system.

Our Delicious Sunlight

Another important source of the life force is sunlight. Light is the least dense form of prana in our universe. It carries the full spectrum of rainbow stimulation to our system as it filters through the subtle bodies and is taken in by nervous system receptors in the eyes and the skin. The nerve receptors in the eye translate this full-spectrum information into optic nerve impulses which conduct it to the various brain centers: pineal, pituitary, and the rest of the endocrine system. Through these systems it indirectly energizes and activates our whole organism and regulates body cycles and rhythms. It was once generally held that humans are immune from the cyclic hormonal regulating effects of light as seen in lower animals, in which the visible spectrum regulates the reproductive cycle and other daily and seasonal rhythms. Research by Dr. Alfred Lewy, a psychiatrist at the National Institute of Mental Health has disproved this assumption. He has shown that exposure to a bright light can specifically turn off the production of melanin in humans.[3] He and others have done exciting research to show that light therapy is a specific treatment of choice for Seasonally Affective Disorder (SAD).[4] People with SAD become depressed as the days get shorter. They become irritable, sleepy, anxious, socially withdrawn, and disinterested in work and play. Exposing them to ultrabright lights three hours in the morning and evening, or five hours in the evening, alleviated their symptoms in two to four days. Preliminary studies have suggested that when workers do not receive enough light or the right kind of light, they develop such problems as increased fatigue, decreased performance, decreased immune defenses, and reduced physical fitness. From the health point of view, Dr. Blackwell at Ohio State University found that worker productivity increased ll.7 percent when employees worked under full spectrum (similar to sunlight) bright lights.[5] Dr. Hollwich of the University-Augklinik in Munster Germany found that 50 people blinded with cataracts experienced a reduction in amplitude of the adrenal and blood cell rhythms and in the basic regulatory system activity involving the hypothalamus, pituitary, and adrenal cortex.[6] When their cataracts were removed these abnormalities disappeared. Other researchers, such as Dr. Alain Reinberg in Paris, have discovered some strong indications that the menstrual cycle in women is also influenced by light.[7]

Clinicians and researchers such as Dr. John Downing (M.S. in vision psychology, Ph.D. vision science, and Ph.D. in optometry, are also discovering that light is broken down into different bands of the spectrum, each with a different healing effect. Dr. Downing, in a personal communication, has shared that the spectrum follows the basic chakra color spectral breakdown and that each of these colors activates different parts of the body.[8] He finds the most effective clinical application of this is accomplished by beaming one of several specific bands in the red spectrum through the eye to activate and heal different aspects of the sympathetic nervous system. For the parasympathetic nervous system, he has found that different bands in the blue color spectrum are healing. The specific band in either spectrum varies with each individual, because the sunlight-to-eye-to-optic nerve-to-brain-to-endocrine system represents a chain of colored light activation which parallels the specific color association with each chakra and its associated system. Illustrative of this color-to-organ and chakra association is a *Scientific American* article by the light research pioneer, Dr. Richard Wurtman.[9] He outlines the specific pathway for light as it affects the ovarian function in rats. Sunlight transmission moves through the optic nerve; part of it goes to the vision centers in the cortex, and part goes to the hypothalamus and superchiasmic nucleus, which is the body's internal clock. From there it travels to the spinal cord and up the superior cervical ganglion to the pineal, which sends hormonal messages to the hypothalamus, which then releases a hormonal message to the pituitary. Finally, the pituitary gland releases a luteinizing hormone to stimulate the ovaries. (See Figure 5 on p. 65.) Researchers have found that light in the orange-red wavelength specifically stimulates this ovarian cycle in rats. It is interesting to note that the sexual function is associated with the second chakra, whose primary color is orange.

Skin receptors take light in directly. Melanin in the skin, like the rods and cones of the eye, is able to absorb the radiant energy of sunlight and to convert it to sound or vibrational energy and back again.[10] This energy can be transmitted as resonant energy or transformed into enough heat energy to affect metabolic processes, and as we well know, sunburn. Sunlight energy is necessary for the production of vitamin D, and it also regulates the production of melantonin, a neural hormone produced in the pineal. Research suggests that melantonin induces sleep, inhibits ovulation, and modifies the secretion of other hormones.[11] Frank Barr, M.D., has hypothesized that melanin is centrally involved in the control of almost all physiological and psychological activity.[12] Needless to say, the nutrient of sunlight directly affects us in many important energizing ways. It is possible that as our diet becomes more refined, sunlight subtly becomes an even more important source of direct life force. Currently it is estimated that humans need between 30 to 60 minutes of midday sun to maintain good health. Since a major entry point of sun energy into our system is through the eyes, it is best not to wear sunglasses during this time. Although the eyes are the major entry point, the more we get a complete sunbath on our skin the more sun energy is absorbed. It is even possible that the red blood cell hemoglobin in our capillaries at the surface of the skin absorb sunlight directly, just as the chlorophyl in a plant does, and that these energized hemoglobin biomolecular structures could be directly taking this sunlight energy to the rest of our system.

"Vitamin O"

Another major source of nutrient energy is oxygen. In some modern yoga teaching, it is said that approximately 90 percent of the energy utilized by the body is from oxygen taken in by the lung and skin system. In the absence of oxygen, our physical bodies can only survive a few minutes.

62

We can live without water for a few weeks and go without food for months. "Vitamin O" is our most important nutrient. This form of energy intake is the most commonly used meaning for the word prana. It is the life force that many experience when they walk into a forest and smile as they inhale the vibrant air. In forests and unpolluted bodies of water the energetic field of the air has been enhanced. The oxygen molecule has been resonantly excited. When we take it into our lungs, its energy is transferred to our bodies. If the air has been circulated through air-conditioning or airducts, out of contact with the sunlight, polluted, or irradiated, it loses energy and less of this resonant life force is available to us. This oxygen energy comes into the lungs which surround the heart chakra and acts as a balancing point between the upper and lower chakras. Yogis and health practitioners in the West have observed that when the breath is steady, the mind becomes calm. This observation suggests an important link between the breath and the mind. Eighty percent of the oxygen we take in goes to the brain. This high degree of oxygen to the brain adds to the downward flow of the Kundalini energy and may partially explain how different pranayama exercises are used to excite the Kundalini.

Oxygen is also taken into our systems directly from our food. Steven Levin, Ph.D., has recently developed a hypothesis relating oxygen deficiency in the tissues (anoxia) to chronic disease, and a high rate of oxygen intake, relative to food intake, to good health. [13] In a simple analogy to a battery, he points out that oxygen is the positive terminal and that the foods we eat are a source of vibrant negatively charged electrons. The electrons move from the negative pole, or food, in a living current of energy to the positive oxygen pole. Trace minerals, iron, manganese, zinc, and other electron carriers, are essential for the conduction of this bioelectricity through the cytochrome oxidase system and through our antioxidant system. Vitamins A, C, E, selenium, and various antioxidant enzymes such as super oxide dismutase and glutathione peroxidase serve to protect this electron energy flow from being disrupted by free radicals which steal electrons from the system. These free radicals come from external pollution and from internal pollution, a result of a poor diet consisting of such things as irradiation-caused radiolytic foods. During this process of electron movement and transfer to the oxygen pole, metabolic energy is released helping to fuel our normal metabolic processes. Optimal quantities of oxygen are required to draw this living current. On the other hand, it is important that we eat fresh natural foods that are vibrant with high electron energy. These foods are those which still retain the high-energy carbon-hydrogen bonds that have incorporated activated electrons in their bonding as a result of electron activation from photosynthesis. It is this sunlight energy stored as activated electron energy in the carbon-hydrogen bonding that we find in organic, whole, vegetarian foods. These foods make the most powerful current with the oxygen pole. This last statement implies the superiority of plant food over animal food. It is highly possible that the direct photosynthesis energy of the carbon-hydrogen bond is either altered or lost for humans when it is metabolized first by the animal, and that the animal gets all the benefit of the direct sunlight plant energy. With the current state of our ability to measure heat release from carbon hydrogen bonds of plant and animal tissues, we may not find any perceptible difference in energy release on a material level. But subjectively the difference is easier to perceive.

If there is a decrease in oxygen in the system, there is less power to pull electrons from the oxygen pole of our bioelectric current, and the bioelectric current diminishes in power. Therefore, our task is to maintain a high oxygen level in our tissues. In our polluted and stressful environment, this is not easy. We are starving for oxygen in our office buildings as we improve insulation to save fuel energy costs. The rapid planetary deforestation is decreasing the local supply of oxygen; air pollution combines with and ties up oxygen in the air; and the combustion of our automobiles and industries take it from the local ground level atmosphere. Stress causes oxygen deficiency within the organism. For example, stress from toxic environmental substances in our air, water, and food uses oxygen for detoxification. Chemical pollutants, chlorine in water, and fumes from combustion of petrochemicals from our cars all require that we use our body supply of oxygen to protect us. Emotional stress produces excessive adrenalin and related adrenal hormones which require oxygen for their metabolism. Physical trauma reduces circulation, and therefore the amount of oxygen to the cells is reduced. Bacterial, fungal, and viral infections require our body immune defense cells, the phagocytes, to produce controlled free radical forms of oxygen to combat them. This cell-mediated activity is the main defense against many pathogens, including the yeast candida albicans.[14] Our activated immune phagocyte cells increase their oxygen utilization by as much as 50 times when they are destroying foreign invaders to our system.[15] This, of course, draws oxygen away from its main function, which is the oxidizing of our foods to produce metabolic energy.

Poor diet is another form of oxygen stress. Foods that are excessively acidic such as meat, coffee, soft drinks, carbonated drinks, and alcohol create acidity in the system. This acidity is an excess of hydrogen ions (H^+) in the system, which deplete oxygen by combining with it to create water. In doing this, they short circuit the system so that the full energy-producing movement of electrons going to the oxygen pole is reduced. When less oxygen is available for metabolism, then there is a build-up of lactic acid, and our cellular environment becomes progressively acidic, resulting in the destruction of cellular function. According to Dr. Levine, hypoxia, or lack of oxygen in the tissues, is a fundamental cause of all chronic degenerative diseases.[16] Low tissue oxygen has been associated with candida albicans infections and the degenerative disease of cancer.[17]

Eating foods high in oxygen content seems to be associated with good health. Water is 85 percent oxygen, so we benefit by drinking water and eating foods with a high water content, such as fruits which can be up

64

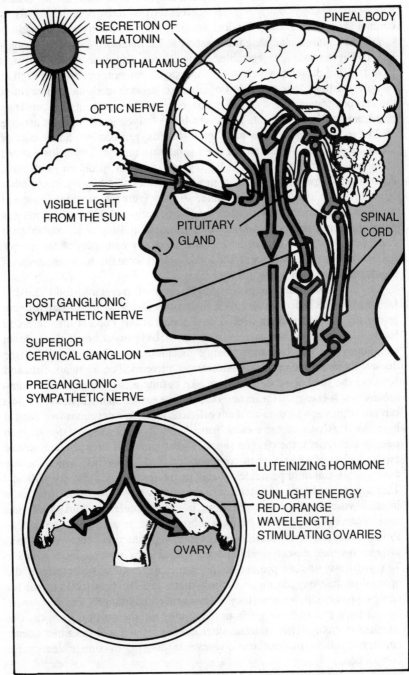

SECRETION OF MELATONIN

HYPOTHALAMUS

OPTIC NERVE

PINEAL BODY

VISIBLE LIGHT FROM THE SUN

PITUITARY GLAND

SPINAL CORD

POST GANGLIONIC SYMPATHETIC NERVE

SUPERIOR CERVICAL GANGLION

PREGANGLIONIC SYMPATHETIC NERVE

LUTEINIZING HORMONE

SUNLIGHT ENERGY RED-ORANGE WAVELENGTH STIMULATING OVARIES

OVARY

Figure 5

to 90 percent water. The next highest oxygen foods are carbohydrates, which are slightly more than 50 percent oxygen by weight. This is computed by using the chemical formula for a carbohydrate, which is CH_2O. The molecular weight of carbon is 12, hydrogen is 1, and oxygen is 16. These foods are vegetables, grains, seeds, and nuts. Seeds and nuts have fats and proteins which lower the oxygen content, but are still high in complex carbohydrate content. For example, sesame seeds have three times the carbohydrate content of red cabbage, mung bean sprouts, green snap beans, and many other fruits and vegetables.[18] Proteins contain an average of 25 percent oxygen. Fats have the lowest oxygen content, an average of about 12 percent. Although we need some unsaturated fatty acids for cell membrane formation, they steal oxygen. Another problem with fats, especially animal fats, is that most pesticides, herbicides, and other environmental toxins are fat soluble, so they increase our environmental toxin load and divert body oxygen for detoxification. For these reasons it is better to consume foods which contain essential fatty acids rather than nonessential fats. Avocados and sesame seeds are examples of these. We need between 10-15 percent of foods which contain high amounts of unsaturated free fatty acids.

It is important to get the right ratio of oxygen-to-food density. Dense foods are those which have a high molecular weight and therefore are physically heavy for their size. Dense foods in this context also refers to foods, such as fats, which require a lot of oxygen to break them down completely for our oxidative energy metabolism. Fatty foods are the densest by these two criteria. Concentrated proteins such as meats, fish, and fowl are the next densest. They are like putting a big log in the fire; they require much energy to ignite and burn. If we eat too many dense foods, we run out of oxygen to oxidize them efficiently and we get more free radical byproducts as part of the metabolism.[19] With an excessive fat-to-oxygen ratio in the system, the oxygen supply is disrupted and diverted and we see the formation of toxic oxygen compounds called "oxitoxins" which include free radicals and lipid peroxides. Lipid peroxides are incipient free radicals. This appears to be the mechanism that explains how a high-fat diet results in cardiovascular disorders. Proteins, in excess, represent "dirty fuel" and require excess oxygen to help us eliminate their nitrogen byproducts. Proteins are not really designed for energy production, but we do need proteins for their essential amino acids. Again, we have to find a balance. Ten to fifteen percent protein in the diet may be quite sufficient for the optimal protein-oxygen mix. Carbohydrates are the best foods to eat for energy production because they burn evenly and require less oxygen to extract the metabolic energy from them; they are the small logs in the fire which burn easily. This awareness has already seeped into the athletic area; athletes regularly practice carbohydrate loading to maximize energy for competition.

Recent work in Japan by Kazuhiko Asai, Ph.D., has found that an unusual mineral oxide called "organic germanium" greatly increases the supply of oxygen to the system and catalyzes many of the detoxification functions of oxygen.[20] Asai has found germanium to be of much help in treating cancer, hypertension, endocrine insufficiency, asthma, and Raynaud's disease.[21] A group of physicians is working with Dr. Levine, who discovered Dr. Asai's work and is now importing organic germanium for use in a complex called pro-oxygen. This pro-oxygen has been found to help in situations such as jet-lag and airplane travel, in which there is limited oxygen available in the airplanes and polluted airports.

Other ways to increase the oxygen in our systems include placing more green plants in our workplaces and homes and doing moderate aerobic exercise five times per week. This can be anything from fast walking to aerobic classes for approximately 20 minutes per session. Use antioxidant supplements or eat foods high in both the antioxidant vitamins A, C, and E and in key antioxidant enzyme cofactors such as zinc and selenium. Such foods include blue-green algae, wheatgrass, seeds, nuts, and complex carbohydrates.

Breathing Exercises

One of the most important ways to increase oxygen in the system is through breathing exercises. Over thousands of years, yogis have developed breathing exercises (pranayama) to energize the system, to calm the mind for meditation, and to activate the Kundalini energy directly. This subject is too vast for this book, but there are some simple breathing exercises which will greatly enhance our "Vitamin O" intake. The reason for these exercises is to help us become aware of how to take a full breath and how to get a full oxygen meal. We breathe all day to stay alive, but most people are using only about ten percent of their breath capacity. When maybe 90 percent of metabolic energy comes from breathing, it merits at least some of the attention we pay to eating our physical food.

Exercise 1 - The Tiger Breath

1. Position yourself on hands and knees.
2. With an incoming breath, sway your back by moving your chest and abdomen toward the floor. Tilt your head back and lift your face at least 30 percent above the horizontal plane. Extend as far back as you can comfortably.
3. On exhalation, slowly breath out through your nose while arching your back and bringing your chin down so it touches or comes close to the V-notch in your collar bone.
4. Move into the swayback position on the next incoming breath.
5. Do not hold your breath after inhaling or exhaling. Keep the cycle moving. Inhalation and exhalation should be the same slow and comfortable duration of time.
6. A good duration for the exercise is three minutes.

Exercise 2 - AUM Breath: Deep Breathing in All Segments of the Lungs

1. Place your hands on your chest with little fingers on the lower edges of your rib cage. Inhale into the area that is covered by your hands. This fills the lower lobes. Sometimes it is thought that abdominal breathing, in which we move the diaphragm in and out, is filling the lower lungs. This is not the case. The lower lobes extend to the bottom of the rib cage and not into the abdominal cavity. To fill the lower lobes it is best to focus on the lower rib cage.

2. Breathe in with the sound of an AAH in your mind and exhale with the audible sound of AAH.

3. Repeat this three times.

4. Place your hands over your breast area and inhale. As you inhale, feel the resonance in your lungs as the middle lobes fill.

5. Inhale to the sound of OOO in your mind and exhale with the audible sound of OOO.

6. Repeat three times.

7. Place the thumb part of your hand over your collar bone and inhale into the area under your hands, filling the upper lobes.

8. Inhale to the sound of MMM in your mind and exhale with the audible sound of MMM...

9. Repeat this three times.

10. In all three of these inhalations, try to expand your lungs as far as possible.

11. After you have practiced each breath for three rounds each, do three cycles of the breaths in sequence to make a complete AUM sound.

12. As we work with our breath, certain emotions may come up. In some of the Ayurvedic medical teachings anger, hate, and envy are said to be held in the lower lobes. The middle lobes are said to store the emotions of attachment and greed. Fear, sadness, and grief are said to be stored in the upper lobes.

Exercise 3 - A Full Breath Rhythmical Cycle

This is the application of the AUM breath to a breathing cycle. It can be done for 6 to 20 minutes; a good average is 15 minutes. It provides a complete oxygen meal. Because many people become energized with it, the best time to do it is in the morning or after returning home from work. If you do it before going to bed, you may become too energized to fall asleep immediately. It is also good for reoxygenating after prolonged time in low oxygen atmospheres such as air travel.

1. Sit comfortably in an upright position with your spine straight.

2. Begin the AUM breath with two counts of time in each lobe position. At the end of the inhalation, hold your breath for three counts and exhale over six counts. As with the inhalation, there should be two counts for each section of the lung.

3. At the end of the exhalation, hold for three counts and begin again.

4. The cycle is three counts inhalation, hold for three, and then six counts of exhalation, hold for three counts and begin the cycle again. Once the timing becomes natural, you don't have to count.
5. In this exercise, do not force your breath. It is better to inhale and exhale in a relaxed way.
6. If the air is not too polluted, this exercise is best done outdoors.
7. With the incoming breath, think about taking in positive energy; with the exhalation, think about discharging negative energy or negative thoughts from your system.

Two Special Energy Portals

The thymus and the spleen represent a special type of energy receptor system. They take in a prana, which is stepped down through the subtle bodies but remains full spectrum, separate it into all the specific colors, and send it individually to each chakra. Leadbeater describes this process in detail in his book on chakras.[22] This is one reason the spleen chakra, rather than the sexual chakra, is described as a major chakra in his system. On an intuitive level, I feel that the spleen chakra becomes secondary to the thymus in this function as a person develops spiritually. This may be why yogis who are already developed to a certain extent haven't recognized the spleen as a major chakra. The reason either organ is able to take in full spectrum cosmic energy may be because the interface between the vortexes of the heart and solar plexus chakras creates open spaces in the subtle body system, allowing cosmic energy to be stepped down while remaining in its full spectrum state.

Sexual Energy

One of the most important energies to be considered is sexual. It is both an internal and an external energy. As a subject, it is too vast to ignore or explore in depth in this book. But there are some clarifying points needed for a balanced perspective. As an internal energy, it is stored in its raw physical form in the sperm and egg. The Tao calls its energy form "ching." Sexual energy is a special form of what the Taoist call "chi" or prana. It is powerful enough to recreate a total human organism. It is estimated in a lifetime of the healthy male enough semen is produced to generate a trillion human lives.[23] When this energy is activated, all the senses are enhanced and men and women feel sexual energy as power or passion. The sperm and egg cells begin to vibrate and create an increased field of sexual magnetic energy. Most of us have experienced this. In the springtime, when mother nature is sending off the energy of creation, these sexual cells and sexual energy resonate with her and increase their energy fields.

When we are in good health, sexual energy is always regenerating for us to use. In Taoist teachings, sexual energy and cell production consume 25 to 40 percent of the raw energy taken in through food, sun, earth, air, and other subtle systems. Every organ and gland contributes nutrients and energy from their SOEFs to produce the sexual seed. In men particularly, excessive loss of semen depletes the total body system of its most precious nutrients. Although men are usually the focus of this concern, in my clinical practice, I have found a close correlation between the health of the women I see and their level of sexual energy. A physically depleted female will often complain of low sexual energy.

Sexual relations between two people who are in love, especially if there is not excessive loss of semen, is a powerful way to replenish and balance the sexual energy. There are a variety of books on this subject. *Taoist Secrets of Love* by Mantak Chia is particularly clear on this subject. It is important to increase our ching, or sexual energy, because it can be transformed into creative and spiritual energy. In our Freudian-Reichian culture, the awareness of transformation of sexual into creative, work, and even spiritual energy has also been established. The Taoists teach that sperm energy is subtly mixed with the prana or chi of the vital organs and refined into spiritual energy. Sexual energy is considered an intermediary link between the raw biological energies and our spiritual energy. This energy is always being transformed automatically and voluntarily into creative and spiritual energy. Yogis also teach that sexual continence aids the evolutionary power of the Kundalini. It has been my experience that there are certain times in the unfolding of Kundalini in which this is more important than others. The process of the Kundalini unfolding usually lets people know automatically when it is the correct time to be celibate. Self-imposed sexual repression as practiced by such diverse groups as Christian and Hindu monks, yoga renunciants, and striving, excessively disciplined couples on the spiritual path may actually block spiritual unfolding physically, emotionally, psychically, and mentally. In many couples who have imposed this discipline upon themselves as an external practice, it often causes a certain amount of stress and relationship imbalance which wastes more energy than it might gain. In the monks, priests, and renunciants the sexual repression often causes personality imbalances and hypocritical sexual activity.

There is a way to maintain the natural flow of love energy on the spiritual, mental, emotional, and physical levels without causing the problems of sexual repression and sexual imbalance. The way is to let go of our false concepts of the way things should or should not be including the issue of celibacy. A recent survey by Jack Kornfiled found that of 54 teachers of different traditions, 39 had sexual relationships as part of their lives.[24] The great modern day saint, Sri Ramana Maharishi, pointed out to his disciples that although celibacy may be an aid, the real issue is where the mind is focused. He taught that the real celibacy is living in God; it is living in the awareness of the bliss of the Self. The main issue is where the mind is focused. He joked that a monk living in the forest thinking about being married is not different from a married person idealizing about being a celibate monk.[25] So the question of whether the concept of celibacy is right or wrong is not the issue. Whichever way which best helps to keep ones mind on the transcendental Self is the issue. Celibacy for people who are very undisciplined in their sexual lives can be a practice that will help them gain some control in their spiritual and personal life. There may be times in the unfolding of the Kundalini energy that it is best to be celibate temporarily. This then is not so much as a conceptual practice, but an attunement to ones own energy flow and needs.

The way for a married person is moderation. Overindulgence in sexual life can deplete or imbalance our body energies. The other key word is balance. There are some people who, by their constitutional needs, are thrown out of balance by too limited sexual activity. For some couples, a frequent exchange of sexual energies may prove to be both balancing for each individual and for the all levels of their relationship. The medieval alchemists and Kabbalistic traditions emphasized the importance of marriage, because the sexual union creates a full cosmic cycle which helps to maintain the energetic and spiritual balance of the aspirants. The balanced exchange of sexual energy between two equally evolved spiritual partners can be a powerful way to co-commune with God. Both male and female will be energized by such a divine exchange. Certain Taoist or Tantric approaches that allow for the exchange of sexual energy and love between two people and yet which conserve the semen may be the middle path that is needed for balance. In the Taoist teaching, these practices are best done as an expression of love between two people in a long-term love relationship rather than as a sexual technique to increase spiritual energy.

A major difference between sexual energy and raw energy such as food and sunlight is that sexual energy is created and stored within our own bodies. We can draw on it at any time. Sexual energy is a more refined energy because it is made within our system so it is easier to absorb and utilize than our raw energy sources, which first must be assimilated into our energetic systems. In the transmutation and refinement of sexual energy into spiritual energy, the path seems to be from the sperm and egg energy to the meridian energy, which brings it to the chakras. These refine it and transfer it to the Kundalini energy moving in the sushumna.

Energy from the Earth's Geomagnetic Fields
The electromagnetic field energy of the earth is another source of energy input into our energetic system. It is usually absorbed through the feet. The Taoists describe a point on the sole near the upper center of the foot, called Yung-Chuany, through which it is specifically drawn up. Lying on the ground can also be a way of recharging. In the Essene and Taoist traditions, the earthly forces are thought of as rebalancing forces to the heavenly forces. It represents the roots of the tree of life penetrating into the earth, or yin, forces with its branches extending to the heavenly, or yang, forces. The earth connection has an important grounding effect. With people whose Kundalini forces seem too strong, I will often recommend working in the garden. When meditating, however, it is best to have an insulator such as a wool meditation pad between ourselves and the

earth, or the energy generated in meditation will be drawn off into the earth. Recently, scientists have observed an earth electromagnetic pulsation called the Schuman resonance. It pulses at 7.83 Hertz per second. NASA discovered that by installing electromagnetic pulsing devices which recreate this Schuman resonance in space ships, the astronauts had less illness. Some people feel that one of the causes of jet lag is that we fly too quickly through the earth's magnetic field. Research using Schuman resonance pulsing devices to create a constant magnetic pulse in air travel has found that they decrease the incidence of jet lag. I try to spend a certain amount of daily time exercising barefoot on the grass. It is a force of nature about which we would benefit by more knowledge. For example, recent Russian work on geomagnetic energies has shown that the growth of children varies with the geomagnetic area in which they live.[26] It is possible that geomagnetic forces have more effect on our energies than we can imagine.

The Densest and Tastiest Nutrient

Although our physical food is the densest and perhaps supplies only ten percent of our energy needs, it occupies much of our interest. Before reading this book, the reader may have thought it was the only nutrient. We have been playing with our concepts of food for thousands of years. In the next round of chapters, our perspective will be how to develop our own individualized diets to support our spiritual lives.

Summary Chapter 8

1. The ultimate nutrient is the God force or cosmic energy.
2. A foundation of the wholistic paradigm is that a nutrient is what we absorb into our overall body-mind-spirit from the different density levels of energy that have precipitated from the pure cosmic energy.
3. The pure cosmic energy is a primary nutrient that we all take into our system through the crown chakra. As our bodies are transformed spiritually, we become open to more of this pure energy.
4. Our system regularly steps down this pure cosmic energy into seven spectrums of energy through the seven subtle bodies. In this way the proper frequency of energy is directed to each of the seven chakras, which are the main intake portals for and are energized by condensed cosmic energy.
5. Our delicious sunlight is the least dense form of cosmic energy in our material universe. It is absorbed primarily through the eyes and the skin.
6. "Vitamin O" is necessary for the basic support of our physical bodies.
7. Two special energy portals are the spleen and thymus.
8. Sexual energy is absorbed in the loving exchange between two people.
9. Geomagnetic forces comprise a poorly understood source of energy which primarily enters through our feet or any other direct contact with the earth. They help us keep grounded. The density variations of the earth's geomagnetic fields also have some unknown effects on us.
10. The tastiest and densest form of energy that we absorb is in our food. This is what we commonly referred to as nutrition before reading this book.

9

The Rainbow Diet

General Concept of the Rainbow Diet

Now we get to the tastiest energy density... food. The vibrations of food are first absorbed visually. The color and arrangement of food creates a certain mental and physiological readiness. For example, depending on what foods are displayed, the content and concentration of our saliva changes. This is further augmented by our conscious responses to the aroma and taste of the food. Depending on what qualities of food we need, we become consciously and unconsciously drawn to the tastes, smells, and colors of the different foods. It is to the meaning of the colors of these foods that the Rainbow Diet awareness primarily addresses itself.

The awareness of the Rainbow Diet starts with acceptance that all comes from God and is nourished by the God Force. This force has been described as OM, universal prana, universal consciousness, cosmic force, and virtual energy state. It is the primordial vibration from which all has been created. Everything, including our food, has a natural system of harmonics in relationship to this primordial vibration. In the Rainbow Diet system of harmonics, all foods have a vibrational alignment to the seven main chakras and their colors, and these colors reflect the spectrum of the rainbow.

Four Main Principles of The Rainbow Diet

1. Each food according to its outer color, which is its reflecting surface, can be related to the specific color and energy of a particular chakra.
2. Differently colored foods are specific for energizing, balancing, and healing their specific color-related chakra.
3. Each colored food energizes, cleanses, builds, heals, and rebalances the glands, organs, and nerve centers associated with its color-related chakra.
4. The purpose of the Rainbow Diet is to help balance, on a regular daily cycle, each individual chakra, its associated organs, glands, and nerve plexes, and the chakra system as a whole.

If we think of our vegetarian food as condensed colored sunlight, we can begin to get a better feeling for the concept of the Rainbow Diet. It does not apply to flesh foods, which primarily stimulate the first chakra. It also does not apply to the colors of junk, fast, frozen, and irradiated foods. Red candy is not the same as a red apple. Food is the principal interface between us and nature on the physical plane, and the colors of our foods are nature's message or clues about the energy and biomolecular content of the specific colored foods she gives us. Through the new paradigm, we have arrived at the concept that food is energy as well as material form. The color of food is key to the energy pattern of food and how its biomolecular nutrients will be bonded to specific cells and tissues in our bodies. The color of a food is its signature. As we become sensitive to nature's efforts to communicate to us through her beautiful colors, we begin to develop a sensitivity to the particular food colors we are drawn to on a specific day as a key to what food energies and nutrients we need to balance our body. The Rainbow Diet is an acknowledgement of nature's effort to communicate with us. It is also a way to use the meaning of this information in an organized fashion to benefit us regularly through our daily intake of food. I will now discuss in more detail the principles of the Rainbow Diet.

By using the vascular autonomic signal (VAS), a technique for measuring the effect of subtle energy fields on the biological and etheric system of the body, I was able to support my intuitive idea that the rainbow colors of nature's foods related to the harmonics of the rainbow colors of our chakras. The VAS pulse was developed by the father of auricular acupuncture, Paul Nogier, M.D. The VAS is a smooth muscle response of our blood vessels, mediated by the hypothalamic region of the brain. Its function is relatively independent from the voluntary control brain centers and therefore less affected by subjectivity than by the popular body-testing systems such as kinesiology muscle testing. When an energy field from a substance is good for the body, the VAS is positive, and the tonus of the arterial wall is increased. This increase was labeled by Dr. Nogier as the "vascular autonomic signal." Basically, it means there is a change in the VAS arterial pulse when a positive energy field enters the body energy field.

Each food has a specific energy frequency and resonance field, which we have described as the vortex manifestation of its SOEF. The body's energy field and the particular vortex resonance energy fields of each chakra are sensitive to the fields of the living substances put in their proximity. Their responses can be measured instantly by the VAS. Laurence Bagley, M.D., feels it is a simple technique to place a substance such as an herb, food, drug, or cell salt into the body field and observe the VAS response.

By putting foods of various colors over each chakra, I was able to determine which colors were most enhancing for each chakra. What I found was a direct correspondence between the colors of foods and chakras -- red foods for the red or base chakra; orange foods for the sexual or orange-colored chakra, etc. I also observed that each food peaked in the intensity of the VAS response at its specific color-resonant chakra. The food also showed a positive VAS, although less marked, at the chakra above and below its specific resonant-colored chakra. This interesting finding supports my earlier statement that the chakras are linked as a total system. It also suggests that foods of different shades will affect the system slightly differently. Additionally, the spectrum phenomenon is more general rather than limited to the exact frequency of the basic color for each chakra. Because I was already testing with the concepts of the Rainbow Diet in my mind and enough research has been done to suggest that even in double blind studies the minds of the subject and the experimenter can affect the outcome, I can't say that the VAS approach proves the Rainbow Diet concept, but it does give us some support for the intuitive "right feeling" of the Rainbow Diet approach. It does supply the reader with another major tool for understanding the relationship between our foods and our bodies so that we can develop our own individualized diet.

Differently colored foods act specifically to energize and balance their particular color-coded chakras. By eating the Rainbow Diet in a patterned way, as described in the next section, we see a regular harmonic balancing of all the chakras as one system. Color healing of chakras and their related systems is not a new approach. It was used in the Golden Age of Greece, in the healing temples of Light and Color at Heliopolis, in ancient Egypt, and in ancient China and India.[1] In America, Dr. Edwin Babbitt's book on *The Principles of Light and Color* and the more recent classic work by Dr. Ott, *Health and Light*, have laid a general foundation for the principles of color therapy in this country. In Chapter 8, I pointed out that Dr. Wurtman's research in beaming orange into a rabbit's eyes showed stimulation of the rabbit's ovarian function, which is connected to the orange second chakra. For centuries, color treatment has been done through different vehicles of light transport, including water charged with sunlight through a colored filter, direct sunlight or other light source treatment through a colored filter on the body or into the eyes, use of colored metals or gems, and of course, colored foods. Colored foods have been used for healing persons of different maladies. For example, red is used for people with low vitality ,which fits with low energy in the first chakra. Red foods are also used to treat people with anemia or a deficiency in the blood vitality. This too is associated with the first chakra. In the Rainbow Diet the focus is not on color therapy as a treatment for disease, but as a natural way through our daily diets to balance and tonify the body, the individual chakras, and the chakra system as a unit. It is for maintenance of health on all levels.

That each food relates to a specific chakra in terms of energizing, healing, cleansing, building, and rebalancing the glands, organs, and nerve centers associated with that chakra is different from chakra healing with colored lights, which is primarily an energizing and balancing effect. For example, rose hips, which are red and therefore particularly important to the first chakra, are high in vitamin C. Vitamin C is important for building and maintaining the connective tissue we need for locomotion, heart muscle, ligament function, blood vessel integrity, and adrenal function. The adrenals, which energize our fight or flight response, have the highest amount of vitamin C in the body. Our muscle system supplies the locomotion for survival. The first chakra, red in color, is linked to these survival organ and gland systems. Another example is leafy greens, which are coded for the heart chakra. They are high in calcium, magnesium, and potassium, which are very important for heart function.

Application of the Rainbow Diet

As stated in the fourth principle, balance is the key to the Rainbow Diet. The application of the diet is based on the idea that all chakras, even though they have different vibratory rates and different types of awareness, are created equal. All of them must be nourished. **The Rainbow Diet calls for the full spectrum of foods for the full spectrum of the chakras throughout the spectrum of the day.**

The morning starts with the first three chakras: red, orange, and yellow-gold. Midday is the third through the fifth chakras: yellow-gold, green, and blue in color. Evening is the fifth through the seventh chakras: blue, indigo, and violet-purple in color. This sequence aligns with the general pattern for the awakening of the chakras. The daily stimulation and balancing of the chakras by the use of the appropriately colored foods maintains a balance which is important in spiritual life. If we only try to stimulate and charge the "higher" chakras, over a long period of time it is possible to become subtly uncentered or ungrounded.

There are exceptions to this spectral pattern. One is the use of a single color food for limited periods of time to energize a specifically weakened chakra and its associated organs, glands, and nerve centers. There are also times when one wants to activate a specific chakra gently for a short period of time by eating those foods that will stimulate that chakra. A beneficial time to do this might be during a fruit fast.

The Rainbow Diet is not a technique for enlightenment. It is simply a support system to aid in a harmonious and centered spiritual unfolding. It is a whole-person, full-chakra approach to nutrition. It is an organizing principle and a level of food awareness for helping us develop our own individualized diets for spiritual life. The principles of the Rainbow Diet are appropriate for any level of intake of vegetables, fruits, nuts, seeds, grains, eggs, and dairy products. In this diet, white foods, which represent the full rainbow spectrum, can be used with any meal. It includes soy products like tofu and vegetables like cauliflower. Although color coding does not apply for flesh foods, one can be a transitional vegetarian, lacto-ovo-vegetarian (the eggshell color is the code), lacto-vegetarian, vegan, or fruitarian and the diet principles still are very functional.

Look at the basics of the Rainbow Diet and the timing of meals:

Morning

Red, orange, and yellow-golden foods are eaten for supporting the first, second, and third chakras. This includes mostly fruits such as apples, oranges, and bananas. Fruits are good cleansers and aid in any unfinished digestion from the night before. The golden colors also include the golden and brown grains such as wheat, rice, corn, buckwheat, oats, and rye.

The yellow-gold color also includes most nuts and seeds such as sesame, sunflower, pumpkin, and almonds. Once nuts and seeds begin to germinate by soaking and sprouting, they become alkaline in their effect in the body and combine well with fruits. In general, fruits are the primary morning food. Soaked seeds and nuts, whole or ground, combine well with them. These soaked nuts and seeds in the morning are particularly good for people with blood sugar imbalances.

Midday

Yellow-golden, green, and blue foods are eaten for enhancing the third, fourth, and fifth chakras. The predominant color for the midday meal is green. This is the time for eating salads and other vegetable dishes - - sprouts, avocados, lettuce, and dark greens. We could also eat fruit meals of green apples, watermelon, or fruits of other colors of the third through the fifth chakras. Although the main color focus is green, it doesn't mean that minor amounts of other colored foods such as tomatoes can't be included. Carrots, which are in the orange-gold spectrum also fit in quite well.

Evening

Blue, indigo, purple, gold, and white foods enhance the fifth, sixth, and seventh chakras. Gold is included in the evening because purple and gold are complements, and the crown chakra is associated with golden, as well as purple, light. The main evening meal colors are purple, white, and gold. In the context of arising early to meditate, light dinners such as fruit, eaten before sunset, are the most appropriate. A fruit dinner might, for example, include papaya and mangos, which are both color and shape signatures for the pituitary and pineal glands. These two are directly associated with the sixth and seventh chakras. Common purple foods in the vegetable kingdom include eggplant, purple cabbage, dulse, and beets, which are said by Rudolf Steiner to stimulate mind-brain function and act as excellent blood purifiers. We can also include some greens and sprouts. The golden foods include the golden grains such as wheat, rice, millet, and oats. Golden nuts and seeds such as sunflower, pumpkin, cashews, sesame and almonds also fit in.

I've avoided giving extensive food lists for morning and midday colors because these colors are easy to find. It is also important not to be confined and make an obsessive religion out of it, so I have minimized the lists. The blue-indigo-purple spectrum does not so readily come to mind, so I've included a list of some of the foods available.

Gold - White Foods

Grains: different wheat varieties, rye, oats, barley, corn, rice, sorghum, triticale, millet, and quinoa

Fruits: dates, maple syrup, golden apples, hazel pear, apricots, golden grapefruit, loes golden dog pear, kumquat, loquat, oil palm, lady finger banana, bread fruit, cantaloupe, mango, papaya, and pineapple

Nuts and seeds: sunflower, sesame, soy, wild hazelnuts, filberts, almonds, European walnuts, black walnuts, butternut, pistachio, brazil nut, Queensland nut, bambarra nut, pumpkin seeds

Legumes: lentils, cowpea, peanut

Vegetables: gold pumpkin, 40 varieties of mushrooms, cauliflower, jicama, white asparagus, white radish, and daikon

Herbs: cinnamon, horseradish, caraway, coriander, dill, Spanish onion, Welsh onion, garlic, and ginger

Purple Foods
Grains: purple corn and amaranth

Fruits: Bill berry-whortberry, blackthorn berry, black cherry, black figs, spartan apple, durondean pear, all varieties of purple prunes and plums, blackberry, dewberry, raisins, all varieties of purple grapes, mulberry, passion fruit, huckleberry, and elderberry

Legumes: scarlet runner bean, Canadian wonder bean, Mexican blackberries, black gram seeds, purple kidney bean, labially seeds (bean), climbing purple padded kidney bean, vanilla bean and adulation bean

Vegetables: eggplant, purple onion, purple cabbage, beet, purple broccoli, kohlrabi, turnips, asparagus, dulse, Norfolk's, Aramaic's, hijacks, and many purple sea vegetables, sea kale, light purple bamboo shoots, artichoke petals, winter radish, King Edward potato, olives, water chestnut, Jerusalem artichoke, sweet potatoes, truffles, and many purple mushrooms

Herbs: mallow flowers, basil, heather, rosemary, sage, betony, thyme, wild passion flower, marjoram, black pepper, and milkthistle flowers

Blue Foods
Grains: blue corn

Fruits: blue plum, blueberry, bilberry, cabernet grape

Herbs: chicory flowers, borage, hyssop, black thorn, brookline flowers, and pansy

This is not an all-inclusive list, but certainly gives the imagination a beginning. It is important to note that some plants change color as they mature. Pineapple is an example of this. In its earlier stages, the VAS test is most active for the green vibration of the heart chakra. As it turns more golden, it tests more positively for the gold vibration of the crown chakra. The outer color at the time the plant is eaten is the main key to use. Some colors do not exactly color match the primary color for a particular chakra, but are a combination of colors or fall midspectrum between two chakra colors. For example, sesame and sunflower seeds have the strongest VAS response between the second and third chakras and at the crown chakra. These findings indicate a gradual color spectrum transition between chakras.

Using this VAS system, it might be possible to select nutrients based on the locations of the 32 vertebrae of the spine and their associated organs, glands, and chakras. Such a system, however, does not have the simple clarity that the Rainbow Diet offers.

The Rainbow Diet is a natural and simple approach to nutrition that focuses on a 24-hour cycle. I find it easy to eat fruits and some soaked and ground seeds and nuts in the morning, a green salad at lunch, and either mango, papaya, purple figs, or blueberries for a fruit meal, or a more beet and dulse focused salad for dinner. For people who eat only one or two meals per day, it would be good to create the rainbow cycle with the colors of snacks. With a one meal per day cycle and no snacks to put the other colors into the diet, it is useful to trust your intuition of which of the chakra groups need the most balancing. On some days certain colors will appeal, and on others we may want nothing to do with the those colors.

For the two meal a day person, the same idea holds. If not snacking to get the color spectrum in, then one can develop a cyclic spectrum over a two-day cycle. Eating foods by their colors is like eating a particular color from the sun. It brings us closer to the forces of nature.

Summary Chapter 9

1. Everything has a natural system of harmonics in relationship to the primordial vibration of the cosmic energy. This includes our foods.
2. All foods have a vibrational harmonic to the seven main chakras, and the glands, organs, and nerve centers associated with their color-related chakras.
3. Each food, according to its outer color, can be related to the specific color and energy of the same colored chakra.
4. Each food relates to a specific chakra in terms of energizing, healing, cleansing, building, and rebalancing the glands, organs, and nerve centers associated with that particular chakra. Each food heals and energizes a particular chakra.
5. The Rainbow Diet uses full color spectrum of foods for the full spectrum of the chakras throughout the spectrum of the day.
6. The Rainbow Diet is an organizing principle in helping us develop our own individualized diet for spiritual life. It can be usefully applied to any level of intake of fruits, vegetables, nuts, seeds, grains, and dairy products.

10

The Human Crystal

Crystalline Properties of the Body

The key to understanding the assimilation of energy into our physical structure is through the awareness of our bodies as a series of synchronous, interacting crystal structures. The human body on this level is a linkage of oscillating solid and liquid crystals that form an overall energy pattern for the total body. Each organ, gland, nerve system, cell, and protein structure -- even the tissue salts in the body are a level of organization with some degree of crystallinelike function. Marcel Vogel, the world-reknowned crystal expert, has pointed out that the human energy field exists as an array of oscillating energy points which have a layered structure and a definite symmetry. He points out that these properties fulfill the definition of a normal crystal in material form.[1]

Our bone structure has long been recognized as a solid crystal structure with piezoelectric properties. A piezoelectric effect is the creation of an electromagnetic field pulse when a crystalline structure is physically stressed or pushed out of its normal shape. Although various esoteric traditions have implied that the pineal and the pituitary have solid crystal structures, our skeletal bone structure is the only proven solid crystal structure in the body. As a solid crystal, it has the ability to convert vibrational energy, such as sound or light, into electrical magnetic and electric energy. Crystals can absorb, store, amplify, transduce, and transmit these vibrational energies. Researchers such as Glen Rein, M.D., at the Soma Psyche Institute International in New York City have also shown that electromagnetic subtle psychic healing energies and crystal energies have similar biological effects on the body. Additional research by Dr. Rein indicates that psychic healing energies alter the measurable electromagnetic pattern of a crystal, suggesting that subtle energies can alter the physical structure of a crystal. His research suggests that subtle energies and electromagnetic energies can be converted, amplified, transduced, and transmitted by a crystal in a form of energy which has biological effects.[2] These properties of a crystal play an important role in helping us develop a model of how the body as a complex crystalline structure helps to absorb energy from our food.

Bone-Generated Piezoelectric EMFs

When physical stress or an electromagnetic field (EMF) is applied to a piezoelectric crystal, the crystal will change shape and generate an EMF.[3]

Bone, quartz crystal, and tourmaline are among the few crystal forms with piezoelectric properties. Studies suggest that the crystallinelike components of the extracellular matrix of bone, such as collagen and proteoglycans, possess piezoelcectric qualities.[4] It has also been established that mineralized tissue such as cartilage, dentin, teeth in general, and relatively nonmineralized tissues such as keratin in skin, elastin, artery tissue, connective tissue (tendons and ligaments), and even some amino acid crystals (glycine, proline, and hydroxyproline) all have piezoelectric properties.[5]

The main forces which create pulsed piezoelectric EMFs in bone are the anti-gravity muscles, the cardiovascular system, voluntary muscles, and impact with the environment. We have also noted the ability of projected electromagnetic fields to create a piezoelectric response in bone. It is important to note that the pulsed piezoelectric EMFs that are created by bone stress have biological activity.[6] The findings suggest that the piezoelectricity created can produce an EMF of sufficient magnitude to produce a wide range of effects on living systems. Theoretically, these piezoelectric fields could affect "cell nutrition, local pH control, enzyme activation and suppression, orientation of intra- and extracellular macromolecules, migratory and proliferative activity of cells, synthetic capacity and specialized function of cells, contractility and permeability of cell membranes, and energy transfer."[7]

Research into the effects of pulsing EMFs on bone physiology has gone on for over 30 years. Recently, much interesting research has been done on the physiological and clinical applications of pulsing EMFs on bone by prominent researchers such as Andrew Bassett, M.D., at College of Physicians and Surgeons, Columbia University (a professor of mine from medical school). In 1968 Dr. Bassett first introduced me to the piezoelcectric properties of bone and the effect of electrical fields on bone growth and destruction. He has put forth the hypothesis that alterations in a cell's electrical environment will create a change in the cell's physiological behavior. He has shown that pulsed EMFs diminish bone resorption to near normal in experimentally induced osteoporic rat bone, and increase the rate of bone formation to be equal to those of healthy free-roaming rats. Under these pulsing fields, he found that the rate of collagen production increased.[8] Dr. Bassett also reports that, depending on the pulse pattern of the EMFs, cells receiving different EMF pulse fields were found to have different biological responses.[9] For example, a pulse burst elevates calcium content in the bone, while a single pulse lowers the calcium content. What can be deduced from this research is that pulsing EMFs affect bone function and that by varying the EMF wave, pulse, and intensity the EMF pattern and the types of bone intracellular and extracellular response will vary. Cells of all types can be influenced by EMFs as weak as 2×10^{-10} amperes.[10]

Bone-Generated Streaming Potential EMFs

Another type of electric or electrical-magnetic field response is also found in bone structure. Called streaming potentials, this electrical field is created by the flow of ions, charged solutes, and cells such as red blood cells through the tissues, carried by extracellular fluids such as blood through the extracellular matrix. When the bone is even subtly bent from pressure by such events as walking or even by the pulse of our arteries, the extracellular fluids are pumped through the bone. An electrical potential is created as a result of the electrostatic interaction of the electrically charged fluids moving past the fixed charge in the crystalline bone structure. These electrical fluids can also interact with the piezoelcectric fields of the bone.[11]

EMF fields in bone may also be produced as a result of bone's semiconductor or solid state properties, which occur when there is a change in pressure on the bone structure. This change has been associated with an increase in electron conductivity, and hence, EMF production.

Nature of Bone-Generated Energy

Depending on the generating sources, EMF intensity, pulse characteristics, and the combination of the electrical interactions within the bone structure and fluids, a particular EMF field will be generated in the bone. These properties play an important role in our theory of how vibrational energy is assimilated from food.

It is also important to understand that the energy that is being discussed is not simply mechanistic, heat, and electron transfer. As pointed out by McClare in *Resonance in Bioenergetics,* there is a level of organization in biological systems -- a tuned resonance between energy levels in different molecules -- that enables bioenergetic systems to operate rapidly and yet efficiently.[12] He points out that energy released via resonance is exchanged so quickly that it is not thermally available, but remains a form of stored energy. This implies that 100 percent of the resonant energy is transferred and that no entropy is created in resonantly transferred energy. This is distinctly different from energy transfer in the mechanistic system, which always involves some loss of energy.

Liquid Crystal Structures in Human Systems

There are other forms of crystallinelike systems in the body, and one of the most important is the liquid crystal. A liquid crystal is technically defined as having form, liquid properties, stored information, and a measurable electromagnetic field. From our perspective, it also has a SOEF, which is reflected in its stored information and EMF. A liquid crystal can act simultaneously as liquid and crystal. The larger liquid crystal systems include fatty tissue, muscle and nerve tissue, the lymphatic system, white blood cells, and the various pleural and peritoneal linings.

Muscle and nerve tissue exist as liquid crystal systems held in shape by bone and skin systems. The muscles, by the nature of their structure, have also been shown to have some piezoelectric properties. Muscle and nerve tissue also exist as liquid crystal systems held into form by bone and skin systems. On a cellular level, all cells and cell membranes are considered liquid crystals. In *Liquid Crystals and Ordered Fluids* , edited by J. F. Johnson and R.S. Porter, it is pointed out that the various cell membranes, membrane components, and intracellular membranes function as liquid crystal structures.[13] These include the plasma membrane, mitochondrial membrane, smooth and rough endoplasmic reticulum, nuclear membranes, and chloroplast membranes.

Bodily fluids also have crystal qualities. The water molecule contains in itself the potential forms of all crystals in its primary form of a tetrahedron. Water can bring all different forms of ions into a crystalline state and hold them in solution. In addition, the more structured the water is, the higher concentration of ions it can hold. One of the most important of these ion solutions is the dissolved cell salts. In Norm Miksell's paper on structured water, the author points out that when the body cells and tissues become diseased or cancerous, the crystalline protein structures no longer have the proper configuration to maintain the water in an optimal structured state. Ions and other solutes in the cell consequently become redistributed by the new pattern of unstructured water.[14] If the water in the cell, extracellular fluid, or blood plasma becomes structured, it will then be able to attract and hold more ions by virtue of its hydration shell patterns. When structured water is organized around a particular ion, as it is with cell salts, it is able to move the ions more easily into the more structured cytoplasmic water inside the cell. Once the ionically structured water is within a cell, it helps attract the same cell salt or ion into the cell. This is probably how the ferrum phosphorum cell salt works to help people who are anemic draw more iron into their intracellular and extracellular fluids.

The Body as a Series of Synchronous Amplified Crystalline Resonant Fields

I believe that the fundamental mechanism by which the cell salt structured water and its enlarged hydration shell are able to attract additional like ions has to do with the creation of an amplified crystalline resonant field by cell salt and structured water. This amplified field is able to attract the weaker but similarly resonating crystal fields of the single ions. The single ions are drawn into and fit synchronistically into the larger resonant field pattern of the cell salt in its structured water.

This structured water and cell salt dynamic represents an important principle. Identical crystal resonant fields emanated by micro-nutrients are attracted to larger resonant fields emanated by the organism's larger crystalline and liquid crystalline patterns. This includes the total system along with individual organs, glands, cellular, subcellular, and molecular structures. This explains how micronutrients, through vibrating crystalline fields, are drawn to the appropriate resonating crystalline sites.

Indirect support for this idea of the overall living system as a complex of synchronistic oscillating crystalline structures has slowly been accumulated by the scientific community. In *An Atlas of Cellular Oscillators* by P.R. Rapp, research in over 450 papers is cited in cataloguing an atlas of biological and biochemical oscillators with a periodicity of one hour or less.[15] This includes oscillations in enzyme-catalyzed reactions such as photosynthesis (molecular crystalline subsystems), oscillations in protein synthesis, and oscillations in cell membranes, secretory cells, neuronal cells, skeletal cells, smooth cells, and heart muscle cells, and cell movement. In a healthy state, the body's structures are a multileveled series of interacting systems and subsystems that resonate harmoniously. From this perspective, disease occurs when this synchronicity is thrown into a disharmony. Appropriate crystal balancing of the total system through the chakras or of subsystems with a particular organ or gland can be very beneficial for healing this dis-synchronicity.

The Human Organism as a Healing Vibratory Transmitter

This understanding also relates to the use of human thought vibratory power, gems and crystals, and their elixirs in healing. Each organ system or subsystem gives off a specific measurable electromagnetic field. The EMFs are measurable, subtle vibratory fields that can have great effect on the behavior of an organism. Dr. Delgado's work referred to earlier has illustrated this point. Each crystal or gem also has a specific EMF which radiates from its piezoelectric structure. For example, ruby and emerald resonate sympathetically with the liquid crystalline structures of the heart muscle system. By amplifying the energies of these gems with light, sound, or with our own healing thoughts we activate a stabilizing resonant EMF. In my work in crystal healing and meditation, it has become intuitively clear that thoughts are vibratory energy. They come from the same undifferentiated cosmic energy. "In the beginning was the Word, and the Word was with God, and the Word was God" (John 1:1). The SOEFs are also vibratory patterns coming from the same source. In this way thoughts and SOEFs are related. When one is able to tune to the SOEF pattern with the mind, it is possible to send resonant vibratory thought form energy to reenergize and reorganize the dissipated SOEF system. Crystals and gems amplify these specific resonant vibrations. This projected stabilizing EMF can help to bring our example of a disharmonious heart muscle and its SOEF back to its normal healthy resonate vibration. The gems or crystals help to fine-tune, stabilize, and amplify the healing vibration of the thought waves required to create the specific healing resonate EMF needed to rebalance and heal the system.

Using this same principle, we can also used specific gems or gem elixirs to energize and rebalance the individual chakras. Dark opal and tiger's eye help to rebalance the base chakra; fire agate works on the second chakra; the solar plexus and third chakra are aided by quartz and pearl; ruby and emerald stimulate the heart chakra; lapis lazuli is good for the throat chakra; quartz resonates with both the pituitary and pineal or sixth and seventh chakras; diamond is beneficial for the crown chakra.[16]

The human organism and mind can be understood as crystal transmitters. When we become a clear channel for the divine God force of unconditional Love, it comes through us in a way analogous to a gem or crystal being activated by our thought forms. In this enhanced state, a strong resonant field is created which is capable of reprogramming the SOEFs, chakras, and organ systems of a diseased person. By increasing the SOEF energy of a person's crystalline structure, we recreate a new and healthy field which then reorganizes the person on a spiritual, mental, emotional, and physical vibratory level. This higher love force helps to release negative thought forms which are stored as dissonant vibrations within a person's system at any of these four levels. A clear example of this is the healing power of Christ whose mere presence or the touching of His robe brought healing. The projection of loving thought forms heals by increasing the SOEF energy, either specifically or generally. Healing groups using this principle act as amplified crystal resonators for the person being healed. Presently, scientists such as Marcel Vogel are involved in preliminary research to show the link between love as a vibration and its effect on healing.

When the Kundalini is awakened, it also acts as an internal healing force by raising the energy level of the SOEFs. When the healthy SOEF pattern is raised to a more integrated and pure level, entropy-producing negative, dissonant thought forms and emotions are forced out. They seem to come up into consciousness and be released. In one meditation group I lead, a women in her late 60s reported seeing a vision of a particular yellow house. In sharing it, she felt a tremendous relief, because that color yellow had always been associated with the pain of her mother's death 60 years earlier. Since the yellow image came up in meditation and was released, she lost her fear and was healed of her grief. In a recent weekend seminar on meditation and nutrition, an overweight person who for many years had been trying to control her ravenous desire for food experienced an awakening of her Kundalini and reported one week later to have lost her intense desire for food. These two examples show how meditation and awakened Kundalini can spontaneously release dissonant patterns from different levels of our being.

This chapter clarifies the point we knew all along...

People are precious gems.

Summary Chapter 10

1. The key to understanding the assimilation of energy into our physical structure is through the awareness of our body as a series of synchronous, interacting crystal structures.

2. Our bone structure is our body's major solid crystal system. A particular EMF is generated from the crystalline bone structure. Its type depends on its generating source (piezoelectric, streaming potentials, or solid-state activity), its energy intensity, its pulse characteristic, and the combination

of all these interactions within the bone structure.

3. The other major crystallinelike system in the body consists of the liquid crystal structures which exist in every cell membrane, organ, gland, nerve, and muscle system.

4. Bodily fluids, because of the ions within them and the ability of water to become structured, also have crystallinelike qualities.

5. An explanation of how micronutrients reach their correct sites in the body is that they are drawn by their vibrating EMFs to the appropriate resonating crystalline sites in the system.

6. Realizing the crystalline nature of the human body gives us a physical basis for understanding the efficacy of human thought vibrations, gems, crystals, flower essences, gem elixirs, and homeopathy in healing.

7. By increasing the SOEF energy of the crystalline structure of a person, we create a renewed and healthy field which reorganizes the person on a physical, emotional, mental, and spiritual vibratory level.

8. We are, indeed, precious gems.

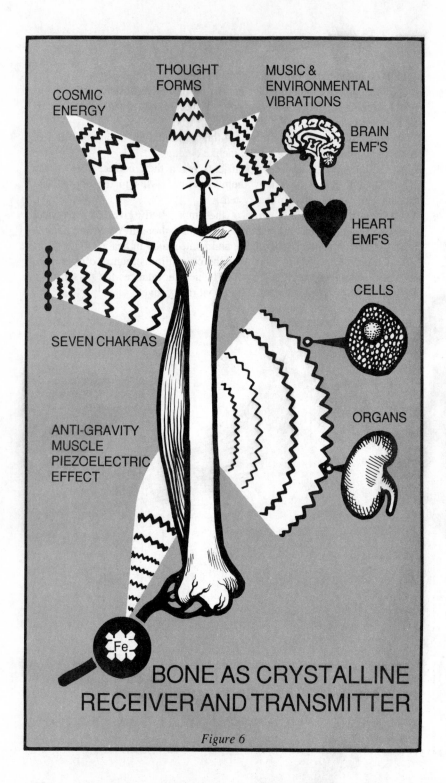

COSMIC ENERGY

THOUGHT FORMS

MUSIC & ENVIRONMENTAL VIBRATIONS

BRAIN EMF'S

HEART EMF'S

CELLS

SEVEN CHAKRAS

ORGANS

ANTI-GRAVITY MUSCLE PIEZOELECTRIC EFFECT

Fe

BONE AS CRYSTALLINE RECEIVER AND TRANSMITTER

Figure 6

11

Bioenergetic Assimilation

When cosmic energy is sufficiently condensed, it arrives on our plates as food. As solid, whole, raw food it maintains its SOEF. To develop a new paradigm of the process of food assimilation requires the understanding of assimilation on both the physical and the energetic level. On a general level, each vegetable and animal substance radiates a unique species-specific subtle vibration from its energy field. Although this is true for both plants and animals, for the rest of this discussion I will refer only to plant foods, as they exist on a more primary level in the food chain than animals. One of the tasks of assimilation is the conversion of food as a foreign body into a likeness with our own body chemistry and vibration, especially on the levels of physical, etheric, and astral bodies. To assimilate food successfully, we must completely absorb the total forces of the food into our own forces. In the process of assimilation, the crystalline vibration of these foods interacts with our total oscillating crystalline system. Anyone familiar with the science of kinesiology knows that when a specific food substance is brought within the body's vibratory field, it may immediately weaken, strengthen, or not appreciably affect the person.

Crystalline Bone Structure and Energy Assimilation

The vibrations of food resonate with our bone structure, which amplifies and transmits resonant energy to the body as a whole. In this process, the bone transforms the vibration of the plant into a resonant frequency that is compatible with our living system. Our crystalline bone structure acts like the crystal in a radio, which picks up radio waves and translates them into audio signals. The sound vibrations resonate with the bone structures in our ears, transmitting these vibrations as electrical vibrations or impulses to our auditory nerves.

Within the plant structure, there are different crystallinelike substructures, similar to the multiple oscillating crystallinelike subsystems in our own bodies. These resonate with the bone and other crystallinelike structures in our bodies. Because bone is the only rigid crystal system in the body, it is the major "antenna" for receiving information into the body and transferring it via its crystalline properties to the rest to the body. It is through the bone resonance vibration that plant EMFs are transformed into specific vibrations that are similar to and hence are able to communicate information and energy to the resonating substructures in the body. In this way, specific vibrational properties of the plant energize and nurture specific organ, glandular, and cellular systems. For example, the dandelion root affects primarily the liver, while the leaf has much less effect on the liver and is best used in salads as a light cleansing tonic. At another level of awareness, it may be that only organs in a state of well-being will draw the right nutrients to themselves and reject inappropriate nutrients. When cells and organs are diseased, their resonant EMF fields seem different from those of healthy cells, so they may not draw the proper nutrients to themselves to create and maintain health. It is documented that the crystal structure and EMF field generated by arthritic bone are different than in normal bone.[1]

Our crystalline bone structure, in general, acts as an antenna for all incoming and internal body vibratory energy and information, including direct thought form energy. It resonates with all levels of nutrient energy, which it either receives directly (music, singing, and chanting), or indirectly, through the EMFs transferred from the chakras as they step down the incoming virtual energy that has entered the system through the seven subtle bodies. The brain, nervous system, and heart also give off EMFs that resonate with our bone and other crystallinelike structures. The crystalline bone structure then amplifies and radiates this energy and information to the rest of the system down to the cellular and subcellular crystalline structures. This is an important way that energy and information is transferred directly to all the cells throughout the body from the chakras as well as through the pure cosmic energy-brain-nervous system linkage.

Dr. Glen Rein has proposed an additional system of how information and energy are directly transferred to the cells.[2] This system is based the fact that the cells are suspended in an extracellular matrix of macromolecular crystallinelike connective tissue components. This matrix is filled with structured water, which also has crystallinelike properties. The water in the extracellular system and the crystallinelike matrix receive the resonant energy and information. In the process of receiving the incoming energy, the electro-chemical formation of this matrix structure changes. This change is then transmitted as an electric current, sending energy and information throughout the whole system. This is a system that provides another pathway by which the resonating bone structure is able to send its biologically transduced vibratory information directly to the whole cellular system. Although there are other crystallinelike subsystems which resonantly take in and transmit energy, the bone structure, because it is the only solid crystal in the system, remains the main transducer. Its solid state enables it to hold memory patterns more permanently as stored EMF frequencies in the bone. Bone and spine traumas, in particular, may be stored in the bone structure, and crystal healing is often very helpful for relieving these traumas. Marcel Vogel calls the bone the storehouse of the mind.[3] Memories are also stored in the crystallinelike structures of the deep connective tissue. This is the biomolecular basis for deep tissue therapies. The bones also vibrate in resonance with other vibratory sources like crystals, gems, mantras, chants, and music. We have all heard the saying "you can feel it in your bones." This helps to explain the powerful effect of religious music like Gregorian chants. As human crystalline systems, we resonate in total unity, harmony, and love with the pulse of the cosmos.

Interplay of Our Tri-System and Crystalline Bone Structure

On another level, plant energy is also assimilated through a dynamic interplay of the crystalline bone structure with the tri-system of our circulatory, nervous, and meridian systems. The Chinese have been familiar with this tri-system relationship for thousands of years. By use of pulse diagnosis on the vascular system, they explain the condition of the various meridians, organs, glands, nerves, and bone systems. A theoretical explanation for how vibrational remedies are taken into the body -- in *Gem Elixirs and Vibrational Healing, Volume II* by Gurudas -- also discusses the interplay of this synchronous tri-system.[4] It helps us understand how energy can be transferred from the physical level to the etheric system of the chakras. In this transfer, meridians act as a bidirectional resonant transfer system between the two levels.

The meridian system also has a direct link with the nervous and circulatory systems, as it is a template for them and the whole physical body. It is the most physical templating energy system organized by the SOEF, carrying more of the body's life force in its crystallinelike structures. In Genesis 4:10 we read of Abel's blood speaking to God from the earth. This can be understood as the crystalline life force sending out its message. The most important of these resonating forces are the hemoglobin structures in the red blood cells and the minerals in plasma. The nervous system carries more of the consciousness mental forces via electromagnetic fields. It helps stimulate and direct cellular growth, including the direction and growth of the blood vessels in the system. Our bone structure is also penetrated by the nervous system. C-fibers and knoblike nerve receptors are found in different types of bone tissue. When the nerve tissues conduct nerve impulses, the physiological changes associated with these pulses create an external EMF.[5] These EMFs may interact with bone EMFs .

Although still theory, there is some evidence suggesting that the meridian, nervous, and circulatory systems form an overall stabilized system that transmits the transformed and amplified energy of the bone to the rest of the body subsystems down to the cellular level. Vibrations from the bone also help to stabilize and energize the meridian system. It is well known that the piezoelectric energies stimulated in the bone by walking create an EMF that programs the maintenance of the bone structure. The pulsating of the heart and blood vessels creates a piezoelectric response in bone that may be creating a stabilizing maintenance EMF in the bone.[6] Dr. Bassett points out that the EMFs from the cardiovascular system might play a major role in some sort of stabilizing signal as they interact with locally generated piezoelectric and streaming potentials.[7] Although the evidence for this sort of relationship is not conclusive, it supports our hypothesis.

Theory of Assimilation

The first step in our assimilation theory starts with the sun activating the chlorophyl in plant cells. Energized chlorophyl, which contains a holographic vibration of the whole plant, is able to transfer its resonant energy and information into the electromagnetic field of the iron in red blood cells. Chlorophyl and hemoglobin only differ by one atom: chlorophyl has magnesium in its structure instead of iron which is in hemoglobin. The newly energized and programmed red blood cells, from their interaction with the chlorophyl, circulate back through the bone system. Red blood cells transmit their new EMF energy and information to the bone via direct resonance and the streaming potential, or electrical fluidium effect. The bone amplifies and transmits it to the rest of the system (Figure 6 on page 88). The red blood cell and hemoglobin systems also transfer resonant plant energy directly to cells and tissues through the resonant transfer of their own EMFs.

In addition to the red blood cell EMFs, the blood plasma charged by plant and body cell EMFs and other input EMFs also transmits electromagnetic fields which are carried by mineral compounds. These plasma crystalline EMFs are transferred to bone, and at the same time charged and reprogrammed by the new bone pattern. They leave the bone structure with the information needed to be drawn by their own EMFs to the appropriate location in the system. The red blood cells and plasma help to stabilize the general patterns of the body. When their charge becomes fatigued, circulation through the bone recharges them. In essence, red blood cells and plasma are both programmers of the bone crystal and programmed by it. The programmed ionic EMFs of the plasma also help to stabilize the meridian system, which in turn helps to program and balance the neurological system (Figure 7). The bone then sends out a pattern harmonic with the whole body. The red blood cells and plasma also leave the bone and carry specific patterns to specific locations in the body and help to stabilize the general EMFs of the body. This tri-system and the crystal energies of the bone are a multiple feedback, self-stabilizing, energy-conducting system. These three systems and the crystalline bone structure interact synchronistically and simultaneously.

Role of Cell Salts in Assimilation

Cell salts play an interesting role in this system. On one level, they are actually a physical micronutrient, but more importantly, they are programmed on a resonant level by the meridian system to act as a template for organizing the formation of micronutrients into tissue building patterns. They also, via their role in structured water, improve the system's vibratory pattern for drawing in specific needed minerals. Each single cell salt may aid the energy flow of the particular meridian it is associated with. The crystalline vibrations from the cell salts in the plasma help to stabilize the meridian system. There are 12 basic cell salts which seem to correlate with each of the twelve major meridians. A person's general health may be aided

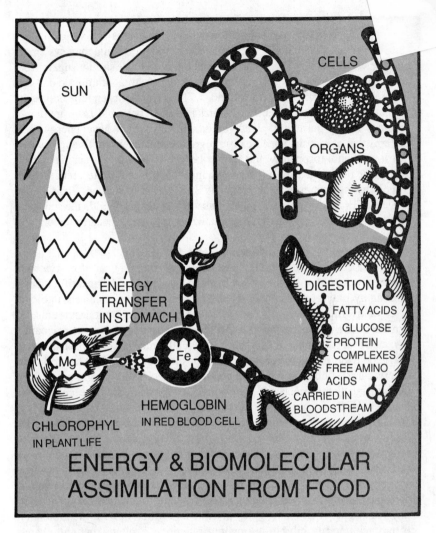

Figure 7

by taking a specific cell salt one day each month. A suggested way to do this is to arrange them by their atomic weight. On the winter solstice, start with the heaviest atomic weight cell salt, which is ferrum phosphoricum. The cell salts listed in order of descending atomic weight are: ferrum phosphorum, calcarea phosphorica, natrum phosphoricum, natrum sulfuricum, magnesia phosphoricum, kali sulphuricum, kali phosphoricum, calcarea sulphurica, calcarea fluorica, kali muriaticum, silicea, and natrum muriaticum. On the 21st of each month, take the next lightest. In this way cell salts can aid both mineral absorption and meridian energy flow.

Energy Transfer from and
Absorption of Molecular Structures

Energy and material are transferred from food into our system in another way as well. This transfer is via the individual simple sugars from complex carbohydrates, crystallinelike proteins, free amino acids, and negatively charged fatty acid formations. These nutrients are crystallinelike formations which carry specific energies and EMF patterns. They are drawn to areas like a particular gland, organ, or cell which have energy field patterns that attract the specifically programmed nutrient by like resonance. These nutrients resonantly and molecularly link into the larger resonating molecular field, releasing their energy into this larger field to reenergize it. This is how the energy of the templating SOEF is recharged. This is one way SOEFs draw nutrients into their templates to build the physical structure. It explains how nutrients get where they are needed in the body.

Micro-Nutrients and Cell EMFs

Bruce Lipton, Ph.D., professor of anatomy at St. George's University School of Medicine in Grenada, has developed a beautiful theory, thoroughly based on current scientific data in the field of cellular biology. It explains in more detail how specifically charged micronutrients, as carriers of energy patterns of a specific food we have ingested, are resonantly attracted to a particular cell's EMF, and actually interface with, transfer their energetic patterns to, and incorporate their material forms into the cell. His theory clarifies how nutrients which are not specifically programmed for a particular cell but are being transported in proximity to the cell by the extracellular fluids, are drawn into the cell.[8]

There are certain facts which are the basis of this understanding. One is that when a protein is exposed to an energy source such as light or radiowave sound, EMFs of the same frequency or a harmonic frequency of the crystallinelike protein, the protein molecule will resonate sympathetically with it. This new resonance vibration has the power to create an electromagnetic energy shift in the protein that can change its physical shape. This change may activate a new function for the protein, or it may temporarily inhibit an ongoing function. Proteins that can change shape like this are called allosteric proteins. In short, proteins, as crystallinelike structures, are able to take in EMF energies and transfer them into a biologically active signal. One familiar example of this is rhodopsin, the crystallinelike protein energy receptor for light found in pigments in the rods of the eye. It takes in the energy of light and transfers it into nerve pulses that transfer this energy into the brain's vision centers. Another common example is melanin, a crystallinelike protein able to absorb light energy and transform it into sound and electromagnetic energy.

The next step that Dr. Lipton adds in his theory is based on evidence that proteins are able to integrate themselves into the cell membrane. There are several different functions for these proteins in the cell membrane. There are receptor proteins involved with reception and detection of incoming electromagnetic frequencies, including EMFs of various nutrients, hormones, ions in solution, neurotransmitters, glucose molecules, free amino acids, free fatty acids, or any other nutrients needed for cellular function which are brought to the cell via the extracellular fluids. These crystallinelike proteins are sensitive to very low levels of energy such as input from single ions, electrons, photons, and protons. On receiving these incoming EMF energies, these receptor proteins convert them into specific biological signals which modulate the cell membrane functioning. These signals directly affect the three other functional protein types in the cell membranes. Receptor proteins may transfer the incoming energy to enzyme proteins which may then become activated to perform enzymatic reactions intracellularly or extracellularly. The receptor proteins may also transfer this energy to transport proteins which transform it into electro-chemical activities that regulate some of the gates and channel systems which let in specific nutrients knocking on the outside of the cell membrane doors. The receptor proteins also act in a direct physical linkage to structural proteins within the cell walls. As the receptor proteins change shape, they create a change in the physical configuration of the structural protein to which they are linked. When the configuration of the structural protein changes, it may also open or shut a particular cell membrane door.

In summary, the receptor proteins are crystallinelike energy transducers which take in the information energy of the multitudinous EMFs impinging on the cell system and convert them into energy message signals to which the cell can respond. These receptor proteins are yet another system that tunes us into the energy of nutrients, as well as the more subtle geomagnetic, earth-atmospheric vibrations such as the Schuman resonance, lunar, solar, and cosmic resonance fields which affect biological life on this planet.

The cell membrane as a total unit vibrates in sympathetic resonance with incoming EMFs. Its resonant vibration is able to induce a harmonic resonance in the intracellular crystallinelike membranes and protein complexes like RNA and DNA. This transfer of harmonic resonant energy is how the cell membrane sends information to the intracellular structures, and therefore has a regulatory effect on them. It is my feeling that the cosmic, earth, food, and bone resonant information energy can also directly transmit energy to the core intracellular structures such as the RNA and DNA. I believe this is particularly true as we develop spiritually through proper nutrition and meditation. We become better and better superconductors of the cosmic energy as we evolve spiritually. As we become better and better superconductors of energy, there is less and less impeded resonance between the microcosm and macrocosm, resulting in the experience of awareness.

There is another piece to this system. The intracellular crystallinelike vibratory structures can resonantly transfer their energy information to the cell membrane and therefore can influence the cell membrane function as well. It is a two-way system. In harmonic resonance with its intracellular structures, the cell membrane sends out EMFs into the extracellular fluids, which attract the specific nutrients they need. This completes the multiple feedback cycles in the overall system of multilevel vibrating crystallinelike systems in the body.

I have outlined several mechanisms of information energy transfer in the system. None are contradictory. Our complex system of energy information assimilation has many checks and balances to keep us attuned.

Concluding Thoughts

In this theoretical system of assimilation, food becomes not only a supplier of nutrients, but also of specific energies that reenergize all levels of our SOEFs. If we think of the development of the human organism as analogous to the development of a seed crystal, another insight is available. Once the adult form of the crystal, the human physical body, has completed its growth, we only need a minimum of nutrients to maintain the homeostasis of the system. The main purpose of nutrition at this point becomes primarily the supplying of energy to maintain the SOEFs of the overall system. If we are not able to decrease the appetites that have served us well for growth, we begin to crystallize spare tires around ourselves. The idea is to eat the minimum necessary to keep the energy and conductivity of the body at a maximum. As we shift toward absorbing less condensed energies into our organism, we need less and less material food even as a source of energy.

Summary Chapter 11

1. To assimilate food successfully, we must completely absorb the total forces of the food into our own forces.

2. The vibrations of food resonate with our bone structure; the bone structure amplifies and transmits resonant energy to the body as a whole.

3. Our bone structure resonates with all levels of nutrient energy as they are resonantly transferred from the chakras, brain, mind, nervous system, heart, and any resonating external frequency such as music, chanting, and thought.

4. Plant energy is assimilated through a dynamic interplay of the crystalline bone structure through circulatory, nervous, and meridian systems.

5. Plant energy is also transferred directly from chlorophyl to the hemoglobin in the red blood cells and the ionic structures in the blood plasma. The red blood cells and plasma transfer the plant energy directly to the cells and to the bone structure, which transmit it to the body.

6. The tissue cell salts aid in the transfer of meridian energy for the patterning of micronutrients in tissue growth. They also help stabilize the meridian energy patterns.

7. Individual crystallinelike simple sugar forms, crystallinelike proteins and free amino acids, and negatively charged fatty acid formations carry specific energies and EMF patterns.

8. In this theoretical system of assimilation, food becomes a supplier of not only nutrients but also of energies that reenergize all levels of our SOEFs.

12

Perspectives on Diet

The purpose of the next series of chapters is to consider certain nutritional questions that will aid the reader in mapping out an individualized diet that enhances the process of spiritual unfolding. This is not a search for the perfect diet, because the only thing that is perfect is beyond the body-mind complex, the Truth of the Self, the Truth of God in All and as All. We already are this perfection, but we have some blocks which keep us from consistently experiencing this Truth. The perfect diet can not even make us 100 percent healthy, because although diet affects the mind and the spirit, its primary effect is on the physical body. For diet to be truly effective, it needs to be in the context of a full spiritual life of meditation, good fellowship, right life, loving our neighbors as our true Selves, and continual love communion with God. On one hand, diet is a powerful discipline that can help us balance our bodies, minds, hearts, and lives in general. On the other hand, diet is an expression of our state of beingness and of our harmony with the universal laws of creation.

My intent is to supply enough perspective that we will be interested in creating an individualized diet that reflects our highest state of awareness and is totally appropriate to our function in the world. This is not so easy because food is the principle interface, on a physical level, between nature and ourselves. The appropriate eating of food is a means of extracting energy from our environment in a harmonious way, and in today's world, this relationship has broken down, becoming mystified and confused. How else, for example, could we, on a national level, have approved the irradiation of fresh fruits and vegetables as a way of "preserving" them? This represents a complete break with nature. What seems normal is abnormal and vice versa. It is as if we are banging our heads against the wall and when we stop, we discover our headache is gone and it is easier to meditate. Meanwhile, modern technology is studying the physiology of how to live normally while banging our head against the wall. Because most people are normally banging their heads against the wall, we are considered abnormal because we choose to stop. We are the funny ones eating "a birdseed and grass diet". It is difficult to change our program in the face of this social pressure and our old programmed habits and belief systems. Nevertheless, it is necessary to examine these patterns and be willing to abandon what is no longer appropriate for maintaining our experience of blissful communion with God and our feeling of well-being, for experiencing a balanced body energy, and for nurturing the spiritualizing force of the Kundalini energy within. Diet itself is not the key to spiritual life, but it helps to open the door to communion with the Divine. To live and eat in a way which enhances this communion is the guideline.

Diet from the perspective of spiritual nutrition is not a religion or an obsessive form of searching for God. It is simply part of a balanced harmonious life in attunement with the universal laws. The primary goal of spiritual nutrition is not a healthy body or longevity; these are byproducts. The primary goal is to eat in a way which helps us more easily nurture, hold, and become better superconductors of cosmic energy, so it is easier to energize the Kundalini spiritualizing force and experience the ecstasy of God within ourselves and in every interaction of our lives. We develop our practice of spiritual nutrition so that when God calls we do not ask for another plate of ice cream.

Creating our own individualized diet for spiritual life requires some artful intelligence in the application of the new nutritional paradigm and the general principles I am sharing. The process is real and basic, rather than esoteric. It involves some trial and error to see what works for us. The criterion is simple: eat what increases your experience of love and communion and let go of what diminishes this communion. It requires some sensitive attention to our daily life needs and to the general purpose of spiritual nutrition which is: instead of living to eat or eating to live, we eat to intensify our communion with the Divine. Let our hunger for the Divine be the overwhelming appetite and guide to our choice of diet.

13

Raw Versus Cooked Foods

Effects of Cooking Foods

Whether or not we should cook our foods is a controversial issue. For many, like myself until about ten years ago, it was not even an issue, because I assumed that it was natural to cook all my food. Some suggest everything should be cooked, some say fruits or grains should be cooked, some say 100 percent raw foods is the way. By applying all levels of the new nutritional paradigm, including its material aspect, we can gain some perspective on this subject. We need to examine the effect of cooking foods on ourselves and on the food. During normal cooking, enzymes are destroyed, the active forms of vitamins and minerals are partially destroyed, pesticides and fungicides break down to form toxic compounds, and there is an increase in free radicals. Cooking foods also coagulates the protein. In addition, eating foods that are too hot can actually disrupt the digestive enzymes in the mucousal lining of the stomach. Eating cooked foods causes an immediate increase in our white blood cell count (WBC).

Importance of Biologically Active Enzymes in Our Diets

On the physical level, all our life processes depend on the functioning of enzymes. They are the physical agents of life, important for digestion, detoxification from internal pollution and external ecological pollution, and maintaining our immune systems and all our metabolic and regenerative processes. It is estimated that there are 75,000 to 100,000 different enzyme systems in the body.[1] Dr. Ann Wigmore calls enzyme preservation the secret of life.[2] Dr. Howell, the pioneer of food enzyme work in this country, says the quantity of enzymes we have in our systems is the equivalent to what we call life energy or vitality, and thinks of our enzyme level as indicative of our health status.[3] There is some interesting evidence associating enzyme reserve with longevity and vitality. For example, the amylase in human saliva is 30 times more abundant in the average 25-year-old than in the average 81-year-old. The total enzyme level in young beetles is twice as great as in old beetles. Fruit flies, grasshoppers, and rats all have more enzymes when they are young.[4] After chronic disease in humans, the enzyme content is depleted.[5]

Raw natural food seems to come loaded with the enzymes needed for much of their digestion. They are released the moment we begin to chew the food and break down cell walls. This is similar to the finding that unprocessed carbohydrates such as grain and raw sugar cane have the right amount of chromium to act as a co-factor in their assimilation. When these are commercially processed into such products as white sugar and white flour, they lose much of their chromium, so in order to assimilate them, we must draw from our own body chromium stores.[6] Over time, this results in a tissue chromium depletion, just as eating cooked foods results in an enzyme depletion.

When we process foods by heating them above 118 degress Fahrenheit for one half hour, there is 100 percent enzyme destruction.[7] According to Howell, it does not matter whether the food is quickly or slowly heated or whether the heat is moist. He reports that in dry heat up to 150 degrees Fahrenheit, enzymes are not destroyed.[8]

The enzymes that are destroyed by cooking are those that predigest the food in the "food enzyme" or cardiac stomach (the upper part of the stomach) for the first 30 to 60 minutes of the digestive cycle. By eating primarily raw foods this predigestion is enhanced. This means that fewer of our own (endogenous) digestive enzymes from the stomach, pancreas, liver, and small intestine are required to complete the digestive work, because there is evidence to show that the amount of endogenous enzyme secretion will decrease or increase depending on how much is needed.[9] This is important because of what Dr. Howell calls the "Law of Adaptive Secretion of Enzymes"[10] which means that enzyme energy goes where it is needed in the body. Dr. Howell believes, as I do, that enzymes represent a certain amount of energy as well as an actual amount of enzyme molecules. If less enzyme energy is needed for digestion, there is more available to enhance other bodily processes. For example, if we are injured or sick, we often experience a drop in appetite because the primary need for the enzyme energy is for the fighting of the illness and for bodily repair.

By eating foods in which the enzymes have not been destroyed, we maintain a continuous exogenous enzyme input into the system and therefore decrease the endogenous depletion of enzyme energy. There is strong evidence that the excess enzymes released from the raw foods or even from enzyme supplements, can be absorbed into the system to increase our enzyme content and energy. Therefore a raw food diet can actually add enzyme energy and material to the system. There are three main methods, on the physical plane, for maintaining or increasing enzyme energy in the system: eating a raw food diet, adding enzymes as a supplement, and fasting. The result of conservation and an increase of enzyme energy in the digestive area is that more enzyme energy is available for our vitality, body detoxification, metabolic function, dissolution of scar tissue and crystallized deposits in the tissues, digestion of excess fatty tissue, and regeneration. This increased vitality and health make more energy available to be present in our spiritual lives and more available to be transmuted into spiritual energy. This is one way raw foods enhance spiritual life. Although certain illnesses can be turned into an important spiritual growth time, it has been my general observation that people with low physical vitality have less energy available for their spiritual focus.

One of the most dramatic illustrations of the importance of raw foods for health and vitality is the famous study by Francis Pottenger, M.D.[11] It was a ten-year, four-generation study of 900 cats. Half the population was fed a raw meat and milk diet; the other half was fed a cooked meat and pasteurized milk diet. The cats who received the cooked food developed degenerative diseases similar to those found in our society. With each generation, there was an increase in congenital bone and other abnormalities, so that by the third generation the cats fed only cooked food were sterile and quite congenitally deformed. The conclusion was that some heat-sensitive qualities were missing from the cooked meat or pasteurized milk, and the only factors we know that are completely destroyed by pasteurization are biologically active enzymes. The study suggests that the absence of enzymes in cooked food made the difference.

In terms of the new nutritional paradigm, cooking, freezing, and irradiating destroy the physical structures of enzymes and other nutrients and disrupt and disorganize etheric SOEF patterns. To revitalize these nutrients for absorption into the system, their SOEFs must be reenergized and reorganized. To do this, energy must come from our overall SOEF system. Drawing energy from our SOEFs increases the entropy and the aging of our system. As discussed in Chapter 3, enzymes represent special high-energy vortex focal points for bringing SOEF energy into the physical plane for all general functions as well as for biological transmutation. The more viable enzyme systems we have, the more avenues are open for us to be energized and revitalized in this way.

Abnormal White Blood Cell Changes with Cooked Food

In 1930, Paul Kouchakoff, M.D., presented a paper at the First International Congress of Microbiology titled *The Influence of Food Cooking on the Blood Formula of Man.* He found that eating raw food did not produce leukocytosis (an increase in the number of white blood cells).[12] Particularly significant about his simple finding was that since 1846, leukocyctosis after eating the normal cooked foods was thought to be normal and was classified as such by Wirchow as "digestive leukocytosis" (a beautiful example of scientists studying the normal physiology of head banging). In physiological reality, eating cooked foods creates a pathological response in the body. When foods are cooked, the energy fields are not able to resonate immediately with the body, so the body responds defensively until it can reorganize the SOEFs of the cooked food into patterns it can resonate with and absorb. He also found that if a food was commercially processed and then cooked, not only did the white blood cell number increase, but there was a change in the ratio of the different white blood cell types to each other.

Kouchakoff found that the critical temperature for initiating leukocytosis was when food was heated at around 191 degrees Fahrenheit for 30 minutes. The highest temperature he found before the leukocytosis occurred was with figs at 206 degree Fahrenheit. Interestingly, the leukocytosis needed as little as 50 milligrams of cooked food to be initiated. An additional finding that should be of interest and relief to some was that if people ate raw food with cooked food of the same type, in a 50/50 ratio, the leukocytosis did not happen. He also found that this was true for a mixture of cooked foods and raw foods that were not the same, as long as the critical temperature change point of the raw food was higher than that of the cooked foods. From the perspective of the new paradigm, these results can be explained by the SOEFs from raw foods transferring their energy by resonance to reenergize and organize the disrupted SOEFs of cooked foods.

The Effect of Cooking on Vitamins and Other Food Components

There is some variation in the results, but most researchers indicate at least a 50 percent loss of vitamin B in cooked foods. Some losses, such as thiamine, can be as high as 96 percent if food is boiled for a prolonged time. Biotin losses can be up to 72 percent, folic acid up to 97 percent, inositol up to 95 percent, vitamin C up to 70 to 80 percent.[13] Viktoras Kulvinskas estimates that the overall nutrient destruction or loss of bio-availability after cooking is approximately 85 percent.[14] Along with this, the Max Plank Institute for Nutritional Research in Germany has found cooked proteins have only 50 percent bio-availability as compared to uncooked proteins.[15] In general, it can be said that cooking foods coagulates the bioactive protein chelated mineral forms, disrupts RNA and DNA structure, and produces free radicals in fats and protein.

In *The Essene Gospel of Peace, Book One* translated from the Dead Sea Scrolls, Jesus is quoted as saying, "For I tell you truly, live only by the fire of life, and prepare not your foods with the fire of death, which kills your foods, your bodies, and your souls also."[16]

Cooking food in these modern times has an added danger. Dr. William Newsome of Canada's Department of Health and Welfare Food Research Division, Bureau of Chemical Safety found that cooked fungicided tomatoes had 10 to 90 times more ETU, a mutagen and cancer-causing compound, than raw tomatoes from the same garden. He found that EBDC fungicides break down under heat to form ETU. He felt that the amount of ETU in chemically treated vegetables is 50 times greater than the same vegetables served raw.[17] The implications of this, with the enormous amounts of chemically treated foods we cook and consume, are worth considering.

Food Temperatures and Body Function

If the food we eat is too hot, it can actually disrupt the enzyme systems in our own gastric mucous as well as injure the gastric mucous directly. A study in *Lancet*, the well know British journal, showed that 15 percent of the people tested who drank tea at 122.5 degrees Fahrenheit and 77 percent of those who drank tea at temperatures greater than 137.5 degrees

Fahrenheit had gastric enzymatic abnormalities.[18]   Dr. McCluskey, in another *Lancet* study, found that constant irritation of the throat and tongue by hot foods, hot beverages, and alcohol was associated with increased cancer of the throat and tongue.[19]   He suggests that we dip our little finger in the hot drink for ten seconds. If it is not scalded, then we can go ahead and drink. The other extreme is that ice drinks and cold foods can slow down enzyme function and peristaltic action. We have the choice to be harmoniously moderate, eating and drinking foods at room temperature, or at temperatures no hotter than what Jesus calls the " fire of life" which is no hotter than temperatures in nature. Harmony is accepting and surrendering to nature's design.

Commentary from the *Essene Gospel of Peace Book One*

"And Jesus continued: 'God commanded your forefathers: Thou shalt not kill.' I say to you: Kill neither men, nor beasts, nor yet the food which goes into your mouth. For if you eat living food, the same will quicken you, but if you kill your food, the dead food will kill you also. For life only comes from life, and death always comes from death. For everything which kills your foods kills your bodies also. And everything which kills your bodies kills your souls also (the link to spiritual nutrition). Therefore, eat not anything which fire or frost or water has destroyed. For burned, frozen, and rotted foods will burn, freeze, and rot your body also. Be not like the foolish husbandman who sowed in his ground cooked, and frozen, and rotted seeds. And the autumn came, and his fields bore nothing. And great was his distress."

Application of Essene Food Principles

One of the greatest human experiments on the raw food diet was done by Dr. Edmond Bordeaux Szekely, who over a period of 33 years guided more than 123,600 people on such a diet with what he terms amazing results in benefitting the quality of people's health compared to control groups.[20] In commenting on his study, Szekely felt that he was on the threshold of great biochemical secrets of life that the Essenes had known thousands of years ago. In the book *The Essenes* by Josephus and his contemporaries, I was able to extract two basic Essene guidelines about food preparation and eating.[21]   These are the keys to these "great Essene secrets." The first is that their diet was raw, living, whole, natural foods. The second was that there was a minimal time lapse between when the food was harvested and when it was eaten. It is called eating in harmony with nature's laws. The Essenes intensely studied and penetrated the meaning of the laws of nature, and their eating patterns came as a result of this understanding. There was no storage, processing, freezing, drying, canning, or irradiating. The food was eaten in its full vital form. They knew that living foods contained a vital force for a period of time after it was picked from its environmental context of the earthly, solar, and cosmic energy. Over time and processing, this vital force is dissipated. The SOEFs lose their energy, and their pattern begins to disorganize. Our modern, scientifically accepted instruments cannot detect these subtle energy differences. There are instruments which can measure these subtle energies, but they are not yet considered acceptable by scientists. Because of the limitations in instrumentation, the actual measurable energy released from the carbon hydrogen bonds of live, whole foods and processed denatured foods would probably be the same in terms of actual calories produced. Our bodies get calories, but not vitality, from the processed cooked foods. Raw, live foods build up our SOEF patterns. Cooked processed foods deplete them. This consideration of SOEF is a major difference between the materialistic-mechanistic paradigm and the paradigm of spiritual nutrition. The only measurement we have is our subjective sensitivity, as when we eat a raw juicy carrot freshly plucked from the garden and compare it to a cooked carrot, or even to the quality of a several-day-old raw organic carrot from the health food store.

In the process of developing his health regenerating diet, Dr. Szekely developed a way of classifying foods that, in terms of the new nutritional paradigm, reflected his understanding of food as having energetic qualities. He saw that using only the materialistic paradigm of food as calories, proteins, fats, and carbohydrates was very limiting. He felt there were four categories of cell-renewing and life-generating foods. The first category he called biogenic.[22,23] These are the most life-generating, high-energy foods. They are alkaline producing and energy charged. They are high in enzymes, predigested complete proteins, chelated minerals, nucleic acids, vitamins, RNA, DNA, and B_{12}. These foods, he found, had the capacity to regenerate and revitalize the human organism. In this category we have all sprouts. This includes soaked and germinated nuts and seeds, sprouted grains, and legumes, as well as the sprouted young wheat grass and other grasses eaten whole or juiced. Sprouting is not a new development. Not only did the Essenes use this technique, but the history of sprouting goes as far back as 3000 B.C. in China with the recorded use of bean sprouts. The process of soaking is used because it activates the proteases which neutralize the enzyme inhibitors that keep the seed, legumes, and grains from germinating at the wrong time.[24] Germinating and sprouting increases the enzyme content by 6 to 20 times.[25] Plant hormones are also activated and phytates are split off, and there is a tremendous increase in metabolic activity. Starches are broken down into simple sugars, proteins are predigested into easily assimilated free amino acids, and fats are broken down into soluble fatty acids. Vitamin and mineral content increases with sprouting; this was one of the original clues of the phenomenon of biological transmutation. Vitamin B_6 is increased by 500 percent, B_5 by 200 percent, B_2 by 1300 percent, Biotin by 50 percent, and folic acid by 600 percent.[26] These biogenic foods have the capacity to generate a totally new organism. It is the life force of these foods which is transferred to people and aids their healing and regeneration.

The second category of foods is called bioactive foods.[27] These are foods which are capable of sustaining and slightly enhancing an already healthy life force. Bioactive foods include fresh, unprocessed, raw fruits and vegetables.

The third category is biostatic foods.[28] These are foods which are neither life-sustaining or life-generating; they diminish the quality of body functioning. They are life-slowing foods that slowly increase the process of aging. These are our cooked foods and foods which, although raw, are no longer fresh.

The fourth category he called bioacidic[29] or life-destroying foods. These are foods which have gone through many processes and refinements and are full of additives and preservatives. They rapidly break down life function.

In the spiritual nutrition paradigm, biogenic foods increase the total SOEF energy of the system and therefore increase the SOEF organization on every level. This results in a reversal of entropy and the aging process. Bioactive foods bring their own quality SOEF energy to the system, which is carried to particular SOEF patterns in our system, and which maintain and slowly energize the SOEF pattern of the organism. The biostatic foods require the human organism to give energy to reactivate the SOEFs of the cooked foods so they can be properly assimilated. The overall result in time is that there is a slow diminution of the total SOEF energy of the organism. This can be offset by other SOEF energizing activities such as meditating, but is this the best and most efficient way to use our SOEF energy? Bioacidic food disrupts and deenergizes the SOEF patterns, analogous to the Kouchakoff study, in which heavily processed foods not only caused a leukocytosis but changed the white blood cell pattern.

General Recommendations of Raw Versus Cooked

For the treatment of illness, Szekely, as do Paavo Airola, Ann Wigmore and Viktoras Kulvinskas, recommends a 100 percent raw food diet. When an individual is in generally good health, Szekely found that the people in his study could maintain themselves well eating 25 percent biogenic, 50 percent bioactive, and 10 to 25 percent biostatic foods. He allows this 10 to 25 percent of biostatic food as a concession, but feels that this should only be lightly cooked tubers and hard vegetables.[30] The world-famous Dr. Paavo Airola has stated that a 100 percent raw food diet would be ideal, but in the recognition that such a diet is difficult for most people to follow, recommends a ratio of 80 percent raw to 20 percent cooked as adequate for supporting general health with a little less raw foods in a colder climate.[31] Viktoras Kulvinskas, one of the top raw food experts in the world, feels a 100 percent raw food diet consisting of 50 percent biogenic and 50 percent bioactive foods will provide maximum quality health, but concedes for city dwellers and others in transition, that 80 to 90 percent raw with 10 to 20 percent cooked root vegetables will provide maintenance health.[32]

The conclusions of the new nutritional paradigm, the teachings of the Essenes of eating in harmony with nature's laws, the message of Jesus in the Essene Gospel, the information about the importance of not destroying enzymes with cooking, the loss of protein bioavailability, the loss of vitamins and minerals with cooking, the danger of fungicides and pesticides breaking down to form toxic compounds with heat, the increase in free radical production, and my own observation of the benefit of a primarily raw food diet for spiritual life make it clear to recommend an 80 percent raw food diet with 25 to 30 percent biogenic foods as basically adequate for general dietary support of spiritual life.

Summary Chapter 13

1. In cooked foods, 100 percent of the enzymes are destroyed, approximately 70 to 85 percent of the vitamins are destroyed, pesticides and fungicides break down to form toxic compounds, protein is 50 percent less assimilable because of coagulation, and there is an increase in free radical production.

2. All our life processes depend on enzyme function. When enzymes are depleted, so is our vital force and health.

3. Eating cooked foods causes a pathogenic leukocyctosis.

4. If food is too hot, it can disrupt our digestive enzymes.

5. When the physical level of the foods is disrupted through cooking, the energy and organization of the food SOEFs are partially disrupted.

6. The Essene secrets o food preparation and eating are to eat raw, living, whole, fresh, natural foods and to have a minimal time lapse between when the food is harvested and when it is eaten.

7. Foods can be classified into four categories according to their cell renewal and regenerating capabilities: biogenic (raw sprouted nuts, seeds, grasses, and grains) which is cell regenerative; bioactive (raw fruits and vegetables) which maintains cell energy at high level; biostatic (cooked, but organic) which creates a slow depletion of cell energy; and bioacidic (processed and adulterated) which is cell degenerative.

8. The general recommendation for a maintenance diet for health and spiritual life is 80 percent raw and 20 percent cooked foods, with 25 to 30 percent of the diet biogenic foods.

9. The recommendation for a healing diet is 100 percent raw.

14

High Versus Low Protein Diet

Fact and Fear

The high versus low protein controversy is more an issue of fear and confusion than fact. The high protein approach to nutrition was initially based on 19th century German research which said that people need a minimum of 120 grams of protein per day. This high protein thinking lingers today, even though the requirement is now considered by conventional nutritionists to be 60 to 90 grams each day. But expert research around the world suggests that the real protein requirement is closer to 25 to 35 grams and less if the protein we eat is raw. In separate research programs, Ragnar Berg, the well known Swedish nutritionist, and D. V. O. Siven in Finland both concluded that 30 grams of protein is sufficient for good health.[1] Dr. Hegsted from Harvard University and Dr. Kuratsuen from Japan independently found that 25 to 30 grams is sufficient.[2] Dr. K. Eimer found that when athletes reduced their protein intake from 100 grams of animal protein to 50 grams of vegetable protein their performances improved.[3] This supports our discussion in Chapter 8 of the superiority of high oxygen complex carbohydrate foods over protein as fuel. Dr. Chittenden, in extensive studies on soldiers and athletes, found that 30 to 50 grams per day is sufficient for maximum physical performance.[4] It is also interesting to note that the average mother's milk protein concentration is just 1.4 percent, sufficient to supply the human organism with all the essential amino acids and protein needed during the most rapid part of its growth and brain development.[5] Apes, considerably stronger than humans, live on a fruitarian diet which averages between 0.2 and 2.2 percent protein, equivalent to the protein concentration in human breast milk. These facts lead one to question: just how much protein do we really need?

Excess Protein and Degenerative Disease

The metabolic combustion of excess protein in the diet does not "burn cleanly," as discussed in Chapter 8, and has been associated with creating an overacid system because of the accumulation of toxic protein metabolic wastes such as uric acids and purines in the tissues. Airola points out that overeating protein "contributes to the development of many of our most common and serious diseases, such as arthritis, kidney damage, pyorrhea, schizophrenia, osteoporosis, atherosclerosis, heart disease, and cancer. " and that a "high protein diet causes premature aging and lowers life expectancy."[6] A high protein diet increases the rate of amyloid deposit in the cells. Amyloid is a byproduct of protein metabolism which is deposited in connective tissues and organs. It has definitely been linked with tissue and organ degeneration and premature aging.

The Russians have had some interesting success in treating schizophrenia with fasting and low protein vegetarian diets. Although they have made a clear connection between a high animal protein diet and certain types of schizophrenia, the exact causes are not clear. One part of the brain dysfunction may be related to certain mineral and vitamin deficiencies caused by a high animal protein diet. A high protein diet includes 20 times more phosphorous than calcium, which depletes calcium in the system, resulting in osteoporosis and tooth decalcification.[7] The schizophrenic condition might be related to B_3, B_6, and magnesium deficiencies which are created by a high meat protein diet.[8] The cited data strongly suggest that most people eat too much protein, and excess protein, especially if it is meat protein, is detrimental to our health.

The Wendt Doctrine

The Wendt doctrine, a result of 30 years of research by Wendt, Wendt, and Wendt, a family of physician researchers, has now received formal recognition by nutritional scientists in Germany. It explains one major factor connecting excess protein consumption to some forms of chronic degenerative disease.[9] The Wendts were able to prove with electron microscope pictures that excess protein clogs the basement membrane, a filtering membrane located between capillaries and cells. It helps regulate the flow of nutrients and waste products between capillaries and the cells and fluid in the tissues they penetrate. The more excess protein there is in the diet, the more protein is lodged in the basement membrane, resulting in a thicker basement membrane with clogged pores. It becomes harder for proteins, other nutrients, and even oxygen to get through to the cells and for waste and breakdown products to get out of the cells. Eventually, the basement membrane becomes so clogged with excess protein that the cells on the inside of the capillary walls begin to store and secrete the excess protein in insoluble forms which accumulate on the inside of the capillaries and arteriole walls, causing atherosclerosis, hypertension, adult-onset diabetes, and what the Wendts term capillarogenic tissue degeneration, the result of clogged basement membranes all over the system. This clogged basement membrane produces cellular malnutrition and results in the anoxia of the tissues. According to Dr. Steven Levine's hypothesis, anoxia is the cause of all degenerative diseases.[10] The key understanding is that excess protein in the diet results in a protein storage disease which slowly chokes off the system. It is much harder to meditate when one is choking on a cellular level and the vitality of the system is slowly dying out.

The Wendts found that this whole process could be reversed by stopping the intake of all animal protein for one to three months, and by eating a low protein diet. They point out that the basement membrane of a fetus is extremely thin and porous, so nutrients can easily pass in and out. Because there is no protein excess in the fetus, they feel that this membrane lets all nutrients into the cells easily. They hypothesize that if an adult were to eat a low protein diet, or do extensive fasting, she or he would achieve the same basement membrane porosity, thinness, and permeability as that of a fetus. This would allow excellent assimilation of nutrients into the cells and export of waste products out of the cells. It would insure the free flow of energy in the system and provide the metabolic energy needed to meditate and keep focused on communion with the Divine.

Protein Combining Is Unnecessary

One of the most unnecessary vegetarian practices is combining protein at meals. This inaccurate concept is that our system only utilizes protein in its complete state and we must eat all the amino acids at once to supply sufficient protein for out system to use metabolically. This fearful type of thinking comes from the idea that we do not store proteins and amino acids. The Wendt doctrine clearly proves that this is not true. Research on individuals fasting from all food shows that their serum albumen(a measure of protein in the system) remained constant throughout the fasting period, yet no protein was consumed.[11] This is because of the existence of an amino acid pool which continually sends free amino acids or protein complexes to where they are needed in the system. In his text book on physiology, the well-known physiologist Dr. Arthur Guyton describes how this amino acid pool works. He states that under normal circumstances all cells contain more protein than they need. When amino acids are needed somewhere else in the body, the excess protein in the cell is reconverted to the protein building blocks called amino acids. These amino acids diffuse into the bloodstream and either go directly to the cells that need them or to the liver, where they are built into new proteins and sent out into the blood to be carried to the appropriate sites. For these three reasons: our amino acid/protein equilibrium system, our cellular protein storage, and the free flow of amino acids in our amino acid pool, food combining to get complete proteins at one meal is completely unnecessary.

The biggest fear generated by pro-meat eaters and new vegetarians is about not getting enough protein. The real problem is just the opposite: we take in too much protein. According to the Max Planck Institute for Nutritional Research in Germany, considered by Paavo Airola to be the most respected and reliable nutritional research organization in the world, there are many vegetable sources of protein which are superior or equal to animal proteins. The Max Planck Institute found complete vegetarian proteins, those which contain all eight essential amino acids, to be available from almonds, sesame, pumpkin, and sunflower seeds, from soybeans, buckwheat, peanuts, potatoes, all leafy greens, and most fruits.[12] Fruits supply approximately the same percentage of complete protein as mother's milk.[13] Airola feels "it is virtually impossible not to get enough protein, provided you have enough to eat of natural, unrefined foods."[14]

Twenty-five to 30 grams of protein are more than sufficient for our protein intake. If the protein is taken in its raw form, even less is needed. In many cases, as our system changes with meditation, fasting, eating lighter, and increasing raw food intake, our basement membranes become clear, more porous, and thinner, so the protein we take in moves into the cells more readily. With reduced blockage, more of the protein we eat pushes itself through the basement membrane into the cells, so our protein needs spontaneously drop. Perhaps over time we might find that no more than the 1.4 percent protein of mother's milk is all we need. The lower limits are not clearly established on the materialistic plane for one who is undergoing a spiritual metamorphosis.

What can be said is that excess protein, whether from animal or vegetable sources, slows the flow of the subtle energy in the system and decreases our capacities as superconductors. It acts as a sludge to our body energy in general and specifically to the Kundalini energy. In fact, when the Kundalini energy becomes too intense for some individuals, I often recommend eating meat or lots of vegetarian protein to slow it down. This mild dietary change has worked well for people, and is one way to regulate the flow of the Kundalini energy. I first noticed this general sludge effect after I changed my diet to vegetarian in 1972. As my basement membranes cleared out of the toxic protein storage load, I began to sense when I was eating too many nuts and seeds to compensate for the supposedly low protein of a vegetarian diet. I would feel toxic, acidic, sluggish, and it was harder to focus in meditation. Through self-experimentation, I found the correct amount of protein intake to feel clear and energized. Over the years, as my basement membranes have cleared, I have slowly decreased my protein intake based on this feedback system. The point I am making is that there are no rules. Through self-observation, as our spiritual practices and bodies change, it is possible to determine what our individual protein needs are. A low protein intake is not the goal or even an idealization. To eat what helps us maximize the flow of energy in the body, the activity of Kundalini, and the experience of our God communion is the purpose of a low protein diet.

Summary Chapter 14

1. Recent scientific evidence suggests that 25 to 30 grams of quality protein are sufficient for good health.
2. Excess intake of protein is associated with many degenerative diseases.
3. The Wendt doctrine shows that excess protein clogs the basement membranes of capillaries, not letting oxygen and other nutrients get through to the tissues and cell, resulting in anoxia and cell destruction and death.
4. With meditation, fasting, and a raw food orientation, there is a gradual detoxification of the basement membrane, so we assimilate more protein while eating less. Our need for protein gradually decreases.
5. An excess of protein slows the flow of the spiritualizing energy of the Kundalini and of the body energy in general.

15

To Be or Not To Be: Vegetarian or Carnivore

Biblical Approach

"Behold I have given you every herb bearing seed which is upon the face of all the earth, and every tree in which is the fruit of a tree yielding seed; to you it shall be for meat" (Genesis 1:29). Ten generations later when Noah was leaving the ark after the great flood and there was no plant food that Noah could find immediately to eat, God said, "Every swarming creature that lives shall be yours to eat; like grass vegetation I have given you all" (Genesis 9:3). This was not a command to eat meat, but a dispensation for the immediate situation. In Leviticus 3:17, the commandment is given that "it is a statute to time indefinite for your generations, in all your dwelling places; you must not eat any fat or any blood at all." This is particularly good advice today, since fat from flesh foods has been implicated in so many degenerative diseases and is a major storage site for pesticides, herbicides, and other environmental toxins which enter the food chain. Up until Noah, the first ten patriarchs lived an average of 912 years. In the ten generation between Shem (Noah's son) and Abraham, the average life span dropped to 317 years. Eating flesh cut their life spans by approximately two-thirds. In Chapter 14, it was suggested that the main toxic and degenerate effect of a high protein diet was from eating meat rather than vegetarian protein. Statistics clearly show that vegetarians suffer less from chronic degenerative disease and cancer and have longer life spans than non-vegetarians. For example, in a study of Seventh Day Adventists, who are the largest single group of vegetarians in the United States, the risk rate of colon cancer was 1.0 for strict vegetarians as compared to 2.7 for beef eaters.[1] A study comparing mortality from breast cancer among strict vegetarian Seventh Day Adventists and those Seventh Day Adventists eating meat more than three times per week, showed that the vegetarians had half as much mortality.[2] Seventh Day Adventists had 40 percent less coronary disease, four times less mortality from respiratory disease, and a general mortality rate of 50 to 70 percent less compared to non-vegetarians living in the same American society.[3] The longest-lived people around the world, Hunzkuts, Bulgarians, East Indian Todas, Russian Caucasians, and Yucatan Indians, are either vegetarians or eat very little meat.[4] Only 5 out of 154 Bulgarian centenarians eat meat regularly.[5]

God's message to Adam was a clear commandment not to kill and eat the animals. At the giving of the Ten Commandments, "Thou shalt not kill" was interpreted by some to mean that one should not kill animals for food. This is certainly what is implied in the teachings of the Essenes and of Jesus in the *Essene Gospel of Peace Book One*. However, because of the direction given to Noah, we cannot dogmatically claim that the Old Testament message gives a totally clear moral direction from God about whether to be a vegetarian. For me, the original message of most complete harmony is in Genesis 1:29. It is my guide for understanding the commandment, "Thou shalt not kill", but I acknowledge that may not be an agreeable interpretation for everyone.

Difference Between Plant and Animal Nutrition

Plant nutrition, when understood as densified sunlight, is distinctly different from animal nutrition. Sunlight, as a cosmic radiation, stimulates the energetic subtle body of the plant and helps to build its structure out of carbon dioxide(CO_2) and water (H_2O) to form activated carbon-hydrogen bonds through the process of photosynthesis which store sunlight energy as excited electrons. Taken into our systems, they stimulate a resonant response from the inner light of our higher spiritual subtle bodies which directly receive the pranic transfer of the stored sunlight. In anthroposophical medicine, this relationship of plant light to the stimulation, formation, and maintenance of the nervous system is important for spiritual development. Rudolf Steiner felt that this outside light was significant because it stimulated the inner light as a spiritual process.[6]

When animals eat plants, they benefit directly from this release of light energy into the system. This light builds up the force of their nervous system and its related subtle astral or personality body. When animal foods are eaten by humans, we not only have to overcome the forces of the animal's biomolecular system, but also of this stronger astral body-nervous system. This puts a strain on our own nervous system development and function. This point becomes increasingly important when people have degenerative nervous system diseases. Dr. Swank's diet of low animal fat for the treatment of multiple sclerosis, a degenerative nervous system disease, is an example of the importance of avoiding or minimizing animal food when we are attempting to heal the nervous system.[7] By assimilating the plant energy directly, we stimulate our own inner light forces and nervous system. By taking in plant energy indirectly through animal foods, we lose the benefit of this stimulation on our inner light and nervous system. As already pointed out, if we do not exercise a biological system, such as our muscles, they weaken. In the same way, eating animal products weakens the nervous system in this indirect way. This is a major difference between plant and animal nutrition. By taking in plant nutrition, we go through the whole stimulation and assimilation process which the animals foods do not require of us. To digest vegetarian foods requires more inner spiritual light and digestive power. Over generations of heavy meat eating, some individuals have lost some this power and may have difficulty assimilating the living plant forces of a vegetarian diet.

Harmony of the Vegetarian Diet

With a vegetarian diet, we avoid the disharmony of killing animals. The vegetables we eat are taken from the ground in their seasonal cycles in harmony with when they are going to die naturally, and fruits are simply the sunshine gift of the living plant to us. There is a natural harmony between plants and humans. Plants take in carbon dioxide as a product of our respiration and convert it to oxygen and carbohydrates; thus we share an important biological life cycle. Each colored plant, as food, is a condensed spectrum band of sunlight color for us to take in for the balancing of our chakras and the physical organ, gland, and nervous systems. When we take in a full spectrum throughout the day, we benefit by having our total chakra system balanced energetically by our plant friends. This is the principle of the Rainbow Diet.

Bircher-Benner, a world-famous European physician, concluded that the closer food is to the natural sun energy, the higher it is in all levels of nutritional value for the human organism.[8] Plant food is at the top of the nutritional scale and animal food at the bottom. Dairy products fall in between. Steiner felt that raw milk only weakly carried the animal astral forces.[9] The Indian Ayurvedic and yogic systems also consider raw milk a high-quality food. Steiner clarifies another aspect of spiritual nutrition in his teaching that plant nutrition connects humanity to initially unrevealed cosmic forces. He feels that nothing clouds the nervous system when nourishment comes from the plant realm, and that it is by the nourishment of plants that humanity can delve into the cosmic interrelationships which take people beyond the constricted limitation of the mundane personality.[10]

Other Issues of Animal Nutrition

Animals may be our friends, but they are not if we eat them. In Genesis 9:3 it says not to eat the fat or the blood of animals. Blood is often filled with adrenaline because of the fear the animal experiences as it and those around it are being slaughtered. When we eat the flesh, unless it is Kosher and the blood is drained out, we take in fear-associated adrenaline. This adrenal-fear energy blocks the awakening of the first chakra into the feeling of trust, and stimulates our system in a way that is adverse to the inner stillness of meditation. In today's marketplace, animals are fed an assortment of pesticides, stilbesterol, hormones, antibiotics, tranquilizers, and even cement.

Because animals are at the top of the food chain, environmental pollution and radiation, such as strontium 90 is most concentrated in their flesh. It has been demonstrated that cancer virus can be transferred from one species to another.[11] In 1974 it was shown that chimpanzees fed from birth with milk from leukemic cows died of leukemia in the first year of life.[12]

In Chapter 8, I discussed how concentrated protein foods *i* not "burn cleanly," partly because of their nitrogen content. The nitrogen is metabolized into uric acid which has a toxic effect when an excess is deposited in the tissues. Our bodies are able to excrete only eight grains of uric acid per day, but one pound of meat leaves a residue of eighteen grains of uric acid.[13] Eating flesh foods makes it relatively easy to build up a uric acid excess in the tissues. One reason some people like meat is that it has an initial stimulating affect from the uric acid, perhaps because its structure is similar to that of caffeine. Meat protein is also very low in oxygen. A high meat diet seems to be related to a disruption of mental function, and in some cases has been found to either exacerbate or cause schizophrenia, according to the Russian research of Dr. Yuri Nikolayev of the Moscow Institute of Psychiatry. They have had some interesting success in stopping the symptoms of schizophrenia with water fasts.[14] When people revert to high meat intake their schizophrenic symptoms often return.

My observations in working with Kundalini and diet is that flesh foods act as "intense sludge" to the purifying and spiritualizing flow of Kundalini. Because of this "sludge effect," it is the primary dietary treatment I recommend when people feel the Kundalini energy has become too intense for them. If one wants to slow down the spiritualizing process of the Kundalini with diet, a flesh food diet is the most effective way.

Summary Chapter 15

1. Because of God's dispensation to Noah to eat animals, we can not dogmatically say that the Bible commands us to be vegetarian, as it did for Adam. Because of God's message to Noah, the commandment, "Thou shall not kill" can't be said to completely forbid killing animals for food. The choice is ours.

2. Statistics show that vegetarians live longer and have lower rates of chronic degenerative diseases such as arthritis, heart disease, and cancer.

3. Plant nutrition, when understood as densified sunlight, is distinctly different from animal nutrition.

4. The light released by the forces of the assimilated plant food stimulates an inner spiritual light which enhances our spiritual growth.

5. Although most people can benefit from a complete vegetarian diet, there are some who may no longer genetically have the digestive power to assimilate all their nutrients from a vegetarian diet.

6. A vegetarian diet creates more harmony because we do not have to kill blooded life forms. There is a synergistic oxygen and carbon dioxide life cycle connection between plants and animals. Plants contain the full rainbow spectrum of condensed sunlight for balancing our chakras and associated glands, organs, and nerve centers.

7. There is an added danger of eating animal products because of all the hormones, antibiotics, tranquilizers, and other assorted chemicals fed to animals. In addition, animals are at the top of our toxified food chain, so they concentrate the toxins in their tissues.

8. Animal flesh acts as an intense sludge to the flow of the Kundalini. Because of this, it is an effective treatment for decreasing the energy of the Kundalini.

16

Ayurveda Tridosha System and Individualizing the Diet

Tridosha Defined

There are many filters which guide our choice of diet. The tridosha system of the science of Ayurveda is particularly useful in helping us maintain our awareness of nutrition as the interaction between the forces of food and our own dynamic forces. According to Ayurveda, the five basic elements of creation -- air, water, fire, earth, and ether -- manifest in the human psychosomatic complex as three dosha essences: vata, kapha, and pitta. We are all born as a constitutional combination of the three. They govern all our biological and psychological aspects. When they are in balance, they maintain the body in a healthy physiological state. If the doshas become unbalanced, the result can range from a feeling of subtle disharmony in the body-mind complex to the development of disease.

When one dosha predominates as a constitutional force, a person is said to have a constitution of that dosha. There are seven basic constitutional types: kapha, vata, pitta, vata-pitta, pitta-kapha, kapha-vata, and kapha-pitta-vata. There are subtle variations of the different constitutional types. Having a feeling for our constitutional type helps us make choices about what foods we should eat, when we should eat, and how to change our diet with the seasons. My purpose here is to give enough of a feeling for the tridosha system so that we can begin to identify our particular constitution as a key in organizing our diet.

Vata Dosha

The vata dosha is roughly translated as air or wind, or ether in the Greek system. It is the principle of movement in the body and the energy that governs biological movement in the body. It is formed of two of the five elements: ether and air. Vata regulates breathing, all movements of the muscles and tissues, the heart muscle, and all biological movements intra- and extracellular, including the single movements of the nerve impulses.

People with a vata constitution are generally thin, with flat chests, and have noticeable veins and muscle tendons. They have a tendency to have dry, cracked skin. Vata people are very creative people who have active, alert, and restless minds. The talk and move quickly, but also fatigue easily. They are quick to grasp things mentally. Their will power is weak, and they tend to be easily knocked off center. They are not mentally stable and tend to be nervous, anxious, and fearful. Their animal archetype is the rabbit, dog, rat, goat, camel, or crow.[1]

When there is an imbalance of vata, I often recognize it on the psychological level as nervousness, fear, anxiety, insomnia, pain, tremors, and spasms. A vata imbalance may also manifest as rough skin, arthritis, emaciation, stiffness, constipation, dryness, thirst, insomnia, excessive sensitivity and excitability, and physical pain. There is a tendency to lower bowel disorders such as excess gas, low back pain, sciatica, paralysis, and neuralgias. Vata personalities are adversely affected by cold, windy, stormy, and rainy weather, which can directly imbalance their nervous system. For example, I once helped a person with a predominant vata dosha stop her insomnia by having her turn off her fan at night. The wind from the fan was causing a vata imbalance. In general, anything which causes excess, such as a strenuous exercise or mental labor, extreme diet, grief, anger, suppression of natural urges, severe weather conditions, or any practices taken to the limit will cause an imbalance in vata.

Vata people enjoy sweet, salty, and sour tastes. They are often thrown out of balance by taking bitter, astringent (dry), or pungent foods. Sesame seed oil on the skin, a little oil in their food, and a stable, calm, soothing environment help to bring the vata dosha back into balance.

Pitta Dosha

The pitta dosha is roughly translated as fire and is experienced as bodily heat energy. It is the force which governs metabolism. It affects digestion, assimilation, and body temperature. It is similar to bile in the Greek system. Pitta is formed from the water and fire elements.

Those who are predominantly pitta are characterized by strong digestion, large appetites for food and drink, high body heat, intolerance to heat and the sun. They have abundant perspiration, moderate strength and build, strong body odor, a more coppery skin with lots of freckles, moles, and blackheads. Their skin is oily, and there is a tendency for their hair to gray prematurely. Hands and feet are usually warm. They crave cold drinks, and sweet, astringent, and bitter foods. Psychologically, people with a predominant pitta dosha have good comprehension and intelligence. They don't overstrain themselves at work. They are, however, ambitious. They have a tendency toward vanity, intolerance, pride, aggressiveness, stubbornness, hatefulness, anger, and jealousy. Their character resembles that of the archetypal tiger, cat, monkey, owl, or bear.[2]

Summer or midday heat will tend to cause an aggravation of the pitta dosha. During the hot season in India, these were the people I observed to have summer colds, heart palpitations, heat prostration, skin disorders like hives and heat rash, and general misery from the heat. It was often quite dramatic. My son, who is a predominant pitta dosha, was completely healthy through all the seasons we were in India until the hot season. Within the first few days of 100 to 120 degree temperatures, he became sick, exhausted, developed rashes all over his body, and was barely able to attend school. As soon as the cooling monsoon season began, his health returned completely. Other signs of pitta aggravation are acidity, fainting, excessive perspiration, restlessness, increased thirst and desire for cold substances, paleness, and in extreme cases, delirium. Other causes for derangement of pitta are anger, grief, excess physical exertion, fear, improper digestion, acid system, too much pungent, acid, salty, and dry food, too much mustard seed, sesame and linseed oil, fish, mutton, stems of green leafy vegetables, and wine. Sweet, astringent, bitter tasting foods help to rebalance pitta, as do moonlight, cold baths, milk, and ghee.

Kapha Dosha

The kapha principle can be translated as biological water, like the Greek phlegm. It is considered to be formed from earth and water elements. Kapha governs biological strength, vigor, and stability, and natural tissue resistance. It lubricates the joints, moisturizes the skin, gives energy to the heart and lungs, helps heal wounds, and fills the spaces in the body. Kapha activates the anabolic or growth forces in the body -- one reason kapha people tend to become overweight. Kapha manifests as mucus in the chest, throat, nose, sinuses, mouth, joints, and cytoplasm.

People with a kapha constitution have well-developed bodies. They have the type of physical constitutions we may stereotype as football linemen. Kapha people have a slow digestion, made even slower by oily or fatty foods. They do well with pungent, bitter, and astringent food, which often help to bring them into balance. They are especially thrown out of balance by sweet (which they often crave), sour, and salty foods. Excessively sweet fruits may also cause a derangement. The one exception to this is raw honey, which is considered the main dietary antidote to a kapha imbalance. All dairy products, with the exception of some goat milk products, tend to cause derangement in kapha. Goat milk has slight astringent qualities that help minimize the kapha imbalance. Kapha people generally are not very thirsty and should not drink the eight glasses of liquid per day that are supposed to be so healthy for everyone.

Exercise is very important for kapha people. They do poorly if they do not get sufficient or regular exercise, or if they nap during the day. It was a relief for me to discover that my predominant kapha constitution was the cause for my need for exercise, my not feeling good after day naps, and my slow digestion, made even slower with oil.

Tolerance, calmness, forgiveness, and love are predominant kapha characteristics. They are also characterized as righteous, generous, steadfast in friendship, stable of mind, given to measured and deliberate speech, enthusiastic, and understanding. They have tendencies toward greed, attachment, envy, and possessiveness. Intellectually, they may be slow to comprehend, but once they grasp a concept they retain it well. Their symbolic animal archetypes are bull, lion, elephant, horse, or football lineman (in college, I was a football lineman). Kapha constitutions are thrown into imbalance in cold and damp weather. For example, during my first year in India, my nose never dripped, but within one half hour of stepping out of the plane into the damp cold London climate my nose began to run. Kapha people benefit most from the mucousless diet. Exercise, fasting, and heat are also important treatments for people with kapha dosha aggravation or constitution. Symptoms of kapha derangement are heaviness, drowsiness, constipation, itching, skin disease, dullness, laziness, depression, and excess mucus production.

The Doshas and the Cycles

The seasons, the time of day, and one's age are also forces affecting the balance of the doshas. From birth to the teen years, the predominant dosha is kapha. It governs growth. The most obvious manifestation of this is the tendency for frequent colds and runny noses we see in young children. From the teens to the sixties, pitta tends to predominate. Later, there is a tendency toward vata disorders such as arthritis, dryness of skin, tremors, emaciation, and memory loss. As we get older, no matter what our constitution, we need to shift our diet and life style to adjust for the increasing power of the vata dosha on the body-mind complex (Figure 8).

In the daily cycle, kapha forces predominate in all of us from sunrise until 10 a.m. Because of this, those with a strong kapha constitution are most easily thrown into imbalance at this time and do well to avoid dairy products in the morning, eating a light breakfast or none at all. From 10 a.m. to 2 p.m., pitta predominates. This is a very good time to eat, especially for kapha people. However, on a hot day those with a pitta derangement or constitution should eat lightly because pitta is aggravated around noon, when the sun is hottest. From 2 p.m. until sunset, vata predominates. Vata imbalances are often experienced as fatigue and bloating in the late afternoon. Kapha again begins to predominate from sunset to 10 p.m.. Because of this, it is better for everyone, and particularly kapha people, to eat about one hour before sunset. If we eat too late, the decreased digestive fire associated with kapha may not be enough to digest food sufficiently. The result is an immediate toxic buildup which may result in disturbed sleep and difficulty arising early in the morning to meditate. Pitta becomes active between 10 p.m. and 2 a.m., and vata predominates from 2 a.m. until sunrise. Vata creates movement and lightness, and helps to wake people up. This is also a good time to meditate (Figure 9).

The cycle of each season has the potential to aggravate a particular dosha. By being conscious of the seasonal shifts of dosha energies, we are able to shift our diets to maintain balanced doshas. This healthy practice of eating with the seasons is not unique to Ayurveda. Elson Haas, M.D., in his book *Staying Healthy with the Seasons* has described this approach from a Chinese acupuncture point of view.[3] I observe that on the equinoxes, September and March 21, and on the solstices, June and December 21, people are vulnerable to health imbalances. During these times, it is harmonious and a good preventive practice to eat lightly and make an extra effort to keep our life styles and doshas in balance.

Figure 8

The fall, September through November, is a time of winds. It is a time of a decrease in temperature and beginning preparation for the winter. During this time vata has a tendency to aggravate. It is important to minimize our exposure to the wind and cold. We can begin to increase intake of foods which have more sweet, sour (acid), and salty tastes, and to increase our intake of rice, wheat, barley, oats, and oily foods.

In the damp cold of winter, kapha is the dosha most likely to aggravate. It is a time when mucous disorders such as colds, congestion, and bronchitis tend to emerge. It is a time to minimize fatty foods, dairy products, and foods with sweet, salty, or sour tastes. The exception to this is a moderate amount of raw honey, which decreases kapha. This is a time to eat more dry, bitter, pungent, hot, and astringent foods, and to maintain an exercise program and not to nap during the day.

In the early spring, the Ayurvedic teachings describe kapha as becoming liquified. This is another peak aggravation time for kapha. As a physician, I notice a sudden upsurge in kapha disorders such as colds, flus, and bronchitis. This is an excellent time to fast. Fasting, which balances kapha, allows us to clean out the winter kapha buildup, rather than have it clean us out by a kapha aggravation. It is an important time to eat lightly and begin to shift to more fruits, vegetables, and other raw foods. The kapha balancing program is still best to follow during this time.

In late spring and summer, as the sun begins to heat and dry the land and our bodies, it is the time of pitta aggravation. We see heat rashes, sunburn, burning feet, rashes, heart palpitations, swollen feet, and mental irritability. Sweet, cool liquids, and foods like watermelon are excellent at this time. Foods with sweet, astringent, and bitter tastes help to balance the doshas. Salty, sour, pungent, and hot foods should be minimized. The highest percentage of the diet should be raw, with a particular emphasis on fruits. Cold baths, minimizing direct sunlight from 10 a.m. to 2 p.m., and avoiding excessive physical exertion help to minimize a pitta aggravation (Figure 10).

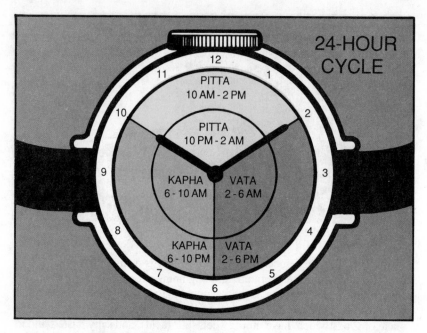

Figure 9

No Single Diet for Everyone

The descriptive science of the doshas illustrates an essential point about nutrition: there is no single diet for everyone at any one time nor a constant diet throughout the year for a single person. Kapha constitution people will be aggravated by a diet high in brown rice and salt. Vata people become grounded with brown rice and salty foods. Some vata people can tolerate a little dairy, while a kapha person may become congested from it. There are a few foods which all would do well to avoid. For example, it is generally best to avoid concentrated processed sweets like white sugar, which are clearly poisonous to the body and mind. Those with a pitta constitution are aggravated by raw honey. However, those with a kapha constitution are balanced by raw honey. For a long period of time, I avoided all sweets, including honey. Recently, in the morning, when kapha has a tendency to aggravate, I occasionally add a half teaspoon of raw honey as an experiment and felt a subtle positive difference. The art of food selection is to become sensitive to the foods which help maintain a dosha balance between our inner constitutional dosha tendencies and the environmental and cyclic effects of nature on the doshas. What I have presented are single dosha archetypes. In reality we are a mixture of all three doshas. Sometimes a single dosha predominates, while sometimes there are two doshas jointly more active, with one slightly stronger than the other. Sometimes all three are of equal strength. In any case, no matter what the combination, we are all affected by cyclic changes and need to pay intelligent attention.

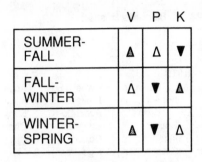

	V	P	K
SUMMER-FALL	▲	Δ	▼
FALL-WINTER	Δ	▼	▲
WINTER-SPRING	▲	▼	Δ

KEY	
Δ	= AGGRAVATES DOSHA
▲	= MINOR EFFECT ON DOSHA
▼	= BALANCES DOSHA
V	= VATA WIND GOAT
P	= PITTA FIRE TIGER
K	= KAPHA WATER ELEPHANT

Figure 10

The Six Tastes and Six Food Qualities

Meals prepared Ayurvedically usually contain different percentages of all six tastes because all six together are said to create a harmonious energy and nutrient balance. The six tastes are sweet (milk, honey, rice, breads, butter); sour (lemon and yogurt); salty (salt), pungent (spicy foods, ginger, cayenne, and cumin); bitter (spinach and other leafy greens); and astringent (beans and lentils). As we can see in Figure 11 the energies associated with different tastes aggravate or balance the doshas in particular patterns.

There are also six major food qualities to consider. Heavy (cheese, yogurt, and wheat); light (barley, corn, spinach, and apples); oily (dairy products, fatty foods, and oils); dry (barley, corn, potatoes, and beans); hot food and drink, and cold food and drink. Figure 12 shows the effect of food qualities on the doshas.

	V	P	K
SWEET	▼	▼	Δ
SOUR	▼	Δ	Δ
SALTY	▼	Δ	Δ
PUNGENT	Δ	Δ	▼
BITTER	Δ	▼	▼
ASTRINGENT	Δ	▼	▼

Figure 11

	V	P	K
HEAVY	▼	▼	Δ
OILY	▼	▼	Δ
HOT	▼	Δ	▼
LIGHT	Δ	Δ	▼
DRY	Δ	Δ	▼
COLD	Δ	▼	Δ

Figure 12

Food Guidelines for Basic Constitutional Types

Note: Guidelines provided in this table are general. Specific adjustments for individual requirements may need to be made, e.g. food allergies, strength of agni, season of the year, and degree of dosha predominance or aggravation.

(+ Aggravates Dosha   - Balances Dosha)

Vata		Pitta		Kapha	
+	**-**	**+**	**-**	**+**	**-**

FRUITS

Vata +	Vata -	Pitta +	Pitta -	Kapha +	Kapha -
Dried Fruits	Sweet Fruits	Sour Fruits	Sweet Fruits	Sweet &Sour	Apples
Apples	Apricots	Apricots	Apples	Fruits	Apricots
Cranberries	Avocado	Berries	Avocado	Avocado	Berries
Pears	Bananas	Bananas	Coconut	Bananas	Cherries
Persimmon	Berries	Cherries	Figs	Coconut	Cranberries
Pomegranate	Cherries	Cranberries	Grapes (dark)	Figs (fresh)	Figs (dry)
Watermelon	Coconut	Grapefruit	Mango	Grapefruit	Mango
	Figs(fresh)	Grapes(green)	Melons	Grapes	Peaches
	Grapefruit	Lemons	Oranges(sweet)	Lemons	Pears
	Grapes	Oranges(sour)	Pears	Melons	Persimmon
	Lemons	Papaya	Pineapple(swt.)	Oranges	Pomegranate
	Mango	Peaches	Plums(sweet)	Papaya	Prunes
	Melons(sweet)	Pineapple(sour)	Pomegranate	Pineapple	Raisins
	Oranges	Persimmon	Prunes	Plums	
	Papaya	Plums(sour)	Raisins		
	Peaches				
	Pineapples				
	Plums				

VEGETABLES

Vata +	Vata -	Pitta +	Pitta -	Kapha +	Kapha -
Broccoli	Asparagus	Pungent	Sweet&Bitter	Sweet&Juicy	Pung.&Bitter
Brussels Sprt.	Beets	Vegetables	Vegetables	Vegetables	Vegetables
Cabbage	Carrots	Beets	Asparagus	Cucumber	Asparagus
Cauliflower	Cucumber	Carrots	Broccoli	Pototoes(swt.)	beets
Celery	Garlic	Eggplant	Brussels Sprt.	Tomatoes	Broccoli
Eggplant	Green Beans	Garlic	Cabbage	Zucchini	Brussels Spr.
Leafy Greens*	Okra(cooked)	Onions	Cauliflower		Cabbage
Lettuce*	Onion(cooked)	Peppers(hot)	Cauliflower		Carrots
Mushrooms	Potato(sweet)	Radishes	Celery		Cauliflower
Onions(raw)	Radishes	Spinach	Green Beans		Celery
Parsley*	Zucchini	Tomatoes	Leafy Greens		Eggplant
Peas			Mushrooms		Leafy Greens
Peppers			Okra		Lettuce
Potatoes(white)			Peas		Mushrooms
Spinach*			Parsley		Okra
Sprouts*			Peppers(green)		Onions
Tomatoes			Potatoes		Parsley
			Sprouts		Peas
			Zucchini		Peppers
					Potato(white)
					Radishes
					Spinach
					Sprouts

*These vegetables are OK in moderation with oil dressing

Figure 13

	Vata		Pitta		Kapha	
	+	-	+	-	+	-

GRAINS

Vata +	Vata -	Pitta +	Pitta -	Kapha +	Kapha -
Barley	Oats(cooked)	Buckwheat	Barley	Oats(cooked)	Barley
Buckwheat	Rice	Corn	Oats(cooked)	Rice(brown)	Corn
Corn	Wheat	Millet	Rice(basmati)	Rice(white)	Millet
Millet		Oats(dry)	Rice(white)	Wheat	Oats(dry)
Oats(dry)		Rice(brown)	Wheat		Rice(basmati, small amount)
Rye		Rye			Rye

ANIMAL FOODS

Vata +	Vata -	Pitta +	Pitta -	Kapha +	Kapha -
Lamb	Beef	Beef	Chicken(wht)	Beef	Chicken(drk)
Pork	Chicken(white)	Eggs(yolk)	Eggs(white)	Lamb	Eggs(scrmb)
Rabbit	Eggs(fried or	Lamb	Rabbit	Pork	Rabbit
Venison	scrambled)	Pork	Shrimp	Seafood	Shrimp
	Seafood	Seafood	(small amount)		Turkey(dark)
	Turkey(white)		Turkey(white)		Shrimp
			Venison		Venison

LEGUMES

Vata	Pitta	Kapha
No Legumes Except Mung, Tofu, Black & Red Lentils	All Legumes OK Except Lentils	All Legumes are Good Except Kidney Beans, Soy Beans, Black Lentils, Mung Beans

NUTS

Vata	Pitta	Kapha
All Nuts are OK in Small Amts.	No Nuts Except Coconut	No Nuts at All

SEEDS

Vata	Pitta	Kapha
All Seeds are OK (in moderation)	No Seeds Except Sunflower and Pumpkin. Sprouted and Soaked Seeds are OK.	No Seeds Except Sunflower and Pumpkin. Sprouted and Soaked Seeds are OK.

SWEETENERS

Vata	Pitta	Kapha
All Sweeteners are OK Except White Sugar	All Sweeteners are OK Except Molasses and Honey	No Sweeteners Except Raw Honey

CONDIMENTS

Vata	Pitta	Kapha
All Spices are Good	No Spices Except Coriander, Cinnamon, Cardamom, Fennel Turmeric, and little Black Pepper	All Spices are Good Except Salt

DAIRY

Vata	Pitta		Kapha
All Dairy Products are OK (in moderation)	Buttermilk	Butter(unsalt.)	No Dairy Except Ghee & Goatmilk
	Cheese	Cottage Cheese	
	Sour Cream	Ghee	
	Yogurt	Milk	

OILS

Vata	Pitta		Kapha
All Oils are Good	Almond	Coconut	No Oils Except Almond, Corn, or Sunflower in Small Amounts
	Corn	Olive	
	Safflower	Sunflower	
	Sesame	Soy	

Over the years, Ayurvedic physicians have developed a list of foods and food types according to how they aggravate or balance the doshas. Figure 13 is a slightly modified list taken from Dr. Vasant Lad's excellent book *Ayurveda, The Science of Self Healing*.[4]

Perspective on Ayurveda Tridosha System

To achieve an optimum diet for our spiritual life, we must be attuned to our own constitutional, diurnal, seasonal, and practical work needs. It requires creating a harmony between our inner needs and the external play of nature. It means not giving up our intuition and power to "this is the answer" diet fads, computer diet programs, any singular diet system that claims to be the only way to health, or even Ayurvedic lists of the right foods for our doshas. No single system, including Ayurvedic, is 100 percent accurate. For example, Rudolph Ballentine, M.D., who uses the Ayurveda in his approach, feels that the application of the system is only 80 percent accurate.[5]

Energy Balancing with Herbs

Ayurvedic science has observed that individual foods and herbs have specific energetic qualities which are suggested to us by the nature of their taste. For example, as a predominant kapha constitution, I've learned to stay away from onions, which aggravate kapha, and lean toward vegetables and greens like carrots, dill, radish, cabbage, cauliflower, lettuce, and spinach, which all decrease kapha. In my raw diet approach, I have added certain herbs to maintain the dosha balance throughout the yearly cycles. For example, as a predominant kapha constitution I use ginger, cardamom, cayenne, and cumin as kapha dosha balancers, particularly in the winter when heat is needed. Vata people may want to include the energy of cinnamon, cardamom, cumin, ginger, sea salt, cloves, mustard, and licorice in their diets at the appropriate times. Pitta people would do better to avoid spices except for cinnamon, coriander, and dill.

The use of herbs in this way reaffirms the principle clarified in Chapter 1 that each food has its own energy essence. Western nutrition's singular focus on classifying foods as simply carbohydrate, protein, and fat increases our sense of separation from food and our harmony with nature.

Summary Chapter 16

1. The tridosha system, by helping us identify our constitutional dosha mixture of kapha, pitta, and vata offers a harmonious diet for spiritual life.
2. Nutrition is concerned with the dynamic interaction of the forces of the foods with the dynamic forces of our own bodies.
3. We can organize and change our diets according to the dosha energy shifts of the cycles of the seasons, days, and our own lives.
4. By using the energies of different herbs to balance our doshas, we add a useful dimension to the raw food diet.
5. Herbs reaffirm the principle that each food has its own energy essence

17

Food Balancing

Three Categories of Food Balancing

In this chapter we will discuss three types of food balancing. The first is alkaline/acid balance, which reflects the physical level of food. The second is yin/yang balance, which recognizes that food has both physical and subtle energy attributes and is the key to understanding energy quality and the general mineral composition of the food. Yin/yang is another system that codes foods according to color, shape, and other characteristics. This of course further supports the concept of the Rainbow Diet. The third form of food balancing has to do with the relationship between the forces of the foods we take into our system and the digestive forces of our system. It is called food combining.

Acidosis

The correct acid/alkaline balance in our food intake is very important. Almost all authorities agree that when the body becomes too acidic, it becomes fertile ground for acute and chronic disease. Airola feels that acidosis, which is a high concentration of acid in the body, is one of the basic causes of all disease, particularly arthritis.[1] Others feel it may even contribute to a cancer-producing cellular environment.[2] There are several reasons why an acidic system produces disease. In Chapter 8, we discussed how the negative pole sends electrons to the positive pole. When there is enough oxygen for this process of metabolic oxidation to take place, we get very effective energy production. If the process is limited by a decrease in oxygen, then there is less energy to power cellular function effectively, and cells begin to break down and die. An acidic system is one that has an excess of hydrogen ions (H^+), which combine with oxygen to form water. Doing so, the excess hydrogen ions short circuit the oxidative metabolism cycle because they use up the oxygen. Anoxia results, and less oxygen is available for its primary function of oxidative metabolism, the production of energy for proper cell function.

The more acidic the system becomes, the less the biochemical buffers in the blood are able to maintain the blood's healthy acid/alkaline balance. The pH, which measures this acid/alkaline balance, begins to become acidic. One way the body compensates for this is to preserve blood alkalinity by depositing excess acidic substances in the tissues and joints.[3] This might explain why acidity increases arthritis. The more acidic a particular tissue area becomes, the more cell degeneration and death there is.

Dead and dying cells make the system still more acidic.

Another mechanism at work at the cellular level is the bioelectric potential that exists between the naturally acidic cell nucleus and the alkaline cytoplasm which surrounds the cell's nucleus.[4] These two poles create a cell battery that maintains the bioelectric potential needed for life function. The degree of polarity between these two poles reflects the vitality of the cell. When the blood and extracellular tissues become acidic, cytoplasm also becomes acidic, and there is less electric potential between it and the cell nucleus. A diminishing of this bioelectric potential means reduced cell vitality and function.

On a grosser level, acid-producing foods seem to create excess mucous, which congests the system and blocks oxygen from entering our system. The result, again, is tissue and cell anoxia. This occurs with an excess of grains, meat, or dairy, all of which are acid-forming foods.

Chemistry of Alkaline-Acid Balance

In understanding the meaning of the alkaline-acid balance, it is important to realize that this balance takes place primarily in the fluid system of our body. Body fluids comprise 70 percent of our body weight: fluid in the cells constitutes 55 percent of our body weight, fluid in our blood is 5 percent, and fluid in the tissues surrounding the cells is 10 percent of body weight. We are a more sophisticated version of the single cell organisms being nurtured by the ocean waters, only the "ocean" is inside of us. Like the oceans and fresh bodies of water which are dying because of pollution, if our bodily fluids become polluted, an acidic acid/base imbalance develops, which kills us too. An interesting study was done by Alexis Carrel, a French physiologist. By carefully maintaining the fluid in which embryonic chicken heart cells were living, keeping it slightly alkaline, he was able to keep these cells alive for 28 years. When he stopped maintaining this extra-cellular fluid in the correct biochemical balance, the cells died. Our fluid alkaline-acid balance is just as important. The normal pH of the blood is 7.4. If it becomes even slightly acidic, the body begins to malfunction. A neutral pH is 7.0; when the blood reaches a pH of 6.95, we experience coma and death, because at this pH the heart relaxes and cannot beat. If pH becomes too alkaline, in the range of 7.7, we become irritable, spasmodic, and can develop tetany and convulsions.

Foods that are high in phosphorous and sulphur produce acid in the system by metabolizing the sulphur and phosphorus into sulphuric and phosphoric acid. In order for the body to excrete these poisonous acids without hurting the kidneys and the bowels, the body neutralizes them with alkaline-forming mineral salts, primarily sodium, potassium, magnesium, and calcium. Foods, such as most vegetables and fruits, which are high in sodium, potassium, calcium, and magnesium usually are alkaline-forming. When these elements are diminished, the system becomes acidic. To maintain the alkaline-forming minerals in the body, and therefore to foster a slightly alkaline condition in the body, we need to eat a certain amount of foods with alkaline-forming elements.

Our bodies are both alkaline and acidic at the same time, with either acid or alkaline predominating. The correct percentage of alkaline- or acid-forming food intake can help to adjust this dynamic equilibrium. The general consensus of Western nutritionists is that the healthiest acid/alkaline balance in the body is maintained by an optimum ratio of 80 percent alkaline-forming foods to 20 percent acid-forming foods.[5] When this ratio is maintained, there is strong resistance against disease. People recovering from an illness are usually more acidotic, and so an even more alkaline diet will hasten the return to health. Airola feels that when the ratio slips to three-to-one, health is endangered.[6] In the yoga system the acid-alkaline ratio for the purest diet is a minimum of 70 percent to 30 percent, for a medium quality diet it is 60 percent to 40 percent, and the most unhealthy diet it is less than 50 percent alkaline- to acid-forming foods.

It is a good idea to maintain a high alkaline mineral salt reserve in order to be able to neutralize emergency situations in which the body becomes acidic. Another reason for eating alkaline-forming foods is that an acidic diet has a low sodium and calcium which consequently reduces the levels of potassium and magnesium in the nerve cells, which results in their improper functioning. If we become too acidic, our cells' functioning diminishes and we lose mental clarity. The mind slows, and eventually coma occurs below the pH of 6.95. An example of this is the diabetic coma that is seen in people who develop severe diabetic acidosis. A slow mind and decreased mental clarity are typical of many whose diet is too acidic.

Definition of Alkaline and Acid Forming Foods

An alkaline-forming food is one which creates an alkaline condition in the body. These are foods which contain high concentrations of sodium, potassium, calcium, magnesium, and iron. Foods that are high in sulphur, phosphorus, chlorine, and iodine are acid-forming foods. They are metabolized in the body to form acids. **Acid-forming foods are not the same as foods such as lemons which contain high concentrations of organic acids and taste acidic.** These mild organic acids act as cleansing agents in the system. They are oxidized into carbon dioxide and water and therefore do not create an acid condition in our system. Because they bring high concentrations of the alkaline-forming minerals to the body, acid fruits increase the alkaline reserve of the body and therefore are alkaline-forming. Foods which decrease the alkaline mineral reserve are considered acid-forming foods.

It is useful to understand that all natural foods contain both alkaline- and acid-forming minerals. If the acid-forming minerals are greater, then the food is acid-forming. If the alkaline-forming minerals are greater, then the food is alkaline-forming. The degree of alkaline- or acid-forming elements in the food can be measured in the laboratory. The nature of the organic matter of the food does not seem to matter in this determination.[7] To determine the acid- or alkaline-forming potential of a food, it is first burned to its mineral ash, then dissolved in neutral pH water. Then the pH of the solution is tested to see if it is acid or alkaline. Chemists are able to measure just how alkaline or acid the solution is, and therefore rate just how alkaline- or acid-forming the food is. There are different charts which give this information.[8,9,10,11]

Acid-Forming and Alkaline-Forming Foods

Most flesh foods are acid-forming, as are most grains, dairy products (especially cheese), a majority of nuts and seeds, beans and peas, simple sugars, fats, and vegetarian protein. Oils are close to neutral. Alkaline-forming foods are vegetables and fruits. Exceptions include asparagus, cranberries, plums, and prunes which are all slightly acidic.[12] In general, the metabolic process of animal organisms is to convert alkaline to acid, and of plants, to convert acid to alkaline. By receiving our needed alkaline minerals from our plant friends we continue the balancing and harmonious cycle between humans and the plant kingdom.

There are some exceptions to these acid- and alkaline-forming generalities. Yogurt and raw milk of goat, cow, and human are considered slightly alkaline, but if milk is pasteurized, it becomes slightly acidic. Cheeses are acidic. Butter is sightly acidic, and because it has so much fat, it is probably more acidic than actually rated chemically. Soybeans are considered alkaline, and tofu is slightly alkaline. Kidney and aduki beans, almonds and brazil nuts, and green corn and millet are alkaline-forming. Asparagus tips, Brussels sprouts, and rhubarb are reported to be acid-forming vegetables.[13]Nuts, seeds, and grains become more alkaline-forming in the process of soaking and sprouting for a minimum of eight hours.

Proteins as a class are the most acid-forming because of their high concentrations of sulphur and phosphorus. Their metabolic breakdown also produces uric acid, which further acidifies the system, and urea, which increases excretion through the kidneys in a way that carries out the much-needed alkaline-forming minerals. Excess protein also clogs the basement membranes, causing cell anoxia and death, which further increases the acidity. Fats as a general class are acid-forming because their metabolism produces acetic acid. Simple carbohydrates like white sugar are acid-forming because they enter the system too quickly and burn too fast. In this unbalanced process, they produce acids such as lactic, butyric, and acetic acid, which acidify the system. Complex carbohydrates metabolize more slowly and evenly and therefore do not form organic acids. Animal research shows that foods with high natural vitamin B content help maintain the correct acid/alkaline balance when there is too much protein consumption.[14] Food containing natural vitamin A helps to rebalance the acidity from overeating fat. Foods high in vitamin C help compensate for acidity from too much sugar and other simple carbohydrates. This research also showed that an excess of synthetic vitamins tends to make the system acidic.[15] Refined foods, medical drugs, psychedelic drugs, soft drinks, and synthetic drugs are acid-forming because they either never contained alkaline-forming minerals or the minerals are leached out during chemical processing and refining.[16] Their intake requires alkalinizing minerals to neutralize their acid end products. This depletes the body stores of alkaline-forming minerals and thus creates an acid shift in the body.

The Yin and Yang of Foods

The terms yin and yang refer to the Oriental philosophical system in which everything in the universe is considered to be a dynamic relationship between yin and yang attributes, which complement each other as part of the whole. Yang attributes are contractive or centripetal, hot, dense, heavy, flat, and low. Yin attributes are expansive or centrifugal, cold, dilated, light, vertical, and thin. Foods and people can be categorized according to the balance of these attributes. For example, basketball players are more yin than football linemen. Men are said to be yang and women are said to be yin. Fruits are yin and beef products are yang. The following foods are listed in relative order from yin to yang: chemical additives, which are considered the most yin, then processed foods, fruits, vegetables, and seaweeds; yang begins to predominate with seeds, nuts, beans, grains dairy, fish, poultry, pork, beef, eggs, miso, and finally salt, which is the most yang.

A way to classify these foods chemically is to measure the difference between the amounts of potassium and sodium in food and compute a ratio. Foods high in potassium are usually yin, and those high in sodium are usually yang. Aihara gives a complete chart and rules for the mathematics of this.[17] The yin and yang balance of foods is also judged by such characteristics as their color, growth patterns, climate in which they they grow best, height, density, and hardness. The color classification of foods is quite interesting; they are classified according to the spectrum of the rainbow. The most yang color is red, which corresponds to the base chakra, or the one closest to the ground. The most yin color is violet, which corresponds to the crown chakra, which is the greatest distance from the ground, and the most yin state. It is important to remember that the more yang-tending or red-orange-yellow fruits are still basically yin in the total spectrum of yang and yin foods. White is a sign of a yin vegetable, and black is a sign of a yang vegetable. Vegetables and fruits which are heavier, harder, shorter, and grow slower and horizontally are considered yang. Yin vegetables are lighter, softer, taller and thinner, and grow faster and vertically. Foods which grow bigger and more abundantly in warmer climates are more yin. Yin foods are predominantly alkaline-forming, but can be either acid- or alkaline-forming. The yin foods which are alkaline-forming are fruits, vegetables, and honey. The healthy foods which are yin acid-forming are beans, nuts, and seeds. The bioacidic foods which are yin and acid-forming are sugar, chemical drugs, soft drinks, and alcohol. Yang foods are usually acid-forming, but can be either acid- or alkaline-forming. The basic yang foods which are acid-forming are grains and animal foods.

Some yang alkaline-forming foods are radish, pickle, miso, and salt. The healthy yang foods tend to be more acid-forming and the healthy yin foods, except beans, seeds, and nuts tend to be more alkaline-forming (Figure 14).

The yin/yang awareness is important because it recognizes that foods have different energies. It is another system that notes that foods are coded by nature according to color, shape, and other attributes in a way that suggests to us what their energy qualities and general mineral compositions are. This supports the principles of the Rainbow Diet.

The proper balance of yin and yang at any one point in time is a relative question. The answer depends on our constitutional attributes, work in the world, our environmental conditions, and spiritual practices. With the awareness of these yang/yin energies, we can create an evolving balance that best helps us develop spiritually. It is my impression that in the spiritual process we spontaneously tend to shift to more yin foods to aid this more expansive (yin) evolution. If we are moving from a more yang diet of flesh foods, the yin/yang balance of 50/50 of a macrobiotic diet as described by Michio Kushi may be one of the first steps in this healing transition.[18] People who are heavily acidified from a high flesh food diet may even require more yin alkaline forming foods in the form of raw fruits and vegetables, and less acid-forming grains than a 50/50 yin/yang balance to rebalance the long-term acidifying effect of eating flesh foods.

As we continue to evolve spiritually and our body becomes healthier, we tend to eat more yin, alkaline-forming raw fruits and vegetables to support the yin expansion of our spiritual life as well as the lighter, more superconductive needs of our body. The mucus-forming, acid-forming, and enzymeless yang grains and cooked foods tend to slow down the transforming spiritualizing energy of the Kundalini, as compared to the effect of the highly purifying and energizing biogenic foods we have discussed. In fact, if a person feels he or she has become too quickly yin from the spiritualizing process, I will often recommend the more yang grains to slow the process. At each step in the evolutionary process, it is important to maintain a life balance that feels harmonious. The judicious use of yin and yang foods can be helpful when we feel a need to gently counterbalance certain yin or yang mental or physical states.

Food Combining

The combining of foods in select ways to enhance the digestive process is historically recorded at the time of Moses. Exodus 16:8 says, "And Moses said: ... the Lord shall give you in the evening flesh to eat, and in the morning bread to the full." This can be extrapolated to mean that one should not mix heavy starch and heavy protein at the same meal. It is also a Kosher law that one does not eat dairy and animal products at the same meal. The principle behind food combining is that different food classes require different enzymes, different rates of digestion, and different digestive pHs for proper digestion. If the foods of the different food classes are combined incorrectly, the specific requirements for their proper digestion

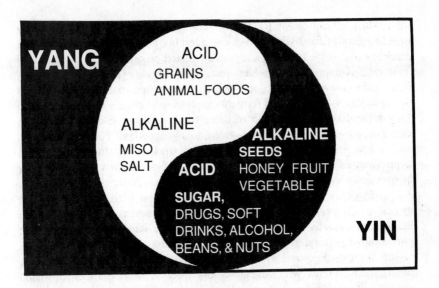

Figure 14

tend to cancel each other. For example, flesh foods require an acid media for digestion, whereas milk is highly alkaline, so it can neutralize the acid required for digesting the flesh foods. It was God's compassion that the Jews should not have to wander in the desert for 40 years and have indigestion at the same time.

Fruit digestion results in the release of an alkaline secretion which neutralizes the acid secretions needed for protein digestion. Because of this, it is not a good idea to eat fruits and proteins at the same meals. Some foods are digested faster than others. If fast-digesting foods like fruits are held up in the digestive system for a longer time than necessary through being combined with foods that digest more slowly, fermentation takes place. For this reason, it is good for digestion to eat fruit and starches which are digested slowly at different meals. Fruits and vegetables require different digestive enzymes, which tend to neutralize each other, so these too are best taken at separate meals.

So many rules for food combining have developed that people become overwhelmed and lose sight of the fact that individuals have to develop their own from direct experiences. **The simplest rule of food combining is to eat foods or combinations of foods that in our direct experience are easiest to digest.** One patient came to me in terror of eating because of all the rules she thought she had to follow. Instead of trusting her inner sensitivity, she had let a book tell her how it was supposed to be. Some people, such as the pitta types, have great digestive power, and these food combining guidelines have little meaning. Others have delicate digestive systems, and the guidelines are very helpful.

In the heart of the food combining guideline in Figure 15 there is a new category of food which gives considerably more leeway to the general guidelines. It is the category called predigested proteins. This chart is from Viktoras Kulvinskas's booklet on *Live Food Longevity Recipes.* Kulvinskas's new food category includes bee pollen, soaked and sprouted nuts and seeds, nut and seed ferments such as seed cheese and yogurt. (See food appendix for explanation of these foods.) These combine well with sweet or subacid fruits, sprouted grains, and vegetables. These soaked nuts and seeds in the morning with fruits work well for people with hypoglycemia. In general, because these predigested proteins are already broken down to free amino acids, they are very easy to digest.

In order to speed personal experimentation with which foods are easiest to digest, some general guidelines with which to experiment are helpful. It is usually easy to digest foods from the same food group or from two compatible food groups. However, too much of even a single food is taxing on the digestive system. Easy to digest combinations include predigested proteins with vegetables or sweet or subacid fruits. Sprouted grains and vegetables, vegetables and low starches, and high and low starches are all generally easy to digest. Relatively easy to digest food combinations to explore are protein and leafy greens, and avocado combined with leafy greens, acid, or subacid fruits. Combinations that are likely to produce putrification and fermentation are protein and starches, oil and protein, protein and sweet or subacid fruit, oil and sweet or subacid fruit, fruit and vegetables, and melons with any other type of food. For some people these combinations may not be a problem if eaten in small amounts. Papaya and lemon go well with any other foods. In the *Essene Gospel of Peace, Book One,* Jesus outlines the ideas for food combining succinctly:

"Take heed, therefore, and defile not with all kinds of abominations the temple of your bodies. Be content with two or three sorts of food, which you will always find upon the table of of of our Earthly Mother. And desire not to devour all things which you see round about you. For I tell you truly, if you mix together all sorts of food in your body, then the peace of your body will cease, and end-less war will rage in you."[19]

The timing of eating foods is also important. If you are having a salad and a protein, by eating the salad first, the hydrochloric acid needed for digesting the protein is blocked. There is better digestion if we eat the salad after the protein or while eating the protein. It is also best to drink liquids at least 20 minutes before the meal, rather than during or after the meal, because liquids dilute the digestive enzymes.

The way we tell if our combinations or timing are good for us is through results. If we get gas, constipation, diarrhea, and feel bloated, nauseated, and enervated after eating, we have a clue that what we are eating

FOOD COMBINING

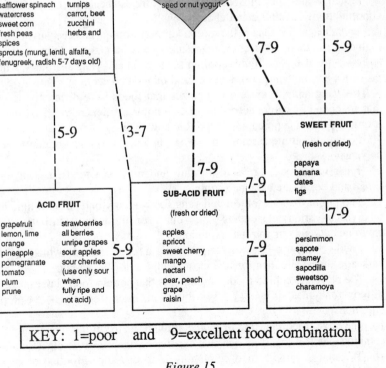

PROTEINS

(mucus forming, acid ash)

animal: poultry, fish, cheese, yogurt (not recommended), nuts (most), soy (bean and sprout), sunflower, sesame, pumpkin, chia, flax, tofu, seed milks, peas, beans and peanuts, miso, yeast, store-bought seed/nut butters

3-7

LOW STARCH

carrot
parsnip
butternut
squash
pumpkin
eggplant
artichoke
corn (old)
popcorn

9

HIGH STARCHES

(acid ash, mucus forming)

grains, garbanzo
(pea or sprout)
potatoes
winter squash
(acorn, hubbard, butternut)
sweet potato
jam
Essene bread
pizza
crisp sourdough rye

9   9   9   9   9   9   9

VEGETABLES

(alkalizing, healing)

leafy greens   mushrooms
weeds   asparagus
buckwheat lettuce   cucumber
radish greens   sweet pepper
sunflower greens   summer
squash
safflower spinach   turnips
watercress   carrot, beet
sweet corn   zucchini
fresh peas   herbs and
spices
sprouts (mung, lentil, alfalfa,
fenugreek, radish 5-7 days old)

PREDIGESTED PROTEIN
(neutral or alkaline ash, low fat)
bee pollen
soaked seeds & nuts
sprouted seeds & nuts
nut & seed ferments
seed or nut cheese
seed or nut yogurt

7-9

SPROUTED GRAIN

For 12 to 60 Hours

(alkalizing, high energy)
wheat milk
grain milks
grain cereals

7-9   5-9

5-9   3-7   7-9

SWEET FRUIT

(fresh or dried)

papaya
banana
dates
figs

7-9

7-9

ACID FRUIT

grapefruit   strawberries
lemon, lime   all berries
orange   unripe grapes
pineapple   sour apples
pomegranate   sour cherries
tomato   (use only sour
plum   when
prune   fully ripe and
                 not acid)

5-9

SUB-ACID FRUIT

(fresh or dried)

apples
apricot
sweet cherry
mango
nectari
pear, peach
grape
raisin

7-9

7-9

persimmon
sapote
mamey
sapodilla
sweetsop
charamoya

KEY: 1=poor   and   9=excellent food combination

Figure 15

133

is not digesting easily and that we need to pay more attention to food combining or food excesses. It is hard to enjoy the flow of the cosmic energies and the peace of meditation when gas warfare is raging inside our stomach and bowels. I find that following the Rainbow Diet -- with just fruit or fruit and predigested protein in the morning, a green salad and soaked nuts and seeds or seed cheese at lunch, and a light meal of purple vegetables at dinner -- is an easy way for me to observe these rules without paying any attention to them. The key to an easy time with food combining awareness is to experiment in developing a routine of eating which naturally has us eating what is easy to digest. In other words, trust your own experience and use your intelligence to make life easy.

Summary Chapter 17

1. The correct alkaline/acid balance is 80 percent alkaline-forming foods and 20 percent acid-forming foods.
2. A system which is too acidic is fertile ground for disease.
3. Acid-forming foods are those high in sulphur, phosphorus, chlorine, and iodine. These minerals are changed to strong acids within the body.
4. Alkaline-forming foods, high in calcium, magnesium, potassium, sodium, and iron, form alkaline mineral salts that neutralize acids.
5. All natural foods contain both acid- and alkaline-forming elements.
6. Proteins are the most acid-forming foods because of their high concentrations of sulphur and phosphorous.
7. Vegetables and fruits are the most alkaline-forming foods because of their high concentrations of calcium, manesium, potassium, and sodium.
8. Foods are also classified according to their yin and yang attributes, which provide a key to their general energy and mineral content.
9. This yang and yin system recognizes that foods have different energies that are coded by nature according to their color, shape, and other attributes. It thus supports the principles of the Rainbow Diet.
10. Foods high in potassium tend to be yin and those high sodium tend to be yang.
11. Most yang foods are acid-forming and most yin foods, except nuts, seeds, and beans, are alkaline-forming.
12. The proper balance of yin and yang foods at any one point in time is a relative question depending on our constitutional attributes, the environment, and our spiritual evolution.
13. Food combining is a way to eat foods in combinations which are the easiest to digest and therefore the most healthiest for the system.
14. The principle behind food combining is that certain food classes require different enzymes, different rates of digestion, and different pHs for proper digestion.
15. The most important rule in food combining is to eat the foods and food combinations that are, from our own experience, the easiest to digest.
16. The key to simple food combining is to develop a routine of eating which naturally has us eating what is easy to digest.

18

The Mind and Nutrition

Diet and Culture

The Greek historian Herodotus, often called the father of history, reported that grain-eating vegetarian cultures surpassed meat-eating cultures in art, science, and spiritual development. He observed that meat-eating nations tended to be warlike and to relate to one another through anger, alienation, and sensual passions. He also commented that meat eaters possessed bravery, courage, and boldness.[1] Rudolf Steiner felt that spiritual progress for humanity depends on a progressive increase in the number of people who followed vegetarian nutrition. He felt that an overemphasis on animal nutrition would eventually pull people away from an interest in spiritual life. There is an implication that a symptom of the Roman downfall was connected to the decadent practice of gluttony. Perhaps this was also true in France before the Revolution. An aristocratic dinner served the night before the French Revolution was reported to have nine courses made from one kind of meat that was prepared in 22 different ways.[2] When one realizes that an estimated 32 million Americans between the ages of 25 and 74 are considered overweight, there is some real concern for the spiritual state of our country.[3] There are some hints that in ancient times those involved in the various priesthoods knew about the effects of certain diets on spiritual development and kept these as secrets to maintain their own power over the populations. A remnant of this may be found in India, where the Brahmin priests eat separately from people of other castes. The implication is that the diet of a social group affects the spiritual consciousness of that group.

Diet and the Mind

In Ayurveda it is established that certain foods affect the qualities of the mind in particular ways. These qualities or states of mind are latent in everyone. In Ayurveda they are divided into three categories called gunas. Anyone who is in the physical body is subject to the subtle forces of the three gunas which are called sattvic, rajasic, and tamasic. A sattvic state of mind is clear, peaceful, and harmonious. It is typified by the pure-living spiritual aspirant. The rajasic state is active, restless, worldly, and aggressive, the mental state of warriors and corporate executives. The tamasic state is lethargic, impulsive, cruel, and morally and physically degenerate. It is typified by our stereotype of the drug addict or thief.

Diet influences the state of mind, and the state of mind influences the diet choice. The warrior class would specifically eat the rajasic diet because it stimulated their minds and bodies into a warlike state. Spiritual aspirants normally choose the sattvic diet and way of life. Consciously or unconsciously, people tend to choose the diet that reinforces and is reflective of their own mental and spiritual state of awareness. The choice of a sattvic diet may either reflect a person's state of harmony or may reflect a person's desire to influence themselves into that state by choosing sattvic foods. The pitfall of pursuing a sattvic diet to create a desired mental state is that it can become a self-righteous religion that traps the aspirants in their own concepts. The object of spiritual life is not to fit a certain conceptual form or way of life. It is simply to be. In that beingness, we create a healthy space for evolution into an individualized diet that is spiritually best for that time. In Ayurveda foods are also thought to have three qualities of density: a fine subtle quality which builds the mind, a less fine quality which builds the body, and a coarse quality that is primarily waste matter.

Sattvic Foods

Foods which have high amounts of this most refined subtle quality are called sattvic. These are considered pure foods which keep the body-mind-spirit complex balanced, clear, harmonious, and strong. They are easy to digest, and their intake does not result in the accumulation of toxins in the system. The intake of these foods helps to keep the mind at peace. These sattvic foods add energy to the SOEFs, rather than draining energy from them for assimilation. Their inherent balanced, harmonious energy is transmitted to us. The experience of a sattvic diet is that of inner strength, harmony, peace, and balance. In the Ayurvedic system, these sattvic foods include all fruits, vegetables, edible greens, grains, grasses, beans, milk, buttermilk, honey, and small quantities of rice or bread preparations. It is completely vegetarian. The alkaline-acid balance is 70 percent to 30 percent.[4]

For our western bodies, a sattvic diet means at least 80% biogenic and bioactive foods and 20 percent cooked or biostatic foods. There is a minimum of stimulating condiments. The diet has an abundance of different sprouts of legumes and grains, immature greens and grasses, fresh fruits and vegetables, and soaked nuts and seeds, as well as raw unsoaked nuts and seeds, all grains and legumes, honey, and sometimes fresh raw milk and yogurt. The alkaline/acid ratio is 80 percent to 20 percent.

Rajasic Foods

Rajasic foods are more stimulating to the nervous system. One will often feel some immediate increased energy from eating them. Coffee, tea, tobacco, fresh meats, and large amounts of stimulating spices such as garlic and onions are examples of rajasic foods. These foods will energize us for our worldly activities, but this energization does not always happen in the clearest and most balanced way. These foods stimulate us to be busy and active, but activity can turn into agitation and restlessness. They tend to push our mind and body beyond its limits. If this is done long enough, we eventually goes into imbalance, and disease begins to manifest. Examples of this are coffee addicts who need more and more coffee to keep pumping their bodies up to do their work. Eventually, the addict becomes more and more physically exhausted until even the coffee will not help. Hypoglycemia, which we will discuss later in this chapter, is a typical result of rajasic imbalance, especially with the overuse of coffee and sugar. Rajasic foods tend to stimulate the body and mind toward a more competitive, warlike, sensual, and pleasure-seeking way of life. In the traditional caste system, the Brahmins, who were the priests, teachers, and spiritual seekers, were forbidden to have rajasic foods. A rajasic diet was considered the diet for kings and warriors.

Rajasic foods include some biogenic and bioactive foods, but they also include flesh foods, and many gourmet, spicy, cooked foods with rich, oily sauces. This diet includes butter, cheese, oils, fried foods, cakes, sugar, and eggs. It is 50 to 60 percent alkaline.[5] The taste stimulation of these foods tends to lead us away from our inner cues, moving us easily toward imbalances such as overeating or coffee and sugar addictions. This diet eventually leads to ill health and chronic degenerative imbalances.

Tamasic Foods

Tamasic foods are stale, decayed, decomposed, spoiled, overcooked, recooked leftovers, and processed foods. These synthetic foods are chemicalized with preservatives, pesticides, fungicides, sweeteners, artificial colors, sulfites, and nitrites and similar chemicals. All the fast foods that are so popular today fall into the tamasic category, as does alcohol, which is a fermented, decomposed food, and all other drugs. Any flesh foods which are not freshly killed are considered tamasic; this includes most meat we find in the marketplace. Only freshly killed wild game and fish are considered rajasic. Tamasic foods have no life force left in them. Their SOEFs have been severely disrupted. It is a diet that is less than 50 percent alkaline.[6] These foods have only minimal quality left in them, and maximum waste. These foods do, however, supply us with toxic chemical breakdown products that affect the functioning of our mind and irritate our nervous system. Because they steal energy from our SOEFs to digest and assimilate, they diminish our life force. These foods lead more quickly than rajasic foods to chronic, degenerate disease. They tend to bring out the worst psychological characteristics because of the irritable lethargic, degenerate state they create in us. At some time, most of us have overeaten some tamasic food and have felt raunchy and toxic. This is the tamasic state, a state in which it is extremely difficult to meditate or to be in harmony with self or environment. A quick assessment of our popular American diet makes it obvious that it is a strong tamasic diet, the results of which are that we rate 21st in life expectancy among the industrialized nations.[7] The tamasic diet may also be contributing to the degenerating moral fiber of our society.

Effects of Specific Food
Excesses and Deficiencies on the Mind

The mind and nervous system are specifically affected by certain vitamin deficiencies such as thiamine deficiency (beri-beri) which causes peripheral nerve damage and damage to certain brain centers, resulting in disorientation, mental confusion, and an off-balance gait. A deficiency of vitamin B_3, or niacin, has been associated with cerebral pellagra, with symptoms resembling schizophrenia. The early work of Drs. Hoffer and Osmond showed that a certain percentage of people diagnosed with schizophrenia overcame the symptoms of their schizophrenia with high doses of niacin. This indicates the importance of nutrients on the function of the mind.[8] Other researchers have found that high doses of vitamins B_6, B_{12}, and C may improve mental functioning in some people. Two new specialties called orthomolecular medicine and orthomolecular psychiatry have developed around the world as a result of all these findings.[9] Carl Pfeifer, Ph.D., M.D., in his book called *Mental and Elemental Nutrients*, points to the role of mineral deficiencies such as low zinc, manganese, chromium, and molybdenum, and excesses in copper, iron, cadmium, lead, and mercury, in disrupted mental function.[10] It has been established that body concentrations of toxic metals can cause hyperactivity or mental retardation.[11,12] The point here is that our nutrients, in excess or deficiency, can affect the function of the mind.

The mind function can also be affected by what is now called cerebral allergies. We usually think about allergies as causing only stuffed-up, runny noses and red eyes, but there is a new medical field called clinical ecology that has shown that some people's mental functioning can be disrupted by the foods they eat and the pollutants they breathe. Symptoms include acute and chronic depression, tension-fatigue syndrome, minimal brain dysfunction, restlessness, anxiety, insomnia, hyperactivity, inappropriate behavior outbursts, fear, panic, unreal feelings, personality changes, schizophrenia, psychosis, hallucinations, and inability to concentrate.[13] If we become aware of our inner responses to foods, we are able to avoid the symptoms of food allergies. Dr. Mandell's book *5-Day Allergy Relief System* includes a good discussion of how to detect and treat these food allergies.[14]

Because of a disharmonious mind and lifestyle, our bodies are shifted into a state of imbalance which may manifest as food allergies or vitamin and mineral deficiencies. For example, by leading a stressful life, we may burn up lots of B vitamins, which need to be replaced in high doses in order to maintain balance. In the long run, the use of high-stress B vitamins to cope with a high-stress lifestyle becomes a rajasic stimulation of our bodies beyond their normal output. It covers up the essential disharmony that is creating the imbalance. For some, the problem may simply be a genetic need for high doses of vitamins according to the principles of biochemical individuality. But for many, this is not the case. This does not mean we should not take high dose vitamins as an immediate effort to rebalance and remedy the situation. It does mean that we need to look at the causes of the imbalance, make deeper lifestyle adjustments, increase our meditation time, and make health-oriented diet changes if they are merited. In this way we can continue our spiritual unfolding in a solid way.

Hypoglycemia

Because a stable blood sugar is important for the normal functioning of the brain and the nervous system, hypoglycemia, said by many to be epidemic in this country, is something that needs to be understood.[15] It has been my observation in treating many meditators that when their hypoglycemia is cured, their ability to meditate and the steadiness of their meditation improves. This alone makes hypogycemia an important condition be aware of.

Hypoglycemia is known as the great mimicker. It can manifest in a variety of symptoms such as chronic fatigue, exhaustion, weakness, depression, headaches, unexplained mood changes and anxiety attacks, concentration difficulties, transitory mental confusion, and even allergies. One problem surrounding hypoglycemia is that only part of the medical establishment acknowledges that it exists. It was originally described in 1924 by Seale Harris, M.D., for which he was given a gold medal award by the A.M.A. in 1949. Then the A.M.A. officially decided in 1973 that hypoglycemia was a nondisease. An interesting story illustrating this confusion is that of Steven Gyland, M.D. He developed the symptoms of hypoglycemia to such an extent that he had to stop his medical practice. In an effort to diagnose the problem, he was examined by 14 specialists and 3 major medical clinics, including the Mayo Clinic. No one ever diagnosed hypoglycemia. After three years of suffering, an inability to work, and seeing a psychiatrist, he discovered the original hypoglycemia paper of Seale Harris. He went on a hypoglycemia diet, and his symptoms disappeared. Interestingly, the medical expert who examined him at the Mayo Clinic has publicly claimed that he has not seen a case of hypoglycemia in 25 years. This claim was made a few years after he had attempted to diagnose Dr. Gyland's problem. If someone does not acknowledge the existence of hypoglycemia, how can they diagnose it ? Like Dr. Gyland, many clients come to me with the complaint that "I've been to several physicians. All my lab tests are normal. They say I am fine, but I feel miserable." It is difficult to be interested in spiritual life when one is feeling miserable. Often these people have some form of hypoglycemia as part of their imbalance.

Classically, the six-hour glucose tolerance test is considered the diagnostic procedure for diagnosing hypoglycemia, but some orthomolecular physicians have found that it may give some false normals. Some people may develop hypoglycemia symptoms during the test but have a normal glucose tolerance curve. It seems that some people are very sensitive to changes in blood sugar, while others may have dramatic shifts in blood sugar and experience no symptoms. The clue to this may be found in Dr.

Roger Williams's book *Biochemical Individuality,* which stresses that we have different biological sensitivities. The diagnosis of hypoglycemia requires clinical judgment. In my work, I also used more subtle testing systems such as acupuncture pulse diagnosis and various forms of muscle testing to help confirm the diagnosis.

Causes of Reactive Hypoglycemia

To understand hypoglycemia, it helps to understand that it is not a disease. It is a symptom of a physiological imbalance in the system which manifests as low or erratic blood sugar. It may be caused by an allergic reaction, some form of endocrine gland disorder, or even some nutritional deficiency of chromium, zinc, pantothenic acid, magnesium, potassium, or vitamin B_6. There are severe causes of it such as pancreatic tumors, Addison's disease, and pituitary or other brain tumors, but these are not causes of reactive hypoglycemia, which is our focus. The allergic cause may be any substance, but often it is white sugar.

The most frequent form of reactive hypoglycemia I see is a subtle or gross endocrine imbalance. It is an imbalance of the glucose metabolism as regulated by the pituitary, thyroid, pancreas, adrenal, liver, and other endocrine glands. A simplified version of the dynamics of the endocrine balance and hypoglycemia will give a feeling for the meaning of hypoglycemia. When we eat white sugar or other sweets the blood sugar rapidly rises. If the endocrine system is toned, it can compensate for this by smoothly lowering the blood sugar with the carefully timed excretion of insulin. If it secretes too much insulin, our healthy adrenals and liver release more glucose to compensate for the excessive drop in glucose. If the endocrine system is not in balance, then it is unable to compensate for the excess stress the white sugar has created, and our blood sugar drops too low and we see symptoms. This does not just mean a pancreas disorder of excess insulin secretion. Hypoglycemia is not simply the opposite of diabetes. Quite often, the pancreas is normal, and some other part of the endocrine system is out of balance. It is important to understand that, like our chakras, our glands function as a total system. It may be the adrenals, thyroid, pituitary, ovary, liver, pancreas, or a combination. This is important because the endocrine glands are reflective of the chakra system balance. It has been my experience in some cases of hypoglycemia that the subtle bodies are disordered in a way that the person is suffering from unusual psychic phenomena that are often frightening to them. On treatment of the hypoglycemia, the chakras rebalance and psychic vulnerability and discomfort go away.

In a study of mine done on 100 people in 1981-82, I found that only 20 percent had exclusively a pancreas imbalance. An additional 36 percent of those with hypoglycemic symptoms had pancreas imbalances associated with other endocrine imbalances. Exclusive adrenal imbalances caused 25 percent of the hypoglycemia, and an additional 36 percent had adrenal imbalances associated with other endocrine imbalances. In 6 percent, the thyroid alone was out of balance, and 21 percent of the time this occurred in combination with other organs. The pituitary, ovary, and liver were only out of order in combination with other endocrine organs. A liver dysfunction is often the main cause of hypoglycemia in alcoholics or people with hepatitis, but I did not have alcoholics in this study. A useful way to understand the epidemic level of hypoglycemia in this country is to think of it as the endocrine system and the chakra system being out of tune. The high incidence of hypoglycemia is another indication of how important it is for the total chakra system to be energetically balanced. Chronic life stress, which tends to imbalance the chakra system and limit the amount of cosmic energy recharging the chakras, can bring about hypoglycemia. I have seen 15 to 20 cases of sudden stress such as a car accident or even childbirth precipitate hypoglycemia in people who were already on the edge of chakra and endocrine imbalance. In people who are leading harmonious sattvic lives and eating a healthy sattvic diet, there is more resiliency to sudden stresses or even some prolonged stresses, but people living on the edge of their resources are more vulnerable to having their chakras and endocrine system become imbalanced by sudden stress.

Another piece to the hypoglycemia puzzle is the concept of variable sensitivity to the changes in blood sugar. Dr. Buckley, a psychiatrist and clinical researcher, has found that there are glucose-sensitive receptors in the hypothalamic brain center which act as a feedback system for a specific anxiety center in the brain called the locus coeruleus.[16] When blood sugar drops below a certain point, the glucose receptor center cannot properly control the anxiety center in the locus coeruleus. This results in anxiety symptoms typified by mental and physical agitation, fear, increased heart rate, and irritability. The degree of biological sensitivity of this glucose receptor is a key to how sensitive each individual may be to drops in blood glucose. The determining factor of this individualized sensitivity seems to be a genetic predisposition. Hypersensitivity to alterations in blood glucose, with associated erratic behavior, may be linked with the increasing number of people suffering from unexplained anxiety and panic attacks.

Epidemic Cause of Hypoglycemia

The remaining question is, what causes hypoglycemia, which various reports estimate to be an epidemic of at least 10 percent of the people in America?[17] And the evidence for the epidemic of hypoglycemia is mounting. For example, Michael Lesser, M.D. reports that 67 percent of his psychiatric patients suffer from hypoglycemia.[18] In another study of a different population, 25 percent of 5,000 so-called healthy military inductees were found to have blood sugars consistent with the diagnosis of hypoglycemia.[19] The cause for a phenomenon with the magnitude of 24 million people is not likely to be simply vitamin deficiencies or food allergies, it is most likely a stressful, overextended lifestyle and a tamasic diet high in white sugar and other imbalancing stimulants.

Hypoglycemia is the result of living the all-American dream of moving faster, of wanting bigger and better things, and of a highly competitive and aggressive lifestyle which is out of harmony with our inner Self and mother nature. To fuel this fast lifestyle we eat processed fast, and plenty of instant-energy white-sugar foods. To both relieve the pain of this lifestyle and temporarily energize we use alcohol, coffee, cigarettes, sweets, and stimulant drugs. Americans consume 125 pounds of white sugar per year per person, which is either hidden in foods or eaten directly, as in our coffee.[20] Paavo Airola once described this as "completely incredible nutritional folly; nothing less than an act of unintentional national suicide."[21] Our bodies were not designed to metabolize this high input of refined sugars continually. The strain of this repeated high sugar intake, like the "normality" of banging our heads against the wall, eventually leads to the headache of a metabolic disorder which we know as hypoglycemia. Other major dietary substances that have been linked to creating hypoglycemic imbalances are coffee, alcohol, and cigarettes. Coffee and other caffeine-containing substances like black tea, cola drinks, aspirin compounds, and caffeinelike compounds in chocolate cause an overstimulation of the adrenal glands which then release adrenaline substances that stimulate the liver to release excess glucose into the blood. This creates a rapid rise in blood sugar in a pattern similar to when white sugar is eaten. Alcohol drinking, particularly of sweet liqueurs and wine, contributes to hypoglycemia. An estimated 70 percent of alcoholics are hypoglycemic. Most do not realize it, but studies have found that blood glucose also increases after smoking a cigarette. All of these toxins act directly to imbalance the endocrine system.

Although hypoglycemia results from multiple causes, the primary epidemic cause is a disharmonious, stressful life style and a tamasic diet high in refined carbohydrates, coffee, alcohol, and cigarettes. This is why researchers have found that so many juvenile offenders improve their behavior when put on a corrective diet for hypoglycemia. For example, one study found that 82 percent of 106 juveniles on probation had hypoglycemia. When put on a corrective diet, almost all of them significantly improved in their social function.[22] There are numerous studies showing that hypoglycemia alters our mental and social behavior toward the tamasic, emotional, mental, and moral tendencies of erratic, violent, and antisocial behavior.[23,24,25] The lifestyle and diet that create hypoglycemia are some of the first things people who are interested in a diet for spiritual life would do well to consider changing.

The Treatment of Hypoglycemia

With the appropriate homeopathic and dietary hypoglycemic treatment of approximately six small meals per day -- a low protein, high natural complex carbohydrate diet with no sweets or sweet fruit, people heal very quickly. For details of the hypoglycemic diet please see the book *Hypoglycemia: A Better Approach* by Paavo Airola. If people have trouble with a high natural carbohydrate diet, I increase germinated nuts and seeds, which act as predigested proteins and help to balance the blood sugar. This can be in the form of seed sauces (food appendix I) or simply soaked nuts or seeds. The more raw the diet is, the quicker the healing. In a study of 100 cases of mine in 1981-82, 53 percent of the people had complete symptom relief in three weeks, and 74 percent had absence of all symptoms after one month. The other 26 percent took one to four months to achieve complete healing. All of these cases remained symptom-free on a regular, but healthier diet in the two and four month follow-up. With the diet alone, the healing in my research takes an average of six months to a year. My definition of healing hypoglycemia means not only a complete absence of symptoms, but the ability to resume eating only two to three times per day and have sweet fruits, dried fruits, and even some honey in the diet without having any return of hypoglycemic symptoms. For healing to be sustained, some basic shift in lifestyle towards more harmony with ourselves and nature is necessary. We need to shift toward a more sattvic diet lifestyle to sustain real healing and increase our spiritual development.

Hypoglycemia, Meditation, and Kundalini
It has been my impression that meditation requires extra blood glucose fuel. Many people I have observed seem to increase their desire for sweets after beginning to meditate. Crystalline glucose is one of the more efficient nutrients for carrying and transferring prana in the system. The mistake meditators often make is to seek more glucose for the system by eating refined processed foods laden with white sugar, which is a tamasic food that unbalances the body toward hypoglycemia and a wide variety of other diseases. A high complex carbohydrate diet with plenty of grains, soaked nuts and seeds, vegetables, and fruits will supply a gradual release of glucose into the bloodstream without the ups and downs of white sugar. This high complex carbohydrate diet will preserve our health much better than eating white sugar. I have had the opportunity to treat a number of monks and other spiritual aspirants involved in intense spiritual practices who developed hypoglycemia because they did not understand this simple point. In almost all of those who followed the treatment program for hypoglycemia, there was an increase in the ability to concentrate and an improved steadiness of the meditation experience was reported. A steadier emotional, awake, and aware state was also experienced. Once healed, these people were able to stop snacking between meals and return to a normal but more sattvic diet. They were able to incorporate the use of sweet fruits and some honey in their diet with no return of hypoglycemia.

When the Kundalini is awakened, there is occasionally a little more pranic energy released than that with which a person might feel comfortable. One of the main immediate treatments to calm the Kundalini energy is to feed the individual honey. My theory for this is that the ability of the glucose to absorb and transmit prana, as discussed in Chapter 11, enables glucose to act as a "pranic energy shock absorber" throughout the system. The Kundalini, when initially awakened, seems to require much from the glucose reserve as it activates and spiritually energizes a person. If an individual does not have enough reserve complex carbohydrate, honey provides extra glucose to keep the nervous system in balance.

The Mind as Food

What we eat is more than nutrients or even the particular energy of the food. We also eat the mental state of those who grew the food, picked the food, prepared the food, and of the one who is eating the food. Food that is grown with love, picked with love, prepared with love, and eaten with love has a different quality than food that goes through those stages with a different consciousness relating to it. There is a story of a monk who lived a pure life, thought pure thoughts, and ate pure food. One day a king who had a greedy nature desired that the monk come and stay in his court. The monk agreed to come for a short time. During this time, the monsoon season came and the king insisted that the monk stay until the end of the monsoon. During this whole time, the monk ate the sattvic food prepared by the greedy cook of the greedy king. In time, the pure mind of the monk began to be pervaded by greedy thoughts. One day, in an impulsive moment, he stole the queen's pearl necklace. His mind now agitated by this, he insisted that he had to leave. Meanwhile, the whole castle was in an uproar about the stolen necklace, but of course, the monk was not suspected. Once he returned to eating his own food, prepared with pure thoughts and love, the monk's mind began to clear. After a few weeks, he began to wonder what he was doing with this useless pearl necklace. When it became clear to him what had happened, he decided to return it to the king. The king demanded an explanation. The monk, having returned to his normal fearless state, explained that the food he had been eating in the king's castle, permeated by his greedy consciousness and prepared by his greedy cook, had temporarily infected him with greed. Once he returned to his pure food, prepared with love, his mind became sattvic again and he returned the necklace.

Food Preparation and the Mind

Food prepared with love and eaten with love generates even more love in the person eating the food. If food is prepared with love as an offering to God and with the consciousness that the person preparing the food, the person eating the food, and the food are one in God, the person eating that food will imbibe that consciousness. In Muktananda's ashrams, food preparers were taught to chant or repeat God's name while preparing the food, so no matter what was prepared, it was always experienced as tasty and filled with love. This left a great impression on me.

When I prepare my own food, I go to the garden to see what is ripe and to what I am drawn. I thank the individual plant for feeding me and pick it with love and as an offering to God. Once this harmonious connection is made with nature, I am inspired to create whatever meal appears to me based on my inner sensitivity to the food and myself. In this way my relationship with food as an interface with nature is personal and filled with love. Food for me is not anonymous. In our supermarket and fast food restaurant world of fast, frozen, irradiated, fried, and multi-processed foods, food loses its roots and the imagery of its source in the Divine Mother. Food lives in a context of mother nature's energies of sun, wind, earth, color, and rain. How do we honor our mother, as the Ten Commandments say, if we eat her offerings without the active awareness that what we are eating comes from her bountiful earth rather than from a grocery shelf or a fast food bag? I try to eat everything with the feeling of receiving life. When I sit down to eat, I reflect on sustenance. Eating is a way of focusing on all levels of nurturing which is ultimately Love.

When food is served anonymously, as in a restaurant, I recreate the energy and imagery from my garden. This helps me to connect in a loving way with the Mother's offering. This brings a poetry to the food which turns it into a conscious experience. I even do this in my own home, where I eat within 20 yards of the garden from which I just picked the fresh vegetables. This process is a blessing of the food in a way that honors mother nature and our harmonious connection with her. Formally blessing the food with love and giving thanks to God sets the tone for us to receive the bountiful grace that is on the table. It helps us be present enough to receive the loving vibrations of each ingredient and the whole. Epicurus became famous as a great eater, but actually he was a great spiritual teacher. One day a wealthy king, having heard of his extraordinary meals, came to visit Epicurus. He was amazed to find him dining on bread and salt. But sitting at his table for the meal he was elevated by the consciousness with which the food was eaten. At the end of the meal, the king so appreciated the meal that he offered Epicurus a gift of anything he wanted. The king received another lesson when Epicurus asked only for a pound of butter. When asked why only that, Epicurus replied, "Just to be is enough, nothing more is needed." His final lesson to the king was that a good meal depends on the eater and how he celebrates it.

Teachings from *The Essene Gospel of Peace, Book One*

"For the power of God's angels enters into you with the living food which the Lord gives you from his royal table. And when you eat, have above you the angel of air, and below you the angel of water. Breathe long and deeply at all your meals, that the angel of air may bless your repasts. And chew well your food with your teeth, that it becomes water, and that the angel of water turn it into blood in your body. And eat slowly, as it were a prayer you make to the Lord. For I tell you truly, the power of God enters into you, if you eat in this manner at His table. But Satan turns into a steaming bog the body of him upon whom the angels of the air and water do not descend at his repasts. And the Lord suffers him no longer at His table. For the table of the Lord is an altar, and he who eats at the table of God, is in a temple. For I tell you truly, the body of the Sons of Man is turned into a temple, and their inwards into an altar, if they do the commandments of God. Wherefore, put naught upon the altar of the Lord when your spirit is vexed, neither think upon anyone with anger in the temple of God. And enter only into the Lord's sanctuary when you feel in yourselves the call of His angels, for all that you eat in sorrow, or in anger, or without desire, becomes a poison in your body. For the breath of Satan defiles all these. Place with joy your offerings upon the altar of your body, and let all evil thoughts depart from you when you receive into your body the power of God from His table."[26]

Summary Chapter 18

1. Diet affects the spiritual life of whole cultures as well as individuals.
2. In Ayurveda there are three basic classifications of diet: sattvic, rajasic, and tamasic. These different diets affect the mind, body, and spirit in different ways. The spontaneous choice of a particular diet type reflects a person's state of being.
3. A sattvic diet is the most uplifting spiritually and physically. It is the diet of choice for most who are on the spiritual path.
4. A rajasic diet is one that is stimulating and activating for performing many worldly activities. It is the warrior's or corporate executive's diet.
5. A tamasic diet is a degenerate diet for body, mind, and spirit.
6. An excess or deficiency in vitamins or minerals can affect the functioning of the mind and body.
7. Food allergies can affect our mental and psychological state.
8. A balanced blood sugar aides the ability to meditate.
9. Hypoglycemia is a symptom of an imbalance in the total endocrine system which results in an imbalance of the blood sugar regulation. The precipitating cause for this may be stress from food allergies, mental or physical stress, or nutritional deficiencies.
10. The epidemic cause for hypoglycemia is our cultural living of a disharmonious, stressful lifestyle, and eating a tamasic diet excessively filled with white sugar.
11. The treatment of hypoglycemia requires a change to a more moderate, harmonious lifestyle and a diet of low protein, high natural carbohydrate, and total abstinence from sweets.
12. The awakening of the Kundalini energy seems to increase the need for glucose. This need can be easily met by increasing the amount of high complex natural carbohydrates in the diet.
13. Sometimes the Kundalini becomes too activated, and the glucose from honey has been found to calm this Kundalini. It may act as a pranic shock absorber.
14. The thoughts of those who gather, prepare, serve, and eat the food affect the subtle quality of the food and the one who eats it.
15. Anonymous food has lost its contact with nature. By honoring our food as a gift from mother nature, we personalize the food in a way that restores our contact with nature.

19

Fasting and Spiritual Life

Fasting, practiced as an essential discipline for the attainment of true knowledge, has its history in the spiritual practices of almost all religions. Socrates, Plato, and the Stoic and Neoplatonist philosophers such as Epicteus and Plotinus used fasting to purify the spirit in order to better perceive the truth. Socrates and Plato practiced ten-day fasts.[1] Pythagoras, the great mathematician, practiced 40-day fasts.[2] Fasting is used in religions such as Judaism, Christianity, Hinduism, Islamic, and Buddhism for a variety of different purposes such as penitence, propitiation, a preparatory rite for initiations and marriage, mourning, to develop magical powers, purification and health, and spiritual development. In Hebrew, the word for fasting is *tsoum*. It means the voluntary abstinence from food with a religious end. This is a good definition of spiritual fasting.

The most important fast for the Jews is the abstinence from food and water for the one day prescribed by the Torah for the Day of Atonement. Fasting was prescribed for penitence for sins, and there are fasts of devotion prescribed on Monday and Thursday. Fasts were done to appease God, to ward off punishments, and to seek God's favor. The most famous fasts in the Jewish tradition are Moses' and Elija's 40-day fasts. Daniel, the prophet, fasted in preparation for receiving his revelations. Ester and all the Jewish people in Persia fasted for deliverance from physical destruction. Judith was said to fast all the days of her life (Judith 8:6). With the exception of these famous fasts, most Jewish fasting was prescribed as part of fulfilling the Torah, until the Alexandrian Jews developed the philosophy that bodily desires interfered with spirituality and fasting helped to release mind energies from the material to spiritual level.

The Essenes, who were ascetic, esoteric, scholarly Jewish communities living near Egypt and the Dead Sea, and who authored the Dead Sea Scrolls, used fasting as an important approach for purifying their bodies and enhancing their communion with God. The prophet Elijah was said to have founded the Essenes at Mt. Carmel. The name Essene means "expectant of the one who is to come." They were well-known as prophets and great healers. Essene also means healer, and their members were often called therapeutai. Many of them lived to be greater than 120 years old.[3] The inner core group of the Essenes fasted for 40 days one time per year.[4] Jesus was reportedly raised in an Essene community in Egypt after escaping from Herod the Great. He carried the teaching of fasting to his disciples through his own practice of the 40-day fast and other references to fasting for purification and healing of body and soul. He taught in the *Essene Gospel of Peace, Book One* that:

> "... the word and the power of God will not enter into you, because all manner of abominations have their dwelling in your body and your spirit; for the body is the temple of the spirit, and the spirit is the temple of God. Purify therefore, the temple, that the Lord of the temple may dwell therein and occupy a place that is worthy of him... Renew yourselves and fast. For I tell you truly, that Satan and his plagues may only be cast out by fasting and prayer (also in Mark 9:29). Go by yourself and fast alone... The living God shall see it and great will be your reward. And fast til Beelzebub and all his evil spirits depart from you, and all the angels of our earthly Mother come and serve you (harmony with nature). For I tell you truly, except you fast, you shall never be freed from the power of Satan and all the diseases that come from Satan. Fast and pray fervently, seeking the power of the living God for your healing."[5]

In the two centuries after this, the first Christians practiced various forms of voluntary and prescribed fasting without any set form of rules. The main fasts were the Paschal fast and the weekly fasts of Wednesday and Friday. From 200 to 500 A.D., the practice of fasting came under ecclesiastical discipline. In this process of organized fasting, as in Judaism, fasting lost its character as a voluntary practice, although in both religions, the tradition of voluntary fasting has carried into modern times. For long periods of time the Baal Shem Tov, the Hasidic master, was said to fast during the week and eat only on the Sabbath. The Hasidic master, Rabbi Nachman, was reported to fast from Sabbath to Sabbath as often as 18 times in one year.[6] According to the Vatican Council II, the Church now only asserts ecclesiastical authority over ceremonial fasting. It encourages voluntary fasting as a legitimate spiritual practice but has chosen not to assert authority over the specifics of the individual fasting practices. There are Christian monks who voluntarily fast as a spiritual practice, as in the practice of Matthew the Poor of the Coptic (Egyptian) Orthodox Church, as a well as the monastic orders of Cistercians, Carmelites, and Carthusians.

In Hinduism fasting is practiced with the idea of union with God as well as to fulfill religious prescriptions. The Upanishads, part of the Hindu Holy scriptures, refer to fasting as a means of union with God. In Hinduism, fasting is used for pentinence, before a marriage, before religious initiations, to receive a blessing or a boon from God, and on the new and full moons. The use of fasting in the Hindu tradition is similar to the Judeo-Christian in that it is considered penitence, a time of remembrance and honoring important events and for sacrifice and union with God.

Fasting to Enhance Spiritual Life

Fasting allows our physical bodies to turn toward the assimilation of pranic energy rather than biochemical energy. By accelerating the purification of the body, it allows the physical body to become a better conductor of the Kundalini energy. This improves the alignment of the chakras and subtle bodies, which makes it easier for the cosmic prana to enter the body and increases the possibility of the awakening of the Kundalini Shakti. By removing toxins from the system, we not only become healthier, but we remove blocks from the body and therefore enhance the movement of all energy in the system, as well as of the spiritualizing force of the Kundalini. Through repeated fasts we also become clearer channels for the assimilation of cosmic energy into our systems. We also increase our sensitivity to the movement of the Kundalini. The more we are in touch with the feeling of this God Force, the easier it is to be motivated to live in a way that will continue to enhance its development.

Although formally defined as complete abstinence from food and water, fasting, in a larger context, means to abstain from that which is toxic to mind, body, and soul. A way to understand this is that fasting is the elimination of physical, emotional, and mental toxins from our organism, rather than simply cutting down on or stopping food intake. Fasting for spiritual purposes usually involves some degree of removal of oneself from worldly responsibilities. It can mean complete silence and social isolation during the fast which can be a great revival to those of us who have been putting their energy outward. Gandhi used to observe one day of silence per week. Fasting helps to manifest a healthy body, mind, and spiritual balance and therefore to bring forth the knowledge of God within as love.

After the first few days of a fast, our appetites usually fade and the attachment to food diminishes. This frees the mind to put more energy on the awareness level of our Divine Being rather than our appetites. In fasting, the tight connection between instinct and bodily desires is diminished allowing us to be free from the physical desires of the body. In this state of renunciation, the mind is free to merge into higher states of communion with God. This is not done to make the body suffer, because in practical reality the body is also becoming healthier with fasting. It is done because, until we achieve a certain level of spiritual communion, the desires of the body-mind complex are often stronger than the desire of God communion. The more we can experience ourselves as free of these bodily desires in the practice of fasting, the easier it is to maintain this freedom in a nonfasting state. Christ alluded to the power of this when he said, "This kind cannot be driven out by anything but prayer and fasting" (Mark 9:29). Matthew the Poor, a modern day Coptic monk of high spiritual attainment who serves as the spiritual father in the Monastery of St. Macarius in the desert of Scete, interprets this statement to mean that by prayer and fasting we are able to drive out Satan (toxins, disease, and bodily desires) from the flesh.[7] Fasting becomes a way to renounce the "pull of the flesh" and enter into the full body enlightenment of the ecstasy of God communion felt in every scintillating cell. In this way, fasting is an act of love.

It is significant that the first act of Christ after his baptism was to begin his 40-day fast in the desert without food or water. The act of baptism grants fullness of the spirit, and spiritual fullness grants, through fasting, victory over bodily desires. This is the direct teaching of Christ's 40-day fast. Liberation from bodily and worldly desires then makes it possible to merge in the contentment, fullness, and Love of God communion. This sequence of baptism, fullness of the spirit, fasting, victory over the bodily desires, and communion with God is the way that Christ taught by his own life practice.

The act of fasting, especially in the 40-day fast, is a mystical sacrifice of the body. Combined with meditation, which on one level is a sacrifice of the mind, fasting becomes a mystical sacrifice of the ego of body and of mind. Fasting, if accompanied by a mystical acceptance of death, is experienced as a partial death of the body. "Whoever loses his life for my sake will save it." (Luke 9:24) In his own fasting, Christ sacrificed his body mystically and showed his willingness to make the ultimate sacrifice on the cross. His sacrifice was not involuntary. Its value was that it was a free offering to God, symbolized by offering his body to his disciples with bread as his body and wine as his blood. Through his 40-day fast and the Last Supper, he was voluntarily crucified before the final offering up of his complete ego-will to God.

The offering of the ego-self in fasting requires us to reach the level Abraham did when he raised his hand to sacrifice his son Isaac at God's command. It was a partial sacrifice with only the lifting of the hand, but it was total in intent. As with Abraham, we cannot offer anything in place of ourselves when we fast. No money, good acts, or words of renunciation will substitute. It requires letting go of our own body-mind-ego complex. Fasting in this inner way overcomes ego and transforms us into the Divine. It is the mystical sacrifice of the body as exemplified by Moses, Elijah, and Jesus. To fast with this understanding leads us to accept the death of the physical body and to overcome our fear of death itself. This is the meaning of spiritual fasting. It is not for our health. It is to complete the sacrifice of the ego-self. Spiritual fasting begins with a sense of communion with God and usually ends with a deeper sense of that communion.

Physiology of Fasting

On the physical level of fasting there are many techniques and approaches. My goal here is to present a general framework for understanding the process of fasting. The definition of fasting varies. It can mean anything from a dry fast, which is abstinence from all food and water, to a fast on foods that are one level less dense than we were previously eating. For example, a fast of this latter sort, for a meat eater, would be a vegetarian diet. Another way of fasting is to abstain from that which is toxic to body and mind, and thus eliminating toxins from the system. The physiology of fasting favors healthy cells. In a process called autolysis, poorly functioning cells are destroyed first in the process of fasting, and their components are broken down and remetabolized. This usually begins after three days of fasting. Another definition of fasting includes any process which initiates this process of autolysis. We stop a fast when the elimination of waste products is complete and the autolysis finishes with the unhealthy cells and begins to break down the healthy cells. This point is usually indicated by a return of appetite and the disappearance of the white coating on the tongue.

Healthy functioning of the body begins to deteriorate when the normal process of cell regeneration and building becomes slower than the breakdown of unhealthy cells in the body. This is usually connected with the accumulation of toxins in the tissues and cells to an extent that it interferes with the proper nutrition and rebuilding of cells. The Wendt Doctrine of excess protein intake, causing a protein storage disease by blocking the basement membrane, is a clear description of how this works. With the basement membrane is clogged, nutrients, including oxygen, cannot get through to the cells, and waste products cannot diffuse out of the cells back into the capillary bloodstream. The result is that the cells begin to malfunction and degenerate. With excess toxicity and without sufficient nutrients, the process of new cell growth slows down. When cells are degenerating faster than new cells are regenerating, we experience aging and disease. It is said that in our industrialized nations many more people die of overnutrition than malnutrition. Fasting helps to clear out the basement membrane so that nutrients can begin to get to the cells and new cell growth can be stimulated. The proteins from the broken down cells are remetabolized and used to rebuild new cells during the fast, so that even without the intake of exogenous protein for cell building, cells regenerate.

During a fast the eliminative systems of the body: the skin, lungs, liver, kidney, and bowels become more active. Because the body is not spending energy digesting and eliminating fresh toxins in the system, it is able to direct all its energy toward the elimination of old accumulated toxins and waste products. The increased release is usually evidenced by foul breath, body odor, dark urine, increased mucous secretion, and foul smelling bowel contents. Because of the extra energy freed by resting the digestive system and because of detoxification and the fresh minerals gained from a juice fast, fasting has a normalizing effect on the biochemical and mineral balance in the tissues and is a tonifier of the nervous system.

Fasting is probably the oldest healing method known. It is particularly good for rebalancing problems caused by excessive eating. In 1986, the U.S. Congressional Joint Nutrition Monitoring Committee reported that 28 percent of Americans (32 million) between 25 and 74 years of age weighed too much, including 11.7 million who were severely overweight. Fasting for this reason alone is important. Fasting has been used throughout history for healing. Such great physicians as Hippocrates, Galen, and Paracelsus used it. In America, because of the influence of the drug therapy approach to healing and because of a basic break in our high technology society with understanding the simple processes of nature, the use of fasting has faded. This has been less true in Europe. In Sweden and Germany there are hundreds of fasting clinics. At the Buchinger Sanatorium in Bad Pyrmont, Germany, more than 80,000 fasts have been supervised.[8]

When to and When Not to Fast

Intentional fasting for short periods of time such as seven to ten days is considered completely safe by many fasting experts. In some Swedish hospital experiments with fasting, patients fasted up to 55 days without any difficulty.[9] Paavo Airola states that water fasting up to 40 days and juice fasting up to 100 days is generally considered safe by fasting medical experts in Europe.[10] Therapeutic fasts from 14 to 21 days are considered common in the European fasting clinics.[11] If one has any sort of serious illness or acute or chronic disease, it is highly recommended to do any fasting in conjunction with a health practitioner who is well versed in the science of fasting. People who have a strong vata dosha constitution, people who are very sensitive to life changes, people who lose weight easily and cannot regain it easily, people with active malignancies, degenerative diseases from which they are suffering malnutrition or extreme emaciation, or people with wasting diseases should probably not fast. If people insist on fasting with these conditions, it should be done under the supervison of an experienced health practitioner. In general, pregnant and lactating women, people who have not reached full physical maturity, and those who are ten pounds or more underweight should not fast. We should also not fast if we are operating heavy machinery, performing dangerous mechanical tasks, or even have to do much driving. During a fast, our minds and bodies become more calm and slower than such tasks usually require for safety.

It is best not to stop a fast in the middle of a detoxification crisis, but gently work our way through it by aiding all the eliminative systems and with techniques such as foot massage to stimulate organs to eliminate. It is important to stop a fast if an extreme nervous or mental condition manifests or a person begins to enter a cycle of high fevers. These are unusual occurrences.

General Fasting Guidelines

One of the most important aspects of fasting is to enhance all the eliminative channels for the toxins leaving the system. I suggest the following guidelines:

1. Take an enema until the bowels are clear at least once per day. Some clinics recommend as many as three separate enemas per day.
2. Brush the skin for 5 to 15 minutes twice daily and follow this with a bath and skin scrub to remove the excess dead cells and draw more toxins out of the system.

3. Take plenty of sunshine and deep breathing exercises to help detoxify the skin and lungs.

4. Get vigorous to moderate exercise during the fast to help activate the system to eliminate toxins. Some people recommend up to three hours per day of exercise such as long vigorous walks and swimming.

5. Take short saunas to enhance prespiration, which helps the detoxification process.

6. Abstain from sexual activity in order to use all energies for healing and regenerating.

7. Use flower essences and gem elixirs during the fast to help balance and align of the subtle bodies and chakras and to awaken the chakras. These can enhance the harmony of the body-mind-spirit complex during the fast. Self-heal, silver sword, papaya, lotus, star sapphire, and quartz seem to be the best combination. Self-heal aids in the natural process of the absorption of prana during fasting. Silver sword aligns all subtle bodies and balances the heart chakra. Papaya is excellent for emotional and sexual balance and allows us to enter the spiritual realms more easily . Lotus stimulates the alignment and balance on all levels of our being, and is outstanding for fasting and meditation. Star sapphire activates all chakras, especially the crown, and specifically stimulates spiritual opening while fasting. Quartz removes negative thoughts and creates emotional calm.[12,13,14] I recommend the gem elixirs and flower essences from Pegasus Products because they are the only ones made with biologically active water.

It is very important to break the fast carefully and consciously. During the fast, the digestive system has shut down and must be carefully restarted. At the end of the fast, the body absorbs everything much more easily, so what we put back into our bodies should be what we really want to rebuild our bodies with. The end of a fast is a very good opportunity to reorganize ourselves around a new quality of diet. I have found that a ratio of one day of breaking the fast for each two to three days of fasting is a good guideline, though everyone's body is different and this needs to be individualized. *How to Keep Slim and Healthy with Juice Fasting* by Paavo Airola gives a step-by-step procedure for fasting and how to break a fast. *Survival into the 21st Century* by Viktoras Kulvinskas is another book that has many tips about different kinds of fasting and fasting procedures. For example, Kulvinskas suggests ending a fast at noon with citrus juice to stimulate the flow of gastric juices and using certain herbs such as ginger and anise to speed up the process of eliminating toxic gas from the system.

Types of Fasts

Airola's book stresses the importance of vegetable and fruit juices plus a special alkalinizing broth as the best way to fast therapeutically and for rejuvenation. He points out that this is the approach used throughout Europe in all the fasting clinics. Kulvinskas is focused more on the water fast for purification and transmutation of the body. Both are correct. There are different levels and purposes of fasting. The concept of different levels of fasting is also a recognition that to fast too severely increases the possibility of a more uncomfortable healing crises from the toxins that are released. One fast does not necessarily completely detoxify and heal the body. Usually we are talking about a purification process that takes years. Since the goal of spiritual life is not to see how quickly we can detoxify, picking the most heroic fast first is not always best. For this reason I suggest several progressive levels of fasting for purification:

Level 1. Those on a meat diet can abstain from meat one week two times per year.

Level 2. Those off blood meats can switch to fasting three days at one time per month, or fast one day per week and twice per year for seven days. This fast can be a mixture of fruits, vegetables, and juices.

Level 3. Those on a lactovegetarian diet can follow the same pattern as level two, but use only fruit and vegetable juice fasts.

Level 4. Those on a vegetarian diet and using fasting as a spiritual practice can follow a pattern of four ten-day fasts per year plus either fasting one day per week or three days at one time per month. These fasts can progress from fruit and vegetable juices, to wheatgrass, and finally to distilled water.

At Level Four we are entering the use of fasting, meditation, and prayer as part of a spiritual path rather than a simple physiological maintenance of the body. It is important to understand the difference. It is also important to become aware of the risk of one's body becoming too pure in our toxic society. The cleaner the basement membrane becomes, the more sensitive we become to our polluted environment because toxins can move right through our systems. A little mucus in the system, for example, can serve to protects us from being so vulnerable to pollution. If we reach a point of purity that we become too vulnerable, we will not be able to function effectively on the physical plane in serving the will of God on this planet. What becomes important, as this balance is reached, is to establish a diet that maintains a level of physiological integrity and purity so that the practice of fasting, which on the physical level, is to compensate for eating too much and for the toxicity of our planet, can be phased out as a tool for detoxification. If we do not overload the system, the body on the right minimal diet can rid itself of almost any toxin and maintain good health. This is a great challenge and will be discussed in detail in Chapter 20. Once this diet has been achieved, then we mainly use fasting as a spiritual practice.

The 40-Day Spiritual Fast

This fast is designed to enhance spiritual life and transmute the body. Although people do therapeutic fasts this long or even longer, it is in a different context and with a different meaning. Jesus Christ and Moses, who both fasted for 40 days without food or water, were not doing it for their physical health. One focus predominated: communion with God. This is the orientation of this fast. It is on this fast that we directly confront death and the offering up of our body, mind, and ego to God. The other purifying fasts help in the preparation for this fast. Even so, it is best to prepare oneself by eating just fruits and vegetables for at least one week before the fast, and have one colonic. The general format of the fast can be as severe as a dry fast of no food and water, though this is usually a little much for most people on their first 40-day fast. The Essenes were said to begin the practice of 40-day fasts by 20 days of juicy fruits, then 10 to 17 days of fruit juices, and 3 to 10 days of distilled water. During the first 20 days, vigorous exercise is recommended. In the second 20 days, lighter exercise is recommended. During the second 20 days a great many more emotional toxic states are released. During this time it is important to be guided by someone who is familiar with this sort of fasting. The last 3 to 5 days of the fast are the most critical, in that our state is clearest and the impressions taken in at this time become deeply imprinted into the total body-mind system. It is best to spend this time in total isolation, preferably out in nature.

With each 40-day fast, the water part of the fast becomes longer and the fruit part becomes shorter. It is said that many of the inner circle of the Essenes did one 40-day fast per year, accompanied by much meditation and an abstention from worldly activities to maximize the focus on God. After five years of 40-day fasts and living as fruitarians with much meditation and other spiritual practices, it is reported that one percent of the Essenes were able to fast on prana as did Jesus and Moses.[15] To live on prana is not my goal, but it does make the point that by a gradual process of fasting and meditation, the body becomes transformed into a perfect superconductor of the prana so that no other form of nutrition is needed.

Also aligned with the 40-day juice and water fast is the idea of the progressive 40-day relative fast each year. For example, for a meat eater, it would be 37 days of vegetarian food followed by three days of juices; for a lacto-vegetarian, 37 days of vegetables and fruits according to the Rainbow principles, ending with 3 days of distilled water; for a vegetarian, thirty days of fruits and vegetables according to Rainbow principles, then 3 days of vegetable juices, 4 days of fruit juices, and 3 days of distilled water. To do only a juice and water fast for 40 days each year requires very experienced spiritual guidance and much previous experience with fasting and should be done with careful consideration. For all these fasts, it is safest to have supervision from an experienced wholistic health practitioner.

Personal Experience of the 40-Day Spiritual Fast

This fast was profound for me. I did not have any specific idea of what I wanted from the fast except to enhance the Divine Love communion. I approached it with some degree of curiosity and a clear sense of an inner direction to do it. Creating the time and space for it to happen in the middle of a busy health practice and family responsibilities was one of the first tasks of my fast. The fast requires slightly more than two months time. I started with juicy fruits, then moved to fresh vegetable juices and then fruit juices, and finally to three days of distilled water. My reason for only three days of distilled water was that the fast was primarily a time of retreat and meditation, and when I am on water for more than three days, which is what I commonly do at the end of other juice fasts, my energy for meditation tends to drop.

My energy after the first two weeks of detoxification became high and stable. It was easy to extend my sitting meditation time. After the first 20 days, my energy began to move more distinctly inward. Over the next two weeks the hours of meditation gradually increased toward nine hours per day. During this time I took long walks to tonify the body. The state of communion with God, of unity awareness, of nonduality, of harmony, and of love seemed to be approaching a higher and higher percentage of my waking awareness. My body was clearly becoming a better superconductor. I could feel the energy pulsing through me frequently during the day. Around the 35th day, I became aware of the flow of what is called the inner nectar in yoga into my psychospiritual system. Physiologically speaking, this is probably connected with the release of the endorphins from the increased prana flowing into the system. This nectar seemed to increase the level of bliss even more. It is a form of inner nutrition.

The critical turning point for the fast was in the last three days on distilled water. This time was spent away from my home in total silence in an isolated mountain retreat. To my surprise, it was relatively easy to meditate the nine hours per day, which is more than I had meditated before. Sometimes four hours of continual meditation would go by in what seemed to be a few minutes. My mind became so devoid of thoughts that in meditation, it would simply dissolve into the light of God for hours at a time. There was no body, no desires, no thoughts, no mind... only God. Unbroken Love communion with God for hours. It was clear that the Essenes knew what they were doing. In these last three days of meditation, only the vague sense of a formless I Am consciousness remained as the last bit of identity. I became a divine lump in this communion. Whether formally meditating or just being, Love existed as the only awareness. Just to Be was totally enough. The flowers bloom, light radiates, and I Am.

During the times between the merging of the mind into the light in meditation, the cosmic prana seemed to penetrate down to the microcosmic DNA of my cells. It was a total sense of resonant unity with the cosmos. My crown chakra seemed fully awakened and activated. The flow of energy into it, which had been increasing over the past 18 months, was coming into the top of my head in an incredible pulseless pulse. The complete crown became one whirling vortex of energy connecting me with the dance of the cosmos. Since that time, it has never diminished. These three days marked the full opening of my crown chakra. During these three days I drank very little water, as this prana and the sunlight became my food. I had no particular concern keeping the fasting protocol, so not having to drink or move my bowels I just rested as a divine ecstatic lump. It is possible that if this continued for too long I might have permanently left my body. The wondrous love communion with God was so strong that death of the body seemed completely secondary. This was my nonconfrontation with death. In transcendence, death is a joke. There is no death for the Transcendent Self; the body may die, but we clearly are not the body or even the mind. To think we are the personality and body is a case of mistaken identity. Many spiritual insights and understandings crystallized for me during this time. It was clear that God had given me three days of transcendence. It was also clear that to lie around as a Divine transcendent lump resonating as the cosmos in unbroken communion with God is not to be my role in this play of the world. **To be a free person is to be the will of God, rather than to be in a particular state, even if this state is the direct ecstatic transcendence of total communion.** Since this time I have discovered, however, that my body-mind complex has been sufficiently transmuted by this 40-day fast, that after a few days of fasting and retreat it is possible to enter into sustained states of the Divine transcendent lump. What exists for me, as my duties in the world are performed, is the solid, intuitive, living, transcendent awareness of the unity, harmony, and oneness of the world as Love, and as my Self.

Simultaneously with this oneness awareness, there is a comfortable working acknowlegment of the apparent duality in which we all live. As the motivation for this fast revealed itself as an attunement with the will of God, rather than as an abstract goal, I do not know if I'll ever feel the inner direction for it to happen again. I can't responsibly recommend either for or against fasts such as mine as a regular yearly spiritual practice. This is because of my lack of experience in repeated 40-day fasts and the lack of any one else with current information on such fasts. I also want to point out that the results of this fast were probably much related to years of meditation and spiritual discipline, and I am not implying that simply by fasting for 40 days all of us will immediately have transcendental experiences.

Summary Chapter 19

1. Fasting has its history in the spiritual and religious observations of almost all the world religions. It is very much part of our Judeo-Christian heritage as exemplified by Moses, Elijah, and Jesus. Fasting and meditation were a major spiritual practice of the mystical Jewish Essene communities, in which Jesus reportedly lived.
2. Fasting in its strictest sense is complete abstinence from food and water. In a larger context, it means to abstain from that which is toxic to mind, body, and spirit. Fasting can also mean to abstain from the densest level of our diet, such as fasting from meat for a meat eater or dairy products for a lactovegetarian.

3. Fasting allows our body to turn to the absorption of lesser densities of cosmic energy rather than the dense biomolecular energy of food.

4. By increasing the amount of cosmic prana entering the body, fasting increases the potential of reaching the critical energy necessary for awakening the Kundalini. The increase in cosmic prana also increases the energy of an already awakened Kundalini.

5. By accelerating the purification of the body, fasting allows the spiritualizing force of the Kundalini to operate more fully in transforming the body.

6. Fasting helps us to overcome the pull of the bodily desires on the mind and makes it easier for the mind to merge in higher states of God communion.

7. The act of fasting, particularly in the 40-day fast with meditation, is a mystical sacrifice of the body and mind to God. It is a mystical death of the ego.

8. The normal physiology of fasting is based on excretion of toxins and autolysis of dead and degenerate cells. Autolysis does not work on healthy cells until all dead and degenerate cells have been destroyed. The normal time to stop fasting is when this first step is completed.

9. During a fast, we must give extra care to supporting the eliminative systems of the body such as the skin, kidneys, liver, bowel, and lungs.

10. Fasting experts feel intentional fasts of seven to ten days is completely safe. Therapeutic fasts in European clinics of 14 to 21 days are the norm.

11. Pregnant and lactating women, people more than ten pounds underweight, those with active malignancies, severe malnutrition, and wasting diseases ordinarily should not fast.

12. Guidelines for spiritual and for cleansing fasts are given, along with recommended schedules.

13. There is a difference between fasting as a general support to spiritual life and fasting as an active spiritual practice.

14. Discussion of the 40-day spiritual fast and author's experience of such a fast are given.

20

The Most Important Single Rule in Spiritual Nutrition: **Undereat !!!**

Importance of Undereating

Moses Maimonides (1135-1204 A.D.), a great scholar and the most celebrated of all Jewish healers taught "Overeating is like a deadly poison to any constitution and is the principle cause of all disease."[1]

Sai Baba of Shirdi a great Hindu-Moslem saint of the early 1900s always gave the advice, "to eat simple and little."

Paavo Airola taught that "systematic undereating is the NUMBER ONE health and longevity secret. Overeating, on the other hand, of even health foods, is one of the main causes of disease and premature aging."[2]

Jesus, in the *Essene Gospel of Peace, Book One* said, "And when you eat, never eat unto fullness. Flee the temptations of Satan, and listen to the voices of God's angels. For Satan and his power tempt you always to eat more and more. But live by the spirit and resist the desires of the body. And your fasting is always pleasing in the eyes of the angels of God. So give heed to how much you have eaten when you are sated, and eat always less by a third."[3] My own awareness of undereating was heightened while serving as a physician in India. On Sundays there would usually be a feast, and just as regularly on Monday, Tuesday, and Wednesday people would come in with diarrhea and dysentery. They would be weak, uncomfortable, their lives were disrupted, and they had trouble meditating as a result of their illness. There is an old Arab proverb which says, "By eating we become sick and by digesting we become healthy". If we are too weak to assimilate the forces and organisms in our food, they overcome us. Those who tended to eat very little at these feasts usually did not get sick because there was less food and fewer bacterial and parasitic forces to overcome. This is one of the secrets of not getting sick while traveling.

One of the most practical reasons for undereating is that it is hard to meditate if our energy is still involved with digesting food. This is especially true if we want to get up early in the morning to meditate and we have eaten too much the night before. I also discovered for myself that even while I was in a cycle of meditating six hours per day, as long as I underate, the food available to me (cooked vegetables and chapatis, a flat bread) in no way depleted my meditation energy. This rule takes precedence over all other dietary advice. This does not mean that we can make a diet out of undereating junk foods and not deplete our energy. If raw, whole, organic foods are available, they are still the choice for optimizing our diet for spiritual life.

Scientific Evidence in Support of Undereating

Dr. Pelletier, in his research on longevity, found that cultures in which people led long healthy lives, such as in the Vilcabambam region of Ecuador, the Hunza of West Pakistan, the Tarahumara Indians of Mexico, and the Russian people of the Abkhasian region, people ate low protein, high natural carbohydrate diets that contained approximately one-half the amount of protein Americans eat and only 50 to 60 percent of the total calories.[4] Airola makes the point in *How to Get Well* that one never sees an obese centenarian.

Dr. Clive McCay of Cornell University found the life span of rats doubled when their food intake was halved.[5] Professor Huxley extended the life span of worms by a factor of 19 by periodically underfeeding them.[6] Research has also shown that undereating increases the life span in fruit flies, water fleas, and trout.[7]

There are many historical cases of the health and longevity benefits of undereating. Saint Paul the anchorite lived to be 113 years eating only dates and drinking only water. Thomas Carn, born in London in 1588, who lived to be 207, and a Mr. Jenkins, born in Yorkshire, England, who lived from 1500-1670, both ate no breakfast, had either raw milk or butter with honey and fruit for lunch (Carn may have had bread also), and had either raw milk or fruit for supper. The Countess Desmond Catherine who lived to the age of 145 ate only fruit. Dr. Szekeley reports that all of these people practiced undereating.[8]

One of the most famous of the undereaters is Luigi Cornaro, who lived from 1464 to 1566. He was a Venetian nobleman and the administrator of the Bishopric of Padua. By his forties, he had nearly eaten himself to death. He was attended by Doctor Father Benedict who advised him in the arts of natural living and undereating. From that point on he simplified his diet to 12 ounces of food and 14 ounces of liquid per day, never deviating from this undereating. He was quoted to have said, "A word to the wise is sufficient." The one exception to this was at the age of 78 when his family insisted he increase his intake. He increased it by 2 ounces and immediately got sick. After this he dropped down to 8 ounces of food and eleven ounces of fluid per day until he died at the age of 102. His writings on undereating can be summed up in two statements: **"The less I ate, the better I felt."** and **"Not to satiate oneself with food is the science of health."**[9]   Szekely points out that Luigi Cornaro is a link in the transmission of the Essene teachings.[10] This transmission came through St. Jerome's translation of the Essene Gospel of Peace, from Constantine the African, who studied these texts in the monastery at Monte Cassino and who taught the Essene natural ways at the Salerno School of Medicine where Doctor Father Benedict was trained.   Part of the transmission of the Essene teachings was Cornaro's emphasis on the practice of sobriety, which he shared with everyone, including the Pope, who became a student of his. Sobriety, the art of eating in moderation, can be reduced to two simple guidelines: first, to avoid eating more than our system can easily digest and assimilate; and second, to avoid food and drink which disagrees with the stomach. Sobriety means to pay intelligent attention to the quantity and quality of foods we eat. In practice, it means leaving the table while still wanting to eat and drink more. There is an old proverb which says, "What we leave after taking a hearty meal does us more good than what we have eaten."

The Art of Spiritual Nutrition

The art of spiritual nutrition is to take just the right amount of food and drink for our individual needs. It means to consume exactly what is necessary to assimilate the energy and biomolecular structures required to maintain our body as a mature human crystal. It is to eat in a way that completely supports our transmutation into a superconductor for the spiritualizing energy of the Kundalini. It is to eat in a way that best allows us to attract, conduct, store, and transmit the cosmic energy entering our system. In the preceding chapters, we have looked at qualitative guidelines for this. The quantitative amounts are quite individual, determined only through trial and error. We become both researcher and the one being researched, an approach that helps to develop an inner sensitivity to our real biomolecular and energetic needs. Through meditation and fasting our body is continually transmuting. As we purify on the body-mind-spiritual levels more cosmic energy is able to enter our system, so we require less energy from nature via our food. Through fasting and lighter diets our basement membrane becomes clearer and more porous. As this happens the nutrients we take in get to the cells more easily so we need less food to obtain the same amount of biomolecular nutrition. This is distinctly different from the concept of minimal eating or progressively decreasing food intake as an obsessive mathematical effort to reach a minimum. This is a deprivation-mortification practice that does not necessarily lead to spiritual growth. It does not have the same effect as the highly intuitive approach of eating the most appropriate amount to maximally stimulate spiritual evolution. This latter approach is not based on the materialistic concept of food value.

The art of spiritual nutrition is to be attuned to the subtle changes occurring over time and to adjust our diet accordingly. There are two relative end points in this process. The first is when, as the result of fasting and appropriate eating, our bodies reach a certain level of purification and homeostasis with our polluted environment, which allows our bodies to detoxify naturally without fasting. The second end point is finding a diet that doesn't make us so pure that we become too sensitive to our polluted environment and cannot function. Once this balance has been reached, spiritual fasting, rather than purificatory fasting, becomes the primary fasting practice if we feel drawn to fasting as part of our spiritual life. The art of spiritual nutrition is a cornerstone in the foundation of our spiritual life. It is important for developing right diet as a support for spiritual life. Once this is achieved, just as with any foundation, we no longer have to focus on it. It becomes incorporated into our way of being. It becomes an expression of our awareness and way of being.

Summary Chapter 20

1. The most important single rule in nutrition is to undereat.
2. Human cultural studies, case histories, and animal studies have shown that undereating prolongs life span.
3. Not to satiate ourself with food is the science of health.
4. The art of spiritual nutrition is to be sufficiently attuned to our inner needs and outer life in a way that we know just the right amount of food to eat. It it requires us to be attuned to the subtle changes occurring over time and to adjust our diet accordingly.

21

Chemistry of Stress, Alchemy, and Meditation

Chemistry of Stress

The vast majority of humanity lives in the chemistry of stress. The world for most has become a very dangerous place: individually and nationally sponsored terrorism, chronic wars, nuclear weapons, crime-ridden streets, air and food pollution, nuclear tests and reactors exploding clouds of radioactive material, whole nations thinking about voluntarily irradiating their own food, flu epidemics, people irresponsibly dumping radioactive and toxic wastes into the water supply, businesses and people breaking down, and the divorce rate near 50 percent as people unconsciously repeat their automatic defense patterns against giving and receiving love. For most, these are tough times. We exist in a physiology of doing rather than being. The doing is centered on thinking that we must accumulate food, wealth, sex, or power in order to survive. Our first three chakras are often completely out of balance, or what we commonly call "off center." In the first chakra, we are fixated on survival and fear instead of on healthier consciousness of trust that whatever God does is for the best. This fear blocks us from experiencing our higher purpose. In the second chakra, we are stuck in sex obsessions instead of the more evolved functions of procreativity and creativity. The third chakra, whose higher awareness is sensitivity and emotional integration, is thrown into reactive emotional imbalance, excess desires, and attachment to power. Until these first three chakras are balanced and our consciousness is merged and integrated with their higher functioning, the consciousness of the heart, or love chakra, and the superconscious fifth, sixth, and seventh chakras cannot completely emerge or be fully integrated in a way to create the chemistry of meditation.

On all levels of our being, stress creates degeneration and aging. In earlier chapters we described the sevenfold subtle body system. Mental, emotional, and physical stress cause the subtle bodies to lose their alignment with each other and block the incoming flow of cosmic energy or prana. As the chakra vortexes are deprived of the energizing pranic life force, their vortexual vibration rate is slowed, and the expansion of subtle body energy which is a function of the chakra vortex becomes contracted. The more the subtle body contracts, the harder it is for the pranic life force to get through to energize the chakras and consequently the life functions of the body. The SOEFs, depleted of prana, are more easily disorganized, enhancing the aging process of entropy. This subtle body contraction is reflective of the body-emotion-mind contraction we experience through fear about survival, distrust, and anger with the world, in relationships, and our general state of alienation. The core of this fear is rooted in our misunderstanding and fear of death.

As a result, we live our lives in the adrenal stress syndrome of the caveman who is being stalked by the saber toothed tiger. We live as if our lives were in immediate danger. The adrenal secretion from this lack of harmony, fear, sense of separation, and alienation from our world directly contributes to the aging process. On the physiological level, we experience it as a constant overstimulation of the sympathetic nervous system, causing excessive adrenalin secretion into the blood. We commonly know it as the "uptight" feeling in mind and body. Muscle tension, nerves on edge, shut down digestion, nervous stomach, and mind racing are all physiological symptoms of this adrenal stress syndrome. In this overstimulated sympathetic state, our physiological digestive system is partially shut down. Not only is the flow of prana into our SOEFs minimized, but we cannot even absorb the food energy from our stomachs. Getting the continual false signal that it is fighting for its life, our mind and body, in continual sympathetic overstimulation, eventually fatigues. If it continues long enough, we slip into body-mind breakdown, increased rate of body aging, and the potential of eventual illness.

The biochemistry of stress is congruent with the overall aging process. It parallels the breakdown of the SOEFs patterns and the dissipation of their energy. Adrenalin is a naturally occurring catecolamine and when released by the body under stress, it breaks down into activated metabolite forms such as adrenochrome, a well-known free radical whose excess concentrations have been, at least loosely, associated with schizophrenia.[1] These adrenalin metabolic free radicals and other free radical-like compounds break down cell membrane structures and disrupt the basic electron transfer system of our cellular energy metabolism. The result of this is an electron leakage from the normal electron transport system which leads to the creation of superoxide free radicals, other activated oxygen free radical producing molecules, and additional free radicals.[2] These free radicals further oxidize in our system. The result is increased free radical damage to cell membranes, enzyme systems, and particularly artery endothelial cells (a possible precursor to atherosclerosis).[3] This free radical mediated, oxidative damage results in an accelerated aging and a chronic, degenerative disease process.[4] It represents the common biochemical end point for all types of stress on the system.

A simplified and useful way to understand this mechanism is that the free radicals, in essence, drain the body's molecular system of energy by stealing energy in the form of electrons. The electron energy that the free radicals "steal" is important for maintaining cell membrane structure. Dr. Levine calls these electrons the "molecular glue" which holds all levels of biological structure together, from DNA and RNA to cell membranes.[5] If one takes away the "glue" that holds the biological structure together, we get disorganization of cell function and cell replication, which manifests as increasing entropy and therefore aging.

It is very important to understand that sympathetic nervous system overstimulation has the same destructive end point effect as all other sources of stress such as physical trauma, bacterial and viral infection, and the environmental stress of pollution that is dumped on us by our society. This common effect is the destruction of oxidative cell membranes due to free radical activity. Some of these other environmental stressors that cause an excess of free radicals are ozone, sulfur dioxide and other smog components, radioactive fallout, chemical and radioactive toxins dumped into our earth and water supplies, and foods that have undergone free radicalization.[6] Food that has been irradiated, microwaved (this is my hypothesis), adulterated, processed, spoiled, or undergone other "fast" food preparations has an increased amount of free radicals and other radiolytic breakdown products. The stress of viral infections has been shown to cause increased free radicals in the system.[7] Physical trauma which results in cell membrane damage, such as swelling from bumps and bruises, causes the same free radical production resulting from the broken cell membranes.

There is a basic biochemical statement that can be made about the meaning of stress chemistry from all causes of stress. It is that under any cause of emotional, mental or environmental stress, the normal oxidant/antioxidant biochemical balance is thrown off. With increased free radicalization, the body's antioxidant capacity or biochemical regenerative energy is depleted. The result is that we experience decreased ability to adapt and survive free radical oxidant stresses. This results in cell membrane and other forms of biomolecular degeneration. From this we have accelerated aging and increased incidence of overt disease. This is evidenced in the epidemic increase in autoimmune disease, food allergies, and chemical hypersensitivities, now often called ecological illness. The imbalance of the oxidant/antioxidant ratio and concomitant sensitization to our own bodies and environment are the biochemical corollary of the essential disharmony and alienation from our environment, the people in it, and ourselves that stress consciousness creates. The question remains, how is this transcended?

Chemistry of Alchemy

Alchemy involves the conscious working with energy to transmute elements. For us it begins with a conscious choice to begin to reorganize our disrupted SOEFs by increasing the cosmic energy or prana coming into our system. It involves aligning ourselves with the natural laws of body, mind, and spirit in order to allow the life force to transmute us. This life force, this cosmic energy, this prana, is the God energy which is absolutely necessary for us to transcend the chemistry of stress. This God energy is the ultimate food, and meditation is the ultimate digestive process.

Meditation aligns and expands the subtle bodies, allowing the cosmic prana to come into our chakras and SOEFs with little resistance.

As this power of God enters our system, we become rejuvenated on all levels. The reversal of entropy begins, and the physiology of stress and aging is reversed or slowed down. Hundreds of studies by Transcendental Meditation researchers since the early 1970s have validated the point that meditation reverses or slows the aging process. These researchers have shown that meditation creates a slower and more balanced metabolism with more sympathetic nervous system rest and a better sympathetic/parasympathetic nervous system balance. Unnecessary oxygen consumption, heart rate, and respiration rate have all been shown to be decreased. Meditators in the studies demonstrated a decrease in high blood pressure, increased exercise tolerance in those with angina pectoris, better cardiovascular efficiency, better nervous system reaction time, improved athletic performance, better response to stress as measured by galvanic skin changes, improvement in the hearing threshold (which reflects an improved level of neurophysiological functioning), improved skills at sensory motor tasks, improved creativity testing results, increased scores on intelligence tests, increased mental speed and accuracy, increased long term memory, increased EEG synchronicity and coherence, and general decreased anxiety.[8]

On the biochemical level, researchers have found that meditators have a decrease in plasma cortisol (which is a major stress hormone), a decrease in adrenalin and nonadrenalin metabolites, and a decrease in blood cholesterol.[9] In the physiology of stress and aging, all these parameters have been found to move in the opposite direction to those found in meditators. This makes meditation look like the elixir of life. It is! A most impressive study supporting this assertion was performed by R. K. Wallace on the effects of meditation on the aging process. He took 47 subjects with an average age of 52.8 years who practiced the Transcendental Meditation technique and the TM-Siddhi techniques. He matched them to a control group and the established normal data for such a group. The testing system he used was drawn from the Morgan Adult Growth Examination which gives reliable indicators of biological age. He found that in the subjects of the same chronological age, meditators who had been meditating less than 5 years had a mean biological age of 7.1 years less than that of the control group data. The mean biological age for those meditating 5 years or more was 15 years younger than the norms. Four of these meditators had biological ages of 27 or more years younger than expected for the normal chronological ages.[10]

How to Create the Alchemy of Spiritual Transformation

When careful gardeners plant seedling trees, they usually surround them with a wire fence to keep animals away. They often tie the trees to a supportive stake so the wind does not blow them over. To overcome the chemistry of stress, spiritual seedlings are best aided by a spiritual protective fence or sanctuary. In ancient times and even now, the few serious spiritual aspirants retreated to caves, monasteries, and ashrams in hopes of finding such a sanctuary. There is even an ancient and incompletely understood Ayurvedic process called kaya kalpa in which the participant lived in complete isolation for periods of 40 days to a year. It was the ultimate rest. During this time, cleansing and then regenerative herbs and foods would be given. This kaya kalpa process is described in the biography of the sage Shriman Tapasviji Maharaj, a great ascetic who lived for 185 years. He used this process three times, and experienced what the biographer describes as an amazing regeneration, including the regrowth of new teeth and hair. It was said that when he did this for the first time at the age of slightly more than 100 years, he came out of it looking like a young man in his late 20s.[11] This, perhaps, represents the ultimate intensity in reversing the aging process. It also is a rare individual who can live in an isolated dark room for a year and not have the mind move into the chemistry of stress. It requires advanced spiritual development.

What is different today is that we are entering a collective age of enlightenment on this planet. This requires an approach that is useful for large numbers of people rather than just the rare spiritual aspirant. We need to transform our own everyday life into a spiritual sanctuary, a harmonious meditative way of life that aligns our physical and all our subtle bodies, a way that allows us to experience the full grace of God, a way that allows the full cosmic energy or prana to penetrate all levels of our body-mind-spirit being, filling our lives with the ecstasy of love. This is full person enlightenment. It is our destiny. It is our ultimate function and purpose. It is the chemistry of meditation which is Love. It is the wonderment of oneness awareness. It is knowing the way by being the way.

How does one go about building a spiritual sanctuary in everyday life? As one who lives in the ordinary life circumstances of an 18-year marriage with two teenagers, one dog, one cat, a monthly mortgage, and regular daily work as a wholistic health physician living in the country just outside a city of 36,500 people, I have been given the opportunity to explore the creation of such a sanctuary. For most people, a peaceful world would make the establishment of an inner experience of peace and harmony considerably easier. As one becomes more rooted in the Truth, the apparently turbulent condition of the outer world fades into the harmonious play of consciousness. Yet, for mass enlightenment to unfold on this planet, the path to inner peace would be easier with a peaceful environment. Ultimately we must start with experiencing the peace of our own Divine self. This poem by Lao Tsu very beautifully describes how to create this spiritual sanctuary by starting with ourselves:

"Tao abides in non-action.
Yet nothing is left undone.
If kings and lords observed this,
The ten thousand things would develop naturally.
If they desired to act,
They would return to the simplicity of formless substance,
Without form there is no desire.
Without desire there is tranquillity.
And in this way all things would be at peace."[12]

In meditation we can directly experience this completely fulfilling inner contentment. It arises from different levels of the meditation experience. It may be from the inner bliss of resonating and being filled with the Divine cosmic energy, or from the ecstasy of the at-oneness with God as the formless and as the creation, or from the sublime beingness of the direct awareness of the Truth. In meditation we may receive the direct experience of Love, know ourselves as Love, and experience Love for our true inner Self and consequently the Self of all that resides in all people. These various experiences of inner bliss, sublime joy, peace, and love fill us so wondrously that we are content beyond desire. Without desire there is peace. The practice of meditation reinforces these experiences. **Eventually the experience becomes our waking awareness and we move from the practice of doing of meditation to a state of being in life as a meditation.** This is true meditation. From this we directly experience the Torah teachings and those of Jesus that we should love the Lord with all our heart and might and love our neighbor as our true Self. It is from these direct meditation experiences and from the eventual stabilized direct awareness of the formless reality of God, that we lose desire for the things and power of the world. Without desire there is tranquility. When there is tranquility based on this awareness, "all things would be at peace." From my own meditation experience and from observing and hearing the experiences of other meditators, I assert that this is absolutely true. A stabilized awareness in the nondualistic Truth may not happen all at once. It may take many years to become the predominant awareness in our life, but with persistence it will happen. It is important to note that we don't become anything. What happens is that we simply become aware of the Truth of who we already are.

Earlier we spoke of transmuting the first three chakras so we could awaken to their highest levels of awareness. In the first chakra we are confronted by fear instead of trust, rooted in the fear of death. In meditation, many people eventually have the direct experience of building an awareness that there is no death for the Self. The Self is immortal. With this awareness, the fear of death is gradually dissipated and we are free to trust. Whole books are written on this question, but I again assert from my own direct meditation experience that this fearless awareness develops.

Right Understanding

It is possible to meditate, to have flashy experiences, and yet never develop a right understanding. This is because people sometimes have deep patterns that resist the understanding that arises in meditation. Sometimes they become addicted to the power and energy of the experiences rather than the Truth that lies behind them. They get trapped in going for the "hit." Right understanding, which is an important part of spiritual evolvement, is the integration of our experiences with daily life; it is meditation as a practice and way of being. It is the wisdom to distinguish the real essence of life from the illusions of life.

Right Fellowship

Right fellowship is extremely important in developing right understanding. It may come in the form of traditional guru/disciple relationships, through people who serve as spiritual guides or teachers, through regular meditation groups, or through spiritual group processes such as the core group process suggested by Barbara Marx Hubbard.[13] Wherever it comes from, it is a very important part of creating a spiritual sanctuary. Shiva Puri Baba taught that the most important external aid for creating a spiritual sanctuary or right life was the fellowship of realized souls. Many, for brief periods of time, have higher awareness experiences, altered sensory states, or altered states of consciousness that do indeed take one beyond the ego, but they do not become stabilized in their daily experience. It is rare that we reach such a stabilized awareness as our primary life orientation. It occurs more easily when the direct and sole intent of our life is to become established in the awareness of the Truth as the nondual, holographic pure awareness of God's Light and Love. This takes spiritual discipline. This is one of the hardest parts of creating a spiritual sanctuary in regular worldly life. There are many who do well in a protected ashram situation but when they go out in the world find that they have not internalized their discipline and it slowly begins to fade. Right company, in any form, helps to inspire people toward maintaining their spiritual discipline and developing right understanding. Right fellowship is a form of God's grace. This is important because, although our inner teacher is always working, we do not always want to follow it. The inner teacher of another at just the right time, may give the right positive reinforcement for our own inner spiritual direction. Right fellowship supports, reinforces, and stimulates the inner teacher. It helps to create a situation in which there can be an exchange of teachings and presence among equals. Surrounding ourselves with good company is an extremely critical part of building a spiritual sanctuary. In this age of increasing mass enlightenment, it becomes an even more important principle.

The attuned awareness of the inner teacher, plus right fellowship, can be said to equal what is known as the Guru's grace in the Eastern spiritual disciples. People often go to a Guru to be awakened, but with the heightening awareness and energy of spiritual seekers in general, the awakening of the Kundalini may occur as a result of the increased energy that happens in a group meditation or even a spiritual group gathering such as a world-wide meditation for peace. We may awaken each other by simply transferring this energy to each other. This energy comes from God's grace of right fellowship. Muktananda once made this point in a humorous way by telling us how his dog, who had accumulated energy from being around him, gave shaktipat to the veterinarian. People often attribute this increased energy and grace exclusively to the teacher, guide, or guru who is focusing the group rather than to the result of the total group spiritual energy. God's grace comes in many forms and ways. It can come through the increased cosmic energy of the outer teacher, through the prana of an individual person, through such practices as meditation and fasting, or through reaching a critical point intense enough to awaken the Kundalini spontaneously. It can come from the heightened prana of a whole group, or from a combination of the pranic energies of the inner teacher, outer teacher, and of a meditation group.

Right Livelihood

Right livelihood is our alignment with God's will. We are already perfect. What we really seek is to become the Divine expression of our inner perfection in the world. This is the essence of right livelihood. The more the cosmic energy flows through us, the more we attune to God's will and are able to be involved in the right work for who we are. We become the creative expression of the divine will. In this process, the second chakra awakens and our mind merges in the evolutionary creative energy that was always ours. Right livelihood is the subject for a book in itself, but there are a few guidelines in creating the spiritual sanctuary that are important to consider. The first is the reminder that although right livelihood is extremely important, our highest function is to rest totally in the awareness of our transcendent reality as our primary awareness. Eventually we reach the stage in which it makes little difference to our spiritual state how much time and energy we put into our worldly work. However, for all but those in the most advanced stages of spiritual evolution, too much time and energy spent in work may dull our growing experiences of the Truth. We may find ourselves becoming self-willed doers rather than being in the state of grace. As a doer, we become attached to the rewards of our work, and in that attachment, the ecstatic experience of our transcendent beingness is lost. By working too many hours we can become depleted of mental and physical energy. In this depleted state it is harder to remain awake. The ancient Essenes had a system by which they only worked four hours at economic livelihood and spend the rest of their days in various forms of communion.[14] Because they lived simply, four hours were enough to meet more than their needs. The Essenes were known for producing an abundance which they shared with others. My observation is that people in general are not designed to spend eight to twelve hours per day at the work place, no matter how special the work. A six-hour work day seems to be close to the maximum that all but a few can safely expend on work and keep conscious. The famous 19th century saint Ramakrishna advised people to keep one hand on God's foot and the other hand in the world. Shivapuri Baba advised us to do our minimum duties correctly and keep our minds on God. Traditionally, service to others helps to balance our creative work. For some it becomes the most creative and evolutionary expression. Mother Theresa is an inspiring example of this.

World peace is a function of our inner peace. By our state of meditation we create peace by being peace. For the whole world to be elevated to a state of transcendent awareness, it requires all of us to participate in creating peace on earth. I believe this mission of world peace is becoming a planetary expression of God's will. By building a spiritual sanctuary out of the world, everyone's spiritual evolution will be quickened. We will be brought closer to the quantum leap in consciousness that we, as all of God's children, will someday make. By serving world peace, we are serving the development of inner peace for everyone. By giving our love to the world, we become that love. As love we become the spiritual sanctuary that we seek.

Right Relationship

As love and only as love can we live in right relationship with our mate, children, and all others around us. Unconditional and unrelenting love is the sole building block of the spiritual sanctuary. In building right relationships it is also necessary to organize our time, space, and energy intelligently so there is enough for individual, couple, family, and societal expressions of this love. People often think about communication problems when we think of right relationship, yet in one of my roles as a family therapist I rarely see a communication problem. People through contractions of the heart and through avoidance and acts of retribution communicate their fear of intimacy and of love quite well. It is very difficult to keep the heart open in the face of rejection and hurt that another projects to maintain a safe intimacy distance. This is the crux of the third chakra issue: how do we rise above the emotional hurt, imbalance, and power struggles to the state of balanced and compassionate emotional sensitivity which reflects the higher awareness of the third chakra? We do this by keeping the heart open no matter what pain we may feel. It is this wound of the heart that leads us into the awakening of the fourth, or heart, chakra and to the awakening of the other spiritually oriented chakras. As we do this, it becomes easier to be in the awareness of the Truth of who we are and to see this play of Truth in all our everyday interactions, turning them into valuable lessons as gifts of God. If we allow our heart to contract, our subtle bodies then also contract and become misaligned. This contraction then decreases the pranic life force available to us. The chemistry of stress sets in and the aging process starts again. But most important of all, we shut ourselves off from the cosmic energy which is the love energy of God. It is the source of our spiritual life. It is the source of spiritual awareness. This is the price we pay for the ingrained habit of contracting our heart. As love, we become the spiritual sanctuary. Without it, the sanctuary survives as a frail shell of intellectual awareness.

Attunement to Mother Nature's Natural Laws

Part of our spiritual sanctuary is already present, waiting for us to notice. It is in the natural laws of the universe, but we are rarely in tune with them as a support for our sanctuary. The Essene communities knew the value of harmony with the natural laws and spent much time studying, being in communion, and ultimately living in harmony with them. As a result, not only was their spiritual life enhanced, but they attained very high levels of health. It is reported that it was quite normal for them to attain ages of greater than 120 years.[15] If we are not attuned to these natural laws, our individual thoughts and actions will not be in balance. This harmony is necessary for full health and spiritual life. This is particularly important because modern society is significantly out of tune with these natural laws on almost every level. We are so out of tune that we may just destroy the whole world under the delusion of protecting ourselves. The problem is that these societal thought forms are so strong that it is very easy to be swept along by this unconscious wave of disharmony. We have become so disconnected from natural synchronousness with universal laws that we need to go to the very source of these laws to begin to regain our attunement. The source is the pure, undifferentiated awareness which is the source of all. By merging our awareness in pure consciousness with meditation, we can avoid a distortion in the manifestation of pure awareness into thought and action. The practice of meditation is the main tool for this harmonizing of our awareness. As this practice deepens, the awareness maintains itself in our awake life without formal meditation. At this point we tend to act spontaneously in communion with these laws. We become as the law rather than under the law.

For most people this state of communion is an idealistic form of sanctuary that is rather difficult to attain or sustain. Nevertheless, by meditating regularly for several times a day, we will build a spiritual sanctuary in which our lives will become more and more harmonious with these universal laws. The whole process is helped by living in some connection with nature. It is more strongly reinforced if we are able to live outside of an urban setting, but even attuning to a simple indoor garden in the middle of the city can be helpful.

Once we begin to understand these laws, it is very helpful to do as the Talmud suggests, "to build a fence around the Torah."[16] This means that we create certain self-warning signals or listen to feedback from the right company gathered around us that tell us if we begin to act disharmoniously. One of the dangers in experiencing higher states of awareness is that we begin to feel we are above any concepts or laws by virtue of our direct contact with the source. The issue is that we are also in direct contact with the tremendously disharmonious societal forces which are always pulling us into disharmony. Swami Prakashanada Saraswati, a spiritual uncle to me, would emphasize that we are not totally free from the urges of the body and mind until we leave the body. A great many of the gurus who have come to the West, as well as the various leaders from all religions, have fallen into disgrace because they have assumed they were above needing a fence to warn them when they were being drawn away from unity with the universal laws. They just assumed that whatever they did was that harmony. That fence in Eastern spiritual traditions is called dharma or righteous life. In the West it is called the Ten Commandments. The Ten Commandments have several levels of interpretation. When one says "Thou shalt have no other gods before me," (Exodus 20:3) it can mean that we should always be immersed in universal God consciousness rather than the diverse consciousness of money, power, sex, and other forces of the temporal world. "Honor thy father and thy mother, that thy days may be long upon the land" (Exodus 20:12) can be interpreted to mean to honor the universal laws of mother earth and the cosmic laws of the heavenly father, so our life will be long and spiritually fulfilling. These are concrete statements of universal laws that act as guidelines for those who are not in fully in touch with the direct source. It is optimal to live our life as the love-inspired spontaneous manifestation of these universal laws; this is the firm and joyous foundation of the sanctuary. The important thing is not to create a fearful, contractive tyranny out of a self-righteous, blind application of our own projection of what we consider the "literal" meaning of these laws. How we live by these laws is a function of our own spiritual evolvement at any point in time. There is no right way forever. It is not that simple. Life is not static. It is more important to be harmonious with the spirit of the law. This requires some intelligence, discrimination, and right understanding. It was on this basis that Jesus acted to break with the strict interpretation of the written law and heal on the sabbath. But to maintain the sanctuary, we need to create a feedback system in order to wake us up if we begin to wander. Ultimately, the feedback system is to **know the way by being the way.**

Alchemy of Bodily Health

The physical body is the final aspect of creating a spiritual sanctuary for the alchemical chemistry necessary for human transmutation. We have considered our sanctuary from the spiritual, mental, and emotional aspects and now need to include the body as part of what I call total person enlightenment. The purpose of the understanding shared in this book is to create a synthesis of the relationship between the physical body, the emotional-mental body, and the spirit in spiritual life. It is to give an outline for how to increase awareness in our life so that we may extend beyond the inner spiritual experiences of perfection to become the manifestation of that perfection in our ordinary daily life. By maintaining the practices of right diet and fasting, we help to turn the body into a better superconductor of the cosmic energy. This cosmic energy or prana comes from God and is the immediate experiential "face of God" that we can experience in every moment of our life. The experience of this cosmic love force uniting us with the resonant experience of the macrocosm is bliss. As we clear the toxins and blocks from our system with diet, fasting, and other sources of natural and vibrational healing such as with homeopathy, herbs, flower essences, and gem elixirs, our body becomes more highly organized. As this occurs, we can more easily feel and be attuned with the direct force of God coursing through us. We do not need our Kundalini to be awakened to have an experience of this attunement. We may experience it as one of those sacred moments of Divine inspiration, ecstasy, and love that so many of us have had at some time in our lives. It may be a moment of a quiet and subtle sense of attunement during which our body, mind, and spirit feel totally harmonious with all of God's creation such as what may occur while watching a special sunset . It may be a continued experience of joyous well being. It may be the experience of the awakening or energizing of the power of the Kundalini. Although these experiences occur more frequently with proper diet and fasting, this does not mean that by diet and fasting alone we become enlightened. It is through the integration of the threefold balancing of body, mind, and spirit that we become aligned, merged, and stabilized in the higher evolutionary spiritual awareness.

Seven Alchemical Healers

There are some basic forces, part of the laws of nature, that help to transform and maintain the body in the most optimal state. H.E. Kirschner, M.D., calls them "nature's seven doctors."[17] They are right diet, fresh air, pure water, sunshine, exercise, rest, and of course mental, emotional, and spiritual peace.

We have touched on some of these throughout the book, but I would like to add a few more touches to deepen our understanding of the simplicity of the natural laws. Fresh air, as we discussed earlier, is a direct source of nutrition. In addition to breathing exercises, it is good to take an air bath everyday. Air is absorbed through our pores and acts as a detoxifier. Dr. Kellogg estimated that each person needs about 3,000 cubic feet of fresh pure air per hour to help us detoxify the toxins excreted from our lungs and skin.[18] How much fresh air are we getting in our sealed-off, high-rise office buildings where millions of us work every day? This is a very simple reason many people are out of harmony with the natural law. It is so easy to do. We are surrounded by all sorts of "normal" lifestyle activities that are disharmonious.

Pure water is another of the seven healers. Because of our national and international persistence in creating chemical and radioactive toxic wastes which seep into our waters, it is almost impossible to find pure water. To get anything near the quality of the fresh spring water, that once existed in this country, we have to process the water by distilling or reverse osmosis. In this processing the water becomes unstructured and needs shaking to reeoxygenate and sunlight to become structured and energized.

Adequate sunlight of 30 to 60 minutes per day on the total body gives our bodies a chance to become directly reenergized. Like plants, we soak up and transmute this nutrient into our energy system. Until we become used to the sun, late afternoon and early morning sun are the easiest to begin with. Although a little sunlight is good, hours of sunlight can be too much for the system and lead to imbalances.

Exercise is another of the seven alchemical healers. There is a simple rule: use it or lose it. Dr. Kirschner teaches that activity is life and stagnation is death.[19] Exercise stimulates all the internal organs and muscle systems, it tones the nervous and digestive system, it improves circulation, and it stimulates the skin system to release toxins. No equipment is needed. In fact, working out in a smelly, poorly ventilated and lighted gym deprives us of the benefits of sunlight and fresh air we get during outdoor exercise. Outdoor walking is the best exercise according to many natural healers. The British educator, George Trevelyan, claims to have just two doctors, his right and left legs.[20] For those who feel more vigorous exercise is necessary, it is interesting to point out that the Ayurvedic system of healing recommends exercising to only 50 percent of capacity. The point is that if we turn exercise into a stress for the body we may get aerobic benefit, but too much physical stress may break down body function. I feel between 50 and 80 percent of our exercise capacity needs to be reached. In my own personal practice, I take a fast walk several times per week and do an exercise called the sun salutation at around eight to nine per minute, for twenty minutes, five times per week. I do this in minimal clothes with bare feet on a lawn in order to make a direct barefoot contact with the ground energy. This exercise also allows me to take in the sunshine and do deep breathing at the same time. In this simple way, many of the natural laws are efficiently acknowledged. The general idea of all these laws is to give the body just the right amount of attention to function optimally for spiritual focus in life. This requires some self-observation along with trial and error, until we find the right balance. Then we can settle into a routine of orderly caretaking and not be concerned about it. Everyone must scientifically find his or her own routine.

Rest is another important alchemical healer. It is so important that God even gave us a sabbath so we could not misinterpret the message. In everyday work life, it is important to acknowledge this time for regeneration. In the process of kaya kalpa, the idea of complete rest is an integral part of the rejuvenation program. It works. Rest implies a break from all daily routines, responsibilities, irritating noises, and so on. A quiet spot in nature is good, especially for city people who are cut off from nature's regenerating forces on a daily basis. Rest can take the form of sleep. There is no magic number for sleep; depending on our constitution, we may need from five to eight hours, or even more per night. The main idea is the regularity of a good night of sleep. For some, a little cat nap in the day is helpful; for kapha types it can feel worse. For sedentary, intellectually active office workers, physical labor like gardening or hiking, game playing, or periods of silence may be the best rest. For others, just the opposite may be best. This may also be combined with light fasting. Daily meditation before, during, and after work creates a rest that helps wake us up from production mentality and is of benefit to us all.

Although aligning with these basic natural forces seems simple, it often requires some social independence. Children, when they have a recess from school, automatically know what to do -- they play. How many teachers do we see outside playing? As a physician, I attend medical conferences which are almost always in sealed buildings where we sit for hours at a time immersed in intellectual activity. At lunch time, instead of sitting around even more at a long lunch, with everyone else, I try to find some open space where I can exercise, breath some fresh air, take in some sun, meditate, and eat a light homemade salad. To many, it might seem strange to acknowledge the participation of these natural laws in our life, but they keep us tuned to the life force. After you do this sort of thing for a while, if you do it a quiet, non-self-righteous way, people become accepting and sometimes even join in the fun. There are many who only need the support of a little good company to let their inner teacher guide them to alignment with the natural laws.

Summation of the Chemistry of Alchemy

The chemistry of alchemy involves the decision to reverse the degenerative life process on the physical, emotional-mental, and spiritual dimensions of our lives. It is a conscious choice to reorganize and reenergize the SOEFs by increasing the amount of cosmic prana coming into our system. To successfully do this, everyday life and the world need to be transformed into a spiritual sanctuary. For this purpose, right diet and fasting, even though they do increase the amount of cosmic energy entering the system, are not sufficient. We need a regular practice of meditation, right company, right understanding, right livelihood, right relationship to significant others and society, and attunement to the heavenly and earthly universal laws. In sum, it can be called right life. It is analogous to Buddha's eightfold path, or the meaning of the Sermon on the Mount. In discussing right life and meditation as the path to enlightenment, Shivapuri Baba, an enlightened teacher who lived to be 139 years old, taught that there are three disciplines which are the only cure for the ills of this life.[21] These are the disciplines of the physical, moral, and spiritual laws of the universe. He simply reminded people to be absorbed in God and their duties (the three disciplines) as God. This is what is meant by right life. It is important to emphasize that there is no automatic list to be followed for right life. It requires a wisdom developed out of personal "trial and error" practice and meditation. For those who have trouble meditating, contemplation is sufficient. For most of us, some of the most profound understanding of right life grew out of our so-called mistakes. As long as we are willing to witness and learn from our mistakes, right life will develop for us. Shivapuri Baba felt that the biggest obstacle to right life is inertia and procrastination. The normal yet often disharmonious ways of our modern society are so much easier to follow. In this regard, Muktananda used to say that the cemetery was his favorite place because it is a reminder that some day we will leave our physical bodies and lose our opportunity to pursue the spiritual path. Therefore the time is now. In right life, no part of our existence is negated. It represents the full awakening of the first three chakras. This awakening is the foundation for the stabilized awakening of the awareness of the higher chakras. It represents a major step in the integration of the body, emotional-mental, and spiritual levels of our being. The combination of right life and meditation is the major process for whole person enlightenment.

Chemistry of Meditation

As prana increases in our total context of right life and meditation, we become superconductors, accumulators, and amplifiers of the cosmic energy. This increase more properly aligns all three levels of our being. Our awareness spontaneously increases because the experience of the prana in itself, as the emanation of God and as the face of God, naturally increases our awareness of the Divine. This experiential aspect of the Divine reinforces our direct awareness of the nondualistic truth of God. At some intangible point in the process, this direct awareness which we often experience in the practice of meditation begins to maintain itself more and more predominantly in our waking state. At this point, our mundane daily life is transformed by the awareness we experience in meditation. **Our waking lives are filled with the awareness of meditation, the direct sublime awareness of God, of love in every aspect of our life. This is the chemistry of meditation.**

As we increase our meditation practice, there is an increased alignment of the physical and all the subtle bodies with the pure vibration of the cosmic prana. Meditation is the divine digestive system of the cosmic prana. The clearer a channel we become for the cosmic energy, the more continuous flow of it we have moving through us. This brings us into a continual at-oneness with the universal life force and therefore oneness with our own Divinity. The closer we become resonant with that energy, the more we simply become that Divine energy. This increased pure prana aligns the SOEFs so perfectly that we become aligned with the cosmic energy down to our very RNA-DNA structure. I feel that the spiral structure of the RNA-DNA double helix reflects the spiral-vortexual pattern of the cosmic prana. As cosmic consciousness penetrates to our atomic and molecular structure, we cannot help but feel the ecstasy of this unity of the ultimate macrocosm of pure prana with the ultimate microcosm of our molecular structure. One feels totally harmonious on every level of being. It is a total mind-body-spirit ecstasy vibrating in every atom of our being with every other atom in the universe. **DNA and RNA are the harpstrings; the winds of pure prana blow through, and the sound is pure joy. This is the physiology of meditation.** The experience of it fills us with love, harmony, and joy. **Love is the ultimate harmonic of the physiology of meditation.** The awareness that comes from the continual experience of this total harmonic of love establishes us in the ultimate holographic, nondualistic truth. The chemistry of meditation begins when the ultimate truth of oneness becomes our predominant waking state awareness, and we motionlessly dance and silently sing in the sublime joy of total person enlightenment.

Summary Chapter 21

1. The chemistry of stress represents an entropy-producing process that dissipates the energy and structure of the SOEFs and consequently leads to an increased rate of aging and increased probability of chronic degenerative

disease.

2. The chemistry of stress is the chemistry of biochemical, physiological, emotional, mental, and spiritual degeneration.

3. It arises out of the toxic stress of our personal and world lifestyle. Its common degenerative pathway on the biochemical level is excess free radical production, which results in cell membrane and other biomolecular destruction.

4. On the spiritual level, the chemistry of stress is most related to our first three chakras remaining unawakened and out of balance.

5. The chemistry of alchemy begins with a conscious choice to reorganize and reenergize our disrupted SOEFs by increasing the cosmic energy or prana coming into our system. It requires aligning ourselves with the natural laws of body, mind, and spirit in order to allow the life force to transmute us.

6. This life force is the God energy, the cosmic pranic energy which is absolutely necessary for us in order to transcend the chemistry of stress. This energy is the ultimate food.

7. Meditation is the ultimate digestive process of this food. It aligns and expands the subtle bodies so that the cosmic energy can come into our mind-body complex.

8. In order to sustain the alchemy of spiritual transformation, it is helpful to build a personal and world sanctuary of inner and outer peace. Our everyday life needs to be transformed into a spiritual sanctuary.

9. Right life is the foundation of this spiritual sanctuary. It arises from right diet, right fellowship, right understanding, right livelihood, right relationship to self, significant others, and society, and attunement to the heavenly and earthly universal laws. It is the living expression for how we integrate our physical, moral, and spiritual lives.

10. There are no rules for right life. The right life at one point in our evolution is different from the right life at another point. It requires an intuitive and practical wisdom that attunes us to the spirit of the law rather than blindly binding us to the letter of the law. Intelligence, contemplation and meditation help us to develop our understanding and practice of right life.

11. Right life is knowing the way by being the way.

12. The combination of the practice of meditation and right life is the process of whole person enlightenment. It involves the integration of body, mind, and spirit as a totality in our spiritual life. There is no negation of any part of our being.

13. The chemistry of meditation begins when the ultimate holographic, nondualistic truth becomes our predominant awake state awareness and we motionlessly dance and silently sing in total person enlightenment.

14. Love is the ultimate harmonic of this awareness.

22

Evolution and Fruition of Kundalini

Review of Kundalini

Kundalini is the inner spiritualizing energy that takes us to the experiences of ecstasy, joy, and love. It is the grace of God which transforms us into the nondualistic holographic awareness of the Truth of God, of I Am That I Am. A major purpose in understanding nutrition for spiritual life is to eat in a way that enhances the spiritualizing force of Kundalini. The awakened Kundalini moves through the physical and subtle bodies removing blocks and spiritualizing the consciousness of the aspirant. It eventually awakens our consciousness to the higher awareness and energy of each chakra. As part of the completion process, we merge with it in the crown chakra. This is the view from outside of the process. In the first part of this chapter, I will present an external view of this process which is based on the intuitive integration of my inner experiences with the Kundalini unfolding. This will then be followed by a sharing of some of my own direct Kundalini experiences of the "knots" opening. After this, a spiritual perspective of the whole process will be discussed.

Mudane and Spiritual Kundalini

A model for the inner Kundalini energy flow needs to be clarified so that we can better understand the Kundalini awakening and unfolding process. Kundalini is often referred to as the "two headed serpent" in that there are two aspects to Kundalini. One is the spiritual Kundalini, the all-pervading cosmic energy, the cosmic prana (shakti, energy). As pointed out before, the whole universe is nothing but the vibration of this cosmic prana, or virtual energy. It is this energy which condenses to create the physical form. After the creation of the form, there is a residual energy left in the body which is classically called Kundalini Shakti. It is said to be "coiled like a serpent" in the first chakra in the subtle body near the base of the spine. It awaits in a potential energy state ready to "spring upward". In this potential state, this Kundalini Shakti (divine power) supplies the vital force energy which runs all the mundane functions of the body. For clarity's sake I have termed this partly active Kundalini Shakti as *mundane* Kundalini, and the cosmic prana as *spiritual* Kundalini. In Chapter 8, we saw that the spiritual Kundalini continually "descends" in its pure form through the crown chakra to energize directly the pineal and pituitary glands associated with it. These glands are located so close together that they create a strong electromagnetic field (EMF) which oscillates within the brain tissues. The spiritual Kundalini tends particularly to move into the right or intuitive brain. From there it moves down the body energizing the different chakras and their associated organs, nerve plexuses, and glands. In this process it energetically interfaces with the force of the mundane Kundalini arising from its source. In most cases, by the time the spiritual Kundalini reaches the stored energetic center of the mundane Kundalini in the base chakra, there is not enough combined energy to ignite the stored Kundalini Shakti. A certain amount energy of the mundane Kundalini is always moving up the spinal cord area in its function as the prime life force energy of the body. As it reaches the brain, the mundane Kundalini primarily energizes the left brain, or the rational ego mind, maintaining its dualistic relationship with the spiritual Kundalini energizing the right brain.

The Awakening of Kundalini Shakti

The awakening of the Kundalini Shakti requires that the combination of the spiritual and mundane Kundalini energies reach a combustion point that then sparks the awakening. To prepare for the sparking of the purifying and spiritualizing fire of Kundalini an integrated approach of right diet, right life, and meditation is important to follow. Right diet prepares and maintains the physical body as a superconductor. Right life quiets the emotions and anxieties of the mind, which helps to align the subtle bodies, allowing more energy into the system. Right life also helps to balance and stabilize the first three chakras as a foundation for sustaining the awakening of the superconscious upper chakras. Meditation guides us in right life and more completely aligns all seven subtle bodies so that the full organism becomes a better superconductor of the spiritual Kundalini. This is an integration of body, mind, and spirit. Right diet, right life, and meditation are the most appropriate general practices to share in our Western culture for enhancement of the mass enlightenment that is beginning on this planet. The love of God is an intrinsic part of this approach. The love of God Divine love, devotion to God, desire to commune with God and surrender to God is inherent in right life, right diet, and meditation. It is the driving motivation behind the three disciplines I have outlined. Without Divine love, without the burning desire to commune fully with God, then right diet, right life, and meditation can become empty mechanical disciplines that have a limited impact on our spiritual evolution. Devotion to God is the major driving force in the Judeo-Christian tradition. It is why people seek a spiritual path. In the Eastern tradition, this love of God is called bhakti yoga. There are many other yogas which may also help to make us combustible for the awakening. Repetition of mantras, raja yoga, ashtanga yoga, techniques of hatha yoga, and Kundalini yoga are just a few. The practices of all religions and spiritual paths may also help to prepare us. They include Zen, Buddhism, Zorastrianism, Advaita Vedanta, Hinduism, Islam, the Tao, the Sufi tradition, Judaism, Christianity, and many others.

The awakening happens as a descent of Grace or descent of Love. It occurs when there is enough spiritual Kundalini descending through the crown chakra to reach the energy center of the mundane Kundalini, resting in its potential state in the base chakra, thus sparking the awakening. In the 1930s, when Jung wrote about the mystery of Kundalini, very few people experienced the awakening of Kundalini or had even heard of the word Kundalini. Now it is happening in mass numbers. The first Kundalini clinic was started to supply a frame of reference and direct aid to people experiencing these awakenings. It was particularly important for those in whom it happened unexpectedly and spontaneously as a result of individualized practices rather than in groups which acknowledged the existence of the Kundalini and had some framework for integrating it.

One reason there is an increase in awakenings today is because of the process of right fellowship. Meditation groups, spiritually oriented workshops, or even large spiritual gatherings such as for peace meditations can stimulate the awakening. The increased spiritual Kundalini energy developed by the group creates enough descent of Grace that, combined with the aspirant's own inner energy and preparation, the spark is ignited. The most consistent way that a Kundalini awakening happens is through the tradition of shaktipat initiation. This occurs when a person with a great amount of the spiritual Kundalini flowing shares this energy with the aspirant. The combination of this energy with the Kundalini energy of the aspirant is enough to reach the critical ignition point. The sharing of this spiritual Kundalini energy may be by look, guru's mantra, thought, or direct touch, such as happened to me when Muktananda blew his cosmic prana into my mouth. The awakening may often be a combination of all these ways of increasing the descending power of the spiritual Kundalini: individual preparation and build-up of the aspirant's mundane and spiritual Kundalini, group spiritual energy, and shaktipat.

The awakening may be the intense and classical variety described earlier, or it may be moderate or mild. It occurs according to the Kundalini energy build-up in each person. It is important to acknowledge the mild and moderate awakening, as well as the classically described awakening, as the criteria for an awakened Kundalini. For the vast majority of people, the awakening is very safe. In my experience at the Kundalini clinic, with Muktananda and his path of Siddha Yoga through which thousands of people were awakened, and in my experience with people in my own meditation groups and workshops, it is rare for anyone to have serious trouble with the awakening of the Kundalini. It is after all the our own energy that is awakened, not some foreign drug. It is of course comforting and helpful to have the awakening in the context of right fellowship with someone who is experienced with the workings of Kundalini. There are some who claim that many patients in mental hospitals are there because of an undiagnosed Kundalini awakening. Having worked in mental hospitals, this has not been my experience. Manic episodes, spaced-out and disorganized thinking, or intense personal and even spiritual crises are not the same as a Kundalini awakening. Labeling them as such may make people feel good but adds confusion to the process of getting proper help. It is more important to redefine and appropriately turn the crisis, whatever it is, into an opportunity for psychospiritual growth. It has been my experience from the Kundalini clinic and in Muktananda's main Indian ashram, where I occasionally performed in the role of a psychiatrist evaluating and supporting people having serious psychological difficulties, that many of the people who had difficulties with their Kundalini awakening had a previous history of psychotic episodes or of a very brittle nervous system. These people would usually be carefully stabilized and compassionately sent back to America to continue their spiritual work in a less intense Kundalini-charged situation. I mention this because people with this sort of background do not need to stop their spiritual work, but should be very careful about practices which artificially force the awakening of Kundalini, intensify the energy after the awakening, or which in general intensify the nervous system energy, whether or not there has been an awakening.

A Tale of Two Siddhis (Powers)

With the awakening, a merging of the two Kundalini energies begins to take place. A polarity still exits between the mundane and spiritual Kundalini, but they begin to act synchronistically. It may be analogous to the image of two north pole magnets facing each other as they spiral up the spine. The energy generated by this synchronistic interaction purifies and spiritualizes the body and helps to charge and awaken the chakras. The energy not only begins to move through the subtle nervous system of the whole body, but also begins to open up the sushumna, the major path for Kundalini flow in the body. This subtle path runs vertically in the etheric body along the inside of the spine.

The more we become a superconductor for the flow of this awakened Kundalini and for the influx of the spiritual Kundalini into the system, the more actively and powerfully this partially merged dual Kundalini force works in us. Because of the energy that is generated and the centers that are awakened, we often have temporary experiences of bliss, ecstasy, love, tremendous well-being, Divine intoxication, peace, profound inner contentment, Divine awareness of the nondualistic truth of God, oneness awareness, and direct experiences of our own Inner Self. It is as if the Divine influence of God has descended to the physical plane of our body-mind-spirit complex. We begin to feel this Divine influence permeating every aspect of our life and being. I like to think of the awakened Kundalini as the hand of God. It is at this point that we stop thinking of God in terms of belief. **To have the direct experience of God's presence takes us to the place of the direct knowledge of God and our own true nature as the Transcendent Reality. God is no longer an abstract idea but is a positive reality.** The experience of the energy of God is a tremendous motivation for continuing the spiritual practices that heighten this communion. It is much easier to meditate, to fast, to follow right diet, and to live a right life when our desire for the communion with God and experience of the ecstatic love of God is being fulfilled. We do not need the Kundalini awakened to experience this communion, but when it is awakened, these experiences usually come more frequently and easily.

Once we are aware of the Kundalini energy, it is easier to know what to do to enhance its intensity. One of the subtle traps of the spiritual path, however, is to become addicted to the bliss of these experiences and begin to think of them as the goal of spiritual life rather than simply part of the wonderful awesome process. The goal is to become stabilized in the nondualistic continual awareness of the truth. When the overall goal of spiritual life is consciously in mind and these experiences of the truth are repeated enough, temporary awareness from these experiences begins to build into a more stabilized continuous awareness of the truth. When the awareness of the transcendent reality of our existence as Divine love, as the non-dualistic, holographic truth of the Self becomes our predominant awareness, a major shift in the enlightenment process has taken place.

The Evolution of the Kundalini and the Three "Knots"

The process of the Kundalini evolution may take only a short time, or it may not complete itself in this lifetime. An important factor affecting this is the intensity of our desire for the complete unbroken love communion with the Divine.[1] The awakening is the first step of the opening of the sushumna pathway which takes us to this permanent communion. In this pathway there are three "knots" which are rarely written about, spoken about, or understood. In the yoga literature there are vague references to the three "knots" and their meaning, but I have found few references in Western literature. Because of my own experiences with them I have been drawn to develop an understanding of their significance. Some yogis talk of them as blockages in the sushumna channel, but we will get a clearer functional understanding if we think of them as evolutionary nodal points.

Classically speaking, these "knots" are located at the base chakra (Brahmagranthi), the heart chakra (Vishnugranthi), and the brow chakra (Rudragranthi). I feel that these points represent the different stages in which there is an intensification of the total Kundalini energy in the system. Each stage or "knot" opening reflects a progressively more integrated synchronization and merging of the two polarized Kundalini energies. With each level of merging, there is an amplification and intensification of the Kundalini energy. In an indirect way, the "knots" regulate the flow of Kundalini in the sushumna, so that excessive energy does not flow through and "burn out" the system. Thus the merged Kundalini energies do not move to the next level until the consciousness and conductivity of the individual has reached the capacity to hold the more intense energy and awareness. This does not mean that people do not experience higher states of awareness, it only means that these states do not become stabilized until the channels are sufficiently strengthened to hold the increased energy of those awareness. It is said that the Kundalini is very intelligent. For this reason, it is better to allow it to unfold spontaneously than to attempt to force it artificially with specific meditations or techniques. In some of the yogic teachings, three intensities of Kundalini energy are reported, which I feel correlates with the opening of each "knot."[2] The first level of energy intensity is called prana Kundalini. It corresponds to the energy released with initial awakening and the beginning synchronization and partial merging of the two polar Kundalini energies associated with the awakening. Chit Kundalini is the name of the next major increase in Kundalini intensity, which corresponds to the Kundalini power that is active after the awakening of the second "knot." Para Kundalini is the name for the most refined, most intense, and purest level of Kundalini which the body is able to conduct.

The first "knot" release of energy happens when the individual awakened awareness of the first three chakras merge into one unified state of awakened awareness. The second "knot" represents the merging of the already unified first three chakras with the awakened love of the heart chakra. Parallel to this is a new level of synchronicity and fusing of the two Kundalini energies spiraling up the sushumna. With each increased level of Kundalini merging, the sushumna channel itself becomes more and more open and conductive of the Kundalini.

The final "knot" in the sixth chakra is released when the awakened awareness of all the chakras are merged into the one nondual awareness of the Truth. It is at this point that the mundane and spiritual Kundalini completely merge into one single Kundalini energy. All polarity of the Kundalini and corresponding duality in our consciousness vanishes. The energy of each chakra merges into this one energy, although a remnant of each remains for body maintenance. The subtle bodies are perfectly aligned and merged in a way that the pure cosmic prana is no longer filtered and can directly enter any chakra. The primary center for energy intake becomes the pure prana taken in through the crown chakra. The very sushumna structure itself essentially dissolves into this one energy, our union in God consciousness. With this complete fusing of the two Kundalini energies, the evolutionary activity of the Kundalini in the spiritualization of body, mind, and spirit is essentially complete. We operate from a sense of pure knowingness, and become absorbed in the pure prana of God awareness.

At this level of the greatly increased nondual Kundalini energy, I feel there is a shift in the very energy balance of our atoms. I hypothesize that the increased energy is translated into an increased spin in the rotation of the axis of the atom and in the electron spin. With this increased energy and axis spin of the nucleus and electron, the mass of both the electron and the nucleus expands, but the orbit does not increase. The nucleus and electron are more closely bound and vibrate faster. The person can hold more energy at the atomic level, and it is harder to pull electrons away from the atom. Therefore the system is healthier, because it is harder for the more tightly held electrons to be pulled off by free radical oxidation.

Experiences of the Three "Knots" Opening

Much of my interest, understanding, and sharing about the three "knots" and the movement of the Kundalini is based on the teaching I received from working out the meaning of my own experiences. The merging of the first three chakras occurred about 11 months after the awakening of the Kundalini. I was at Muktananda's Ganeshpuri ashram in India. From the time of the awakening, having tasted of the Divine communion, I pursued deeper and deeper communion, like a bull in heat, as some people joked. It pained me not to be in union. My love for God was so intense I could barely stand it. In one stanza of a poem from my journal at that time (October 5, 1976) I wrote:

"How can I desire anything but you,
Once having joined you for even a moment
In the bliss of I am free
There is nothing higher or more sacred than
To be in total union with you."

My way of response to this intense desire for communion was to increase my spiritual practices. I particularly increased my meditation time to the maximum that my structure could tolerate. I had received Muktananda's permission to meditate more than the customary one hour a day, so I increased to four hours per day, which was a lot for me at that time. This was in addition to the hours of chanting songs to God in which the entire spiritual community participated. At this intensity, most of my three meditations per day were filled with the ecstatic bliss of love communion with God. Frequently merging into the blue light of consciousness within myself, I was introduced to experiences of the non-dualistic reality that imprinted on my awareness, bringing me into a peaceful and content state except for my desire for God. I felt like a plane reaching speeds and energies at which the wings were about ready to come off. My whole body, ego-mind, spirit integration was undergoing intense transformation. With very little formal training or knowledge in any sort of yoga, I was aware that I had embarked, with much trust in God, on a voyage into the unknown. Muktananda's subtle guidance was my only safety line. I was going for it, except that I did not know what I was going for. The following journal entries can best illustrate the intensity of this undertaking. Journal entry October 31, 1976:

"Well today is another turn of sadhana (spiritual practice). It started last night when going to bed. I was lying there repeating my mantra when I began to feel some increased energy. What I perceived as my vas deferens began to twitch and spasm, then I got a partial erection and a feeling of a thin column of energy going directly inside of me vertically from the perineal knot (this is a physical body knot joining the muscles at the base of the perineum). It was painful, but not terribly painful. The night was spent in more of a meditation half sleep.

In my morning meditation I felt calm, peaceful, and enjoyed the play of chiti (conscious). Baba (Muktananda) came in a blue pearl and took me off somewhere. Much blue light. Much energy. I seemed to be all light inside .Kundalini rising. Then the pain at the base of the muladhara (base chakra) began, twitching and spasming of the vas deferens -- sushumna energy stream, which is usually narrow, begins to broaden and increases the intensity of the flow of upward energy. All this alternated with visions of Baba -- and much celestial feeling. I am feeling very gentle and mellow, but I know a process is beginning that is very unusual and beyond my body concepts. I urge myself to let go of any control of the body and let the Kundalini be in complete control. I am determined to go all the way. Shakti is purifying me.

In my afternoon meditation, it started again with lots of energy. Nice visions of Baba alternating with different energy forms. I was feeling joy and light. Then a brief sense of a negative energy feeling -- vision came and quickly passed. Obviously the play of consciousness -- it almost seemed psychedelic. Then the vas deferens spasm began; much pain, hot, painful erection. My whole pelvic area to lower solar area on the inside became flaming red hot. My body began to undulate in orgasmic movements. Self-consciously I am relieved that I am the only one sitting in the mediation hall at that time of the day. But I had tinges of self-consciousness sitting in half lotus having spontaneous preorgasmic undulations. Then I realized that it wasn't going to stop. I was going to have an orgasm right in the middle of the meditation hall! I couldn't believe that this was happening. I wasn't even having any sexual thoughts or feelings. I then began vigorous dry ejaculation spasms with my whole lower pelvis involved. No semen was coming out. What a surprise! With each orgasmic spasm, I could feel and see (in meditation vision) the semen shooting directly up the sushumna, broadening it and extending the sushumna channel opening all the way to my ajna (brow chakra). It filled me with intense energy. It went on for what might have been 15 to 30 minutes. It took another 15 minutes for the erection to go down. It was another one and a half hours before the perineal pain subsided."

The next day, the nails of both my little toes spontaneously came off. If was as if the energy was so intense that my system could barely contain the energy. This whole process was very sobering. I felt a quiet joy in surrendering to a process that was more powerful than I and which was beyond my comprehension. But it is one thing to revel in the bliss of the Divine communion, and another to surrender to having my internal anatomy reorganized.

Following this night- and day-long experience, whenever I even had the glimmerings of a sexual thought, that painful ten- to twelve-inch rod of energy would begin to activate. It seemed as if it were a shish kabob skewer piercing through the round discs of my first three innocent chakras. After returning to America, it did not take long to discover that I had undergone a process of spontaneous celibacy because of this shish kabob effect. My wife was distinctly unhappy about this. With some help from my friend Dr. Lee Sannella and the strength of our own love, we began to take our relationship to new levels of love and compassion. At the time we were living in a rural setting in northern California, and I was immersed in organizing my life according to the principles of what I now call right life. I was working half time, which was enough to cover expenses, and spending the rest of the time working on the land, being with family, meditating, and performing other spiritual practices. My life had never been so attuned and in balance. It was a special time for our whole family. As I analyze it now, I see that all three basic chakras were being awakened to their higher awareness and integrated into my life practice. It was also a time in which the spontaneous celibacy served as a protective space for the Kundalini to complete its work on the awakening and merging of the first three chakras. After about six months, a note from Muktananda arrived suggesting that this period of spontaneous and complete celibacy was nearing completion. When we finally felt it was the time to make love, we both spontaneously and simultaneously merged into the wonderment of the blue light of total communion in the oneness of God. It was clear that we had both been transformed by the spiritualizing power of the Kundalini.

Awakening of the Second "Knot"

The merging of the first three chakras with the heart chakra was not as dramatic or painful. It began about six months after the sequence of time associated with the first "knot" opening and integration. The second opening was marked by a vision experience of the detailed anatomy of the heart chakra, of an increase in the total energy of the Kundalini spiritualizing my system, and the sudden cessation of most of my daily meditation visions. Instead, there was the continuous experience of white light and merging into this formlessness. Sometimes it would be so bright in the early morning meditations that I would think I had meditated into the day time. My whole essence would be vitalized by this light. I became aware of a broad white light energy emanating from my heart chakra. It was a broad vortex that connected me with an impersonal love and empathy with everything and everyone in the universe. Whether meditating or not, on the in or out breath, it was easy to dissolve into the white light. This would happen even while jogging. During this time I would often experience a blue flame in what my left-brained medical mind thought was the bottom of the right auricle of the heart. It was slightly to the right side of my heart. Sometimes this blue light would transform itself into an image of Muktananda or Nityananda. Less frequently, there would be a similar blue flaming light in the brow chakra that seemed aligned with the blue light in the heart area. I don't consider these as visions, since whether I saw them or not I felt their presence. This second "knot" state expanded in awareness over a period of five years before the final merging of chakras began. During this time the daily repeated meditation experiences of my true self as the formless white light of consciousness slowly began to etch itself into my more permanent awakened awareness. An "I Am," or witness awareness, was becoming part of my ground of being.

Awakening of the Third "Knot"

The cycle for this awakening began to build in late October of 1981, about ten months before its culmination. After four years of gently stabilizing and expanding the awareness of the second awakening, the spiritual desire began to get very hot again. I kept thinking of a teaching Muktananda once gave in a lecture, that when God offers you his kingdom, why settle for a handful of dust? My program increased in intensity. I was getting up at 2:30 a.m. to add an extra hour of meditation time, which now was closer to four and one-half to five hours. In early December, the first two experiences of Nirvakalpa samadhi occurred in which even the "I Am" awareness, or witness consciousness, dissolved into the void. All duality was gone. Everything was gone. These lasted for about an hour each. My wife came in during one of them and thought I was dead. Apparently my breathing had stopped for a while. The Kundalini does kill off the illusion of the one you think you are. It was getting more intense. The following is part of a journal poem written on December 27, 1981:

> "Ah -- the bliss of my life,
>> of the world,
>> of my children,
>> of my wife.
> If I die of a broken heart,
> It will not be out of sorrow,
> but because it is so full of Love,
> that I could not say no to more...
> and it just burst out of love."

Journal entry February 12, 1982: "The bliss of the Self, the pulsating oneness, the inner joy has simply grown greater than the contraction of my ego. The critical point has past...the power of the Bliss of God is greater than the safe contraction of the ego. It dies as my liberation grows. The last stage is beginning."

Journal entry May 29, 1982: "Somewhere in this last year I have recognized...I Am That! I am is more a part of my awareness than not. Destiny unfolds on the empty field of my Being. I Am the spectator watching it in the quiet ecstasy of the play; knowing I Am. Just to Be is enough."

By late August of 1982, my meditation had reached a steady six hours per day for several months. My family had returned to the United States three weeks earlier. The kids had to get ready to start school and someone had to find a home in which to live. I am very grateful to my wife, Nora, for being so understanding at this time. It is this awareness, love, and compassionate understanding by a mate that makes it possible for a complete spiritual unfolding to happen for a family person. To completely surrender to the unfolding of the Kundalini requires the right life consent of our social context, so Nora's consent was very important. Spiritual life for family people is made easier when both husband and wife are evolving in their spiritual life.

I did not leave India with my family because I had a sense that something very important was going to happen for me, and I was unable to leave Ganeshpuri at that time. As a wise person once said, "You can't cross a chasm in two small jumps." At this time, the energy of the Kundalini was centered in the I Am awareness of the sixth chakra. Although the gentle throbbing of the Kundalini in the sixth chakra had gone on for years, it now became particularly intense during meditation, feeling as if it were going to explode. After a few weeks of this intensity, it began to occur to me that the third knot was about to be expanded and the Kundalini was going to merge in the crown chakra. The traditional teachings often said that one needed the Guru's permission for this final step of Kundalini to take place. I wondered how this was going to happen. My relationship to Muktananda did not involve a lot of personal talking contact. Other teachings said that the permission of the inner Guru, the Self of all, was sufficient. So I waited for inner guidance.

Finally, during one of my evening meditations, the energy became so intense that I spontaneously got up and wobbled over to the meditation hall that was outside of Muktananda's room. Sometimes in the evening he would come out and walk around this hall. About 30 seconds after I sat down, Muktananda, dressed in his longjohns, opened the door and came out. He walked directly over to me. I know because I peeked! He immediately began to work his fingers over the short path from the sixth to the seventh chakra on my brow forehead and crown area. As he worked on me, the streams of the totally merged Kundalini energy began to flow upward in a v-shaped pattern to my crown chakra. I could feel his other hand gently placed over my head. It seemed to be pulling the Kundalini energy up through the crown. Just when I felt the flow firmly established, he calmly turned and walked back into his room, his function of grace for me completed. He had initiated the expansion of consciousness into the seventh chakra.

Since that time, the awareness of the Kundalini energy has rarely left the crown chakra. A steady pulse of increasing energy continued to flow in the crown chakra, yet the experience of the sushumna channel seemed to fade. About two weeks later in meditation, Sai Baba of Shirdi, a very well known saint who died in 1918 and with whom I had a special connection, appeared. From the palm of his right hand a thunderbolt of energy shot into this now opened pathway. From this I experienced a great widening of the Kundalini path to the crown and the dissolution of the sushumna entirely. It all seemed to dissolve into the merged Kundalini energy in the crown chakra. From this time on, I frequently became aware of a vortex of energy pulsating at the top of my head. A continuous experience of this vortex pulsation did not occur, however, until the end of my 40-day fast seven months later. At that time the top of the crown chakra seemed to disappear, leaving an open, swirling vortex of pure prana. It is through this open vortex that I continually feel the pulsation of the cosmic energy entering my system. The energy felt in the other chakras seems almost nonexistent compared to this channel.

In choosing to share these experiences, I had to let go of old taboos and concepts of spirituality about how this sort of information and our experiences should be keep secret and therefore limited to a select few. There is a story about Ramanuja who when he received a secret mantra from his guru was told that whoever receives this mantra will go to heaven, but if it is given to anyone else without the guru's permission, he will go to hell. Ramanuja immediately went up to a roof top in the village and began to shout repeatedly "Om Namah Shivaya" and explained to the people that who ever repeats this mantra will go to heaven. His guru heard him and shouted up to him, "What are you doing? Don't you know you will go to hell?" Ramanuja called back, "If all these people will go to heaven, I certainly do not mind going to hell." His guru, realizing his true motive, then blessed him for his act of love.

It is important to understand that we will not all have the same experiences in this evolutionary process. A danger in sharing is that we tend to ego-compare experiences. A key thing to remember is to learn, listen, and be inspired by each other's experiences, but to be content with the particular grace that God gives us and to know that our experiences are specifically appropriate for our own spiritual development. It is not necessary to have such an intense awakening and expansion of the three knots in order to evolve spiritually. It is more important that we be willing to experience all of God's grace in whatever form it comes to us. The lightening flash of God's grace needs an attracting focus on earth which is our intention to be fully open to this grace. This willingness draws the grace. Without our desire for God's grace, its effect on us is minimal.

Commentary on Evolutionary Kundalini Process

For most of us the unfolding of Kundalini is a gradual process over years of consistent practice. At different points where the chakras merge and the two Kundalini energies become more synchronous and more fused, there is an increase of the overall Kundalini energy in the body-mind-spirit complex. The time before and after this merging is often experienced as one of more intense spiritual desire and longing accompanied by increased awareness. In between these points are times of integration and stabilization of the newly experienced awareness in our everyday life. With the understanding of the different cycles in the Kundalini unfolding, such practices as complete celibacy for periods of time may be appropriately followed when we are guided by the Kundalini working within. Following the inner guidance of the Kundalini seems more healthy than blindly following extreme practices according to the concepts of different teachers or spiritual paths. This does not mean we sit around and wait for the Kundalini to awaken before doing any spiritual practices. Such things as meditation, right life, right diet, and other general practices that help us to lead a more sattvic, balanced, and harmonious life are clearly part of general spiritual development.

Without the integration of our experiences into everyday life it is difficult to maintain higher awareness. This is why it is so important that the awakened and merged awareness of the right life of the first three chakras be stabilized and integrated as the foundation of daily life. Without this foundation it is difficult to hold the energy of superconscious experiences or to stabilize them in a mature spiritual awareness.

The awakening and spiritualizing power of Kundalini often brings many spiritual experiences. The bliss, ecstasy, complete contentment, peace, and love for God that is often associated with these experiences can be a great motivation for continuing our spiritual life practices. These experiences often bring us into the direct knowledge of our own Divine Self and give us profound inner teachings. The more often we experience this awareness in our meditation, the greater is the reinforcement of Truth to establish itself permanently in all states of our consciousness. These profound spiritual experiences act as a sort of Divine behavior modification program, helping us to be constantly aware of our transcendental reality. These experiences encourage us to follow a purifying and elevating spiritual life practice in order to experience these states more often. The subtle trap with spiritual experiences is that we begin to focus on the "hit" of the experience as an ego feather or even as the goal of spiritual life rather than as part of the process of the Kundalini evolution. All of it is a gift for our spiritual development. If we are able to understand this, we adopt an attitude that is neither for or against experiences. We are simply free to relate to them appropriately for our spiritual benefit.

The intensity of spiritual effort is the most important factor in stimulating the Kundalini unfolding.[3,4] This has been true in my personal experience and in my general observations of people on the various spiritual paths who have attained some real awareness. The guidance, protection, and grace from a teacher, guide, or guru, or even from active spiritual visions, such as I shared with Sai Baba of Shirdi and which many people experience with Christ, is essential. Grace alone, however, is not enough. Salvation is not a one-sided gift from a teacher. It requires our intense effortless-effort as the first wing of the bird. Grace is the second wing. Without both, we do not fly very well. The issue is subtle in that this motivation for self-effort and devotion is affected by the cycles of Kundalini evolution. It is difficult to maintain an intense effort if it is not our time. It is also important to understand that although will power and self-effort help, they do not automatically guarantee a higher awareness. There is an ego trap of doership lurking when we rely solely on self-effort. Through our own will power we may have proudly mastered all the hatha yoga positions or develop many magical powers, but we may have only aggrandized our egos and consequently blocked our spiritual growth. Power or skill is not the same as spiritual awareness. There seems to be an appointed time, which is beyond my understanding, for it all to unfold. It is as if we suddenly understand our spiritual purpose and experience love and devotion for God that we did not see or feel before. There is a divine and sublime mystery in the timing and unfolding of the spiritual process. For us to be attuned to the subtleties of this we are best served by an attitude of being rather than doing. This is a state of effortless-effort. This is part of the implication of my crown chakra being opened by the physical manifestation of grace through Muktananda, through Sai Baba of Shirdi in meditation, and through the act of being inspired to fast for 40 days. These are all forms of God's grace intermixed with various manifestations of self-effort.

The idea of self-effort is paradoxical. Another way of understanding self-effort is as surrender to God. There are times in our spiritual evolution, whether or not the Kundalini is awakened, when there is a clear message from our inner teacher that it is time to take the next step. It may not be convenient or easy. Self-effort is choosing to follow that message no matter what the price. It may mean meditating long hours and eating very little and only light biogenic foods. It may mean a 40-day fast. It may mean working as a taxi cab driver for a few months. This is surrender to God's will. It is saying yes when the flaming Kundalini shish kabob is painfully piercing 10 inches up through the perineum and you do not know what strange thing is going to happen next. Self-effort is when God offers the Divine nectar and you chose not to reach for another plate of ice cream. Self-effort is when God calls and you chose not to turn up the television. Self-effort is the will power required to say yes to grace no matter what the circumstances. In this way self-effort and grace become one.

The issue of self-effort and focusing inward is important because there is a continual desire by people to look only outward for salvation and to avoid self-effort. We search for a Guru or teacher to do this for us. New people would often ask Muktananda in essence, "Are you the best?" as if this would insure their salvation. It also would entitle us to "bragging rights" about our path or guru. Not only does the path or guru then become an extension of our pride, thus blocking our growth, but this becomes a foundation of cults of "my guru" or "my path." Today we see this cult phenomenon in both Eastern spiritual groups and our Western Christian groups, as highlighted by the tragedy of Jonestown. Focusing only outward also confuses us about the importance of our own inner teacher and effort. A great spiritual teacher once said we create our Gods and gurus, but the only thing we can not create is the Self; this is why we should know the Self. Shri Nisargatta, a liberated seer from Bombay, taught that the physical guru is a milestone along the way, but the inner guru is with us for the full journey.[5] Jesus taught the kingdom of God lies within. Kundalini Shakti, a holographic energy pattern of universal consciousness which resides within us, is awakened within us and unfolds within us as a spiritualizing force. It gives us the direct experience of Jesus's message.

After the Merging of the Kundalini
"A quiet completeness pervades.
Completeness...Beingness...Wholeness.
It is enough to Be.
Knowing the Way by Being the Way.
Totally regular... a quietly ecstatic nobody.
A servant of God,
Just Being in the world as the world, yet not of it.
Free to Be God's Will.
The illusion of Doership is gone.
The personality is a mere result of mistaken identity.
There is nothing to Do,
But to Be the sublime celebration of the unfolding of God's creation .
In the Peace of Being, a gentle Love prevails.
We are but one Heart,
Throbbing in the all-pervading harmonious energy of Love,
That is the basis of all existence.
The Truth is Love,
We exist as Love,
To Be as Love,
Just to Be...
Love."

From Journal of August 15, 1986. Kundalini rising is an arrow returning upward to the Heart of God. After the Heart of God has been pierced there is but one complete throbbing energy globe of God's Love, infinitely expanding in all directions from a completely still center. It is the awareness that there is only That One. There are no divisions into mine and thine, you and me, or this or that. It is direct knowledge that we are all fingers on the hand of God. All is experienced as One in the ground of Being of God. It is to know completely in every fiber of our Being, the Truth of the first commandment: "Thou shalt have no other gods before Me" (Exodus 20:3) and "Hear, O Israel: The Lord our God, the Lord is One." (Deuteronomy 6:4.). This is the nondualistic Truth of God.

This awareness is beyond duality. Our binary brain simply cannot cope with it or express it on an intellectual basis. We fall into dualistic words like perfect, which implies its dualistic opposite, imperfect. Of course not only is the word perfect dualistic, it carries within it all our dualistic conceptions of perfection. These perfectionistic conceptions limit our clarity in fulfilling God's will and our understanding of others who are free to Be God's will. To be free to be God's will means we are liberated from any of our concepts or any other person's projections of perfection. It may mean expressing Love by compassionately and fiercely yelling at someone for them to wake up. It may mean allowing yourself to become caught in someone's state or problem to receive an insight in order to be of service. It may require using anger as a spiritual teaching such as Christ did with the money exchangers in the temple. We must allow whatever teaching that must come through and trust that we are an extension of God's will. We realize that although we are not our personality, that as a vehicle of expression in the world our personality must be used as a tool regardless of its own peculiarities. It does not mean that no concepts are left, but instead we recognize them as such and at any time we can transcend them. The merging of Kundalini does not make us perfect, it shifts us into Being as a way of life. We become as the law rather than under the law.

In this state of wholeness, we do not experience ourselves as different or separate from anyone else. There is a continual communion of equality awareness. An example of this occurred after Christ transcended: he came back and broke bread in humble communion with his disciples. Because of the influx of charismatic gurus and teachers in America, people mistakenly have come to judge a person's spiritual state based on how much charisma or psychic power they have. Power is not awareness, it is just power. The manifestation of these qualities such as power may have purpose in a person's mission, but should not be confused with the spiritual state itself. One may appear completely regular in daily life. The great Chinese Master, Chuang Tzu was said to appear as totally plain. In Hasidism, a form of ecstatic mystical Judaism, there is a tradition of the hidden tzaddic. The original leader, the Baal Shem Tov, kept himself hidden for years as a poor householder. In India this is also common. My spiritual uncle, Swami Prakashanada, a person who in 1961 was acknowledged by Swami Muktananda to be in a liberated state, lives very simply in one or two rooms. He sits quietly, just being in his state of Love. Spiritual seekers as well as spiritually advanced monks come from the surrounding area to experience his love or share his right fellowship. There are no tours or public relations promotions which are so common in the West, and of course, no money is asked for or taken. We do not think about power when around him, only about the love and spiritual wisdom of his simple Beingness. In Zen it is taught that we simply continue our daily tasks like chopping wood and carrying water. The point is that this post-Kundalini awareness can be found in the simple regular ecstatic nobodies who are often not recognized because of our own projections and expectation of a spiritual teacher, or it may found in the highly public, charismatic figures that fit our fantasies. But to be a highly charismatic, powerful teacher does not mean to be in this awareness, no matter how the teacher's style fits our expectations and projections of a liberated being. This is a subtle area to understand. I bring these issues up to help us not get caught in concepts. The most important focus is our own inner state.

In this post-Kundalini state one becomes intensely human. There is another stage of heart awareness that opens in which one is subject to the heart pain of the world and of each individual. No matter how people project their pain and alienation on you, you have no choice but to keep the heart open.

March 7, 1985: "As the process of increased prana intensifies in the

body...its main effect seems to be a subtle accumulatio⟨...⟩
heart that is radiating within me most of the time. Not⟨...⟩
love, but a solid awareness of the love that connects ⟨...⟩
love of any one thing, even God. ... It is just Love for Love⟨...⟩
ground of my existence."

This love is an unrelenting love. This sensitivity does not mean o⟨...⟩
is attached to emotions, it means that the emotions go through, one
experiences them, and they pass. One is not the yogic idealized rock that
emotions bounce off. It is more the Taoist water that absorbs all. In the
oneness of a compassionate world connection, even the rock is eventually
absorbed by the water. A poem from the Tao Te Ching, verse 49 makes
this point nicely:

> "The sage has no mind of his own.
> He is aware of the needs of others...
> The sage is shy and humble--- to the world he seems confusing.
> Men look to him and listen.
> He behaves like a little child."[6]

Like everything else on the spiritual path, the nondualistic awareness
does not become 100 percent immediately... or perhaps, ever. Whether it
ever becomes 100 percent is beyond what I can experientially talk about or
judge. In our dualistic thinking, many would like it one way or another.
During my experience of the merging of all the chakra energy and the
Kundalini energy into one divine energy, there was a profound shift to an
essential identity as That, as I Am That I Am, as Being rather than Doing,
as living in the nondualistic awareness of the Truth, of Being in a subtle
state of unity identification with all of creation. It became my predominant
and overwhelming inherent awareness. Yet it was not and is not an
unbroken awareness of that Truth. It appears to be an ever-increasing
awareness of the non-dualistic state moving from a predominant awareness
toward a constant awareness of the state. Shriman Tapasviji Maharaj, the
185-year-old saint, once wept for three days when a close disciple of his
died. When his amazed disciples asked him what was going on, he said that
no matter how great a saint may be and that people call him enlightened,
his mind may sometimes become deluded by the idea that one is separate
from the world or that there is duality and that someone actually dies or is
lost. Although this state is temporary in such a one, Maharaj pointed out,
the grief is felt for the time that it lasts.[7] He taught that no human, even
if liberated, is truly and continuously free from all attachments, grief,
desire, and every trace of dualistic, I-ness or my-ness, thinking. Maharaj
gives a beautiful analogy by comparing the situation to that of a large tree
hit by a strong wind. The trunk moves a little and then regains its
immobile state. The branches shake longer and are affected by lesser winds.
The trunk is analogous to one who is liberated from the basic false
identities and dualistic thinking of the mind. The easily movable branches
are like the workings of the normal dualistic mind.

Some enlightened souls feel one may stop spiritual practices once a particular level or state of awareness has happened. In America there are many forces such as fame, sex, wealth, and power which encourage us to become unconscious of the essential Truth. As our newspapers and consciousness journals have pointed out, many fine gurus, guides, and teachers have fallen to these subtle temptations. Because of this and because it has become a part of my way, I have continued much of my spiritual practices such as right diet, right life, fasting, and hours of meditation. Swami Prakashananda who spontaneously acknowledged the shift in my predominant awareness on two occasions before I left India and who is part of my network of right association, gave me this feedback on my approach in a letter discussing this question. "Baba (Muktananda) has given you everything and you've realized the innate perfection. In this perfection you know everything so what is there to say? It is true that sometimes even then, ignorance arises." In another letter Prakashananda supported these practices, "You are quite right in your estimation of the fast and meditation. There is nothing like it to purify oneself in spite of your being complete as I have always mentioned to you. It is indeed very good for the soul, and you are absolutely right that when you say that as long as one is in the physical body, we need this therapy from time to time." Because I acknowledge occasional wobbling in my nondualistic awareness, the practices continue. They reflect my of state of Being, as my expression of how to live as a family person in the world. It is my way of "putting a fence around the Torah." This way of life is not to suppress the ignorance of duality that arises -- these states are not binding. They are just temporary modifications of the Transcendent Truth of who I am. Even the Way of life may change. In a predominant non-dualistic awareness we become as the law, rather than under it. All laws and concepts, including my own, are games played in order to participate in society.

In this state of Being I feel entirely free to live out my Essene-sattvic archetype. But I do not believe that this particular archetype is the only way. We are all the expressions of the enlightenment process, and I choose to honor the Ten Commandments by killing neither love or joy with my concepts. I share them because they may help or be a guide for some people who share these archetypes. We can only live the Truth as we experience it. If I imitate other people's concepts, how can I Be? I can only manifest my own unique expression of the unmanifest. This is why the Torah repeatedly says, "The God of Abraham, the God of Issac, and the God of Jacob." Each of these great ones was the individual's own unique manifestation. We are all in an enlightenment process that will lead to the potential of a total enlightenment. I can only share with you my experience of that process at my particular stage of awareness. Perfectionistic concepts of either/or belong to the dualists who want to judge, grade, and create separateness. God's kingdom has many mansions and I am just traveling through those palaces like everyone else. We are all flowers of love, infinitely expanding step by step in the pulseless-pulse of the infinite universal awareness. One of my inspirations for this teaching is the great Hasidic master, Rabbi Nachman. It was said that as soon as he achieved a new level of awareness he would immediately with a humble heart begin again like one taking his first step into the realm of holiness.[8] He was said to be driven by an intense yearning for a deeper and deeper perception of God. Bassui Tokusho, a Rinzai Zen master born in 1327, felt so strongly about the need for awakened awareness to ripen that although proclaimed by many as enlightened, he continued intense practices for years as a roving monk before he reached a level of spiritual awareness that he felt was necessary to teach others.[9]

Throughout history some of the great spiritual leaders have experienced what appear to be short breaks in their continual communion with God. Since these great ones exist as a teaching for us in all their actions, it may be that these breaks in oneness awareness are to teach that to apply concepts of perfectionist spiritual standards for those of us in the body is not appropriate. In the Judaic tradition, even the greatest spiritual leader Moses was chastised by God at the waters of Meribah (Numbers 20:12) for not sanctifying and remembering God in the drawing of the water from the rock. For this lapse in awareness, Moses was not allowed to lead the people into the promised land. In the Eastern traditions, the great avatar Rama cried when he discovered that his wife had been abducted. At another time, when he saw his brother unconscious on the battlefield he became grief stricken. Krishna, the master of yoga, and also proclaimed as an avatar, was said to have experienced grief when his father died. These are important examples and teachings to suggest that the concept of totally unbroken cosmic unity awareness while in the physical body may just be a play of the need of our dualistic minds for the safe, comfortable, and neat concept of perfection.

Nevertheless, it is possible that a totally enlightened, unbroken transcendental state exists for someone living in the human body. I have raised this issue to shake up the concepts of the dualistic perfectionists who create misery for themselves and others by their states of non self-acceptance, and by their critical judgment of the spiritual states of others. For me it is simply a divine happening. I am in a natural unfolding that I nurture with my way of life, and which is my way of life. I feel very ordinary, natural, regular, and essentially connected to everyone else in the ground of Being of that regularity. At this point I am focused on neither the conceptual goal of total enlightenment nor on the process. It is enough to simply self-abide in the delight of Being... to know the Way by Being the Way.

Summary Chapter 22

1. Kundalini is the grace of God which transforms our awareness into the nondualistic holographic awareness of the Truth of God.
2. In this Kundalini process we may experience ecstasy, contentment, love, and communion with God.

3. Depending on how we perceive them, these experiences may be an ego trap or serve as Divine behavior modification for encouraging us to follow practices that enhance the spiritualizing energy of the Kundalini.

4. The more often we enter these states of deep communion, the deeper they are etched into our consciousness until they become our awareness.

5. There are two Kundalini energies, the mundane, or the Kundalini Shakti; it rests in the first chakra and is the energizer for the whole body function. The other is the pure prana which enters through the crown chakra; it is called the spiritual Kundalini.

6. When there is sufficient energy in the interaction between the two Kundalini energies, the Kundalini Shakti energy awakens.

7. With the awakening there is a partial fusing and synchronicity of the two energies. As awareness develops there is an increase in total Kundalini energy, synchronicity, and fusing until the two Kundalini energies become fused as one holographic energy in the crown chakra. Our consciousness shifts into a predominant nondualistic awake state awareness of God.

8. The classical "three knots" are nodal points of a quantum jump in increased Kundalini energy in the system. The first "knot" expansion of consciousness and energy occurs with the merging of the first three chakras. The second is associated with the merging of the first three with the heart chakra awareness. The third expansion comes with the merging of all the chakra awareness into one whole, nondualistic, unity awareness of the Truth of God.

9. In the spiritual unfolding there seem to be periods of much intense motivation and periods of less intense times, depending on the needs of the Kundalini process. For this reason, although general practices such as right diet, right life, and meditation are always appropriate, our other spiritual practices may vary.

10. A proper balance of grace and self-effort are necessary for the overall evolution of the Kundalini to effectively take place.

11. Self-effort is not mere will power. It is a paradoxical effortless-effort. It is the ability to say yes when God's grace occurs and we might not feel ready for whatever form it takes.

12. After the merging of Kundalini, we expand beyond a vertical evolution to an infinite expansion in all directions as the one heart of God, as Love, as nondualistic equality unity awareness.

13. In a state of Being rather than doing, we are free to Be the Will of God.

14. For me, it is but the start of another level of expansion in one of God's many mansions. We all share in this unending and gradual unfolding of the many stages of enlightenment.

15. Although our dualistic perfectionist thinking would like us to have an either/or possibility of a perfect unbroken state of awareness, this represents an idealistic concept. We can stop judging ourselves and others, and know that it is enough to just to Be...

16. The simple gift of Kundalini merging is to ...Know the Way... By Being the Way.

23

Nutrition, Kundalini, and Transcendence

Transcendence

Transcendence is the extension of regeneration. It is the process in which the SOEF organization of the body reaches a higher, more purified, and better organized level of energy. It is when the body is liberated from its traditional cellular confinement. Historical examples of actual physical transcendence are those of Elijah, Enoch, Jesus, and the Indian saint Tukaram.

Transcendence is easier to comprehend in the context of the cosmic cycles of involution and evolution. In Chapter 2 we discussed the precipitation of the SOEFs from the faster-than-light virtual energy field into particles moving at the speed of light and finally into our dense human physical form. This is the process of involution. The process of evolution begins with the awakening of the Kundalini Shakti, which is the residue of the involutionary energy stored in the chakra at the base of the spine. The awakening of Kundalini Shakti starts us on a transcendent evolutionary path which we call spiritual evolution. A major step in this path is the complete synchronistic merging of the chakras and Kundalini into a single energy. This happens when the level of spiritual awareness and pranic energy in the system reaches a certain intensity. At this point we transcend duality in both our subtle energy system and in our spiritual awareness. The difficulty in discussing this transcendence pattern is that our brains are binary or dualistic, but the states we are discussing are neither the one nor the many. Although the description appears to be linear, it fits neither the linearity of our western minds or the circularity of the eastern mind. The process is spiral and vortexual.

Spiritual evolution is happening simultaneously on all levels, yet it culminates in an awakened aware balance at various stages of integration at different times. Although there may be no total explanation for this process of involution/evolution, except for that of the play of God, we can partially explain it as the existence of the law of cause and effect on the subtle planes. An analogy is the cosmic vacuum in which energy precipitates spontaneously into matter and then returns back to its original state of virtual energy. The process happens in every level of cosmic existence, including our food. In the book *Oahspe* all energy within matter is called "vortexual".[1] The energy precipitating from the cosmic prana does so in a spiral whirlpool pattern which resides within matter as the potential subtle energy. For example, at a certain moment during the assimilation process, a dissolution of the material food occurs and "vortexual" energy is liberated. The tendency for the corporal is to disincorporate itself.[2] This is the way transcendence works for all of creation, us included. In the process of transcendence our physical material form slowly transmutes into more subtle physical forms, and finally transmutes into subtle energy forms which absorb back into the cosmic energy.

Vortex Pattern and Kundalini

The pure prana or spiritual Kundalini is drawn directly into the system through the crown chakra where there is no subtle anatomy to filter it. It is then drawn into the vortex of the sushumna which is either a major or minor organizing vortical force in the body depending on whether the Kundalini has been awakened. The cosmic prana spirals down to the heart center, which acts as the center of the sushumna vortex, and then broadens again (Figure 16). The vortexual energies of all the chakras are linked to this central Kundalini vortex. The chakras are a less refined energy and draw part of their energy from the Kundalini vortex. Doing so, they deplete the energy of the vortex and hence slow down its spiral energy action. Until the awakening of the Kundalini, the body density regularly pulls energy from the Kundalini vortex downward into the physical structure. Once the Kundalini is awakened this vortex is increasingly energized by its rising. The crown chakra also becomes more activated and more pure prana comes into the system to further energize this central vortex.

When the vortex energy reaches a certain intensity, it begins to draw matter into the etheric or next level of purified and more tightly organized SOEF energy. It works much like sugar being drawn up into the more tightly organized vortex of stirred water as it is dissolved into this moving vortex. With the awakening of the Kundalini, we begin the first movement toward the transmuting of our physical form back to its source - - the transcendent energy of God. The tendency of the energized vortex field is to transmute everything to a higher level of energy existence. This does not deplete the body energy because it is an open system which draws energy from the physical plane via the food. The better superconductor we are for the energy, the more active the Kundalini vortex, and the more the process of transcendence takes place.

The food we eat is very important in this process of transcendence. If we eat high-energy, lighter foods such as as the biogenic foods we have discussed, the Kundalini vortex is more energized and thus more active in transmuting us from matter to energy. The watery fruits, because of their higher conductivity and their structured water energy, particularly enhance the activity. The closer we move to pure prana in our food, the easier it is for the pranic energy of the system to be drawn into the upper vortex field. The dense flesh foods and low energy tamasic foods decrease the energy of the Kundalini vortex. Meat is so much denser than biogenic foods that it

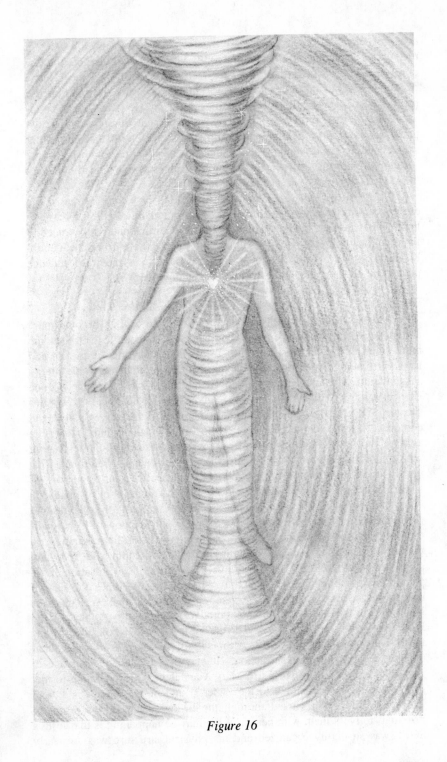

Figure 16

does not enter the pranic field as efficiently. It then acts as a sort of metaphoric sludge to slow down the vortex vibration and therefore to slow or reverse the process of transcendence. The sludge effect of the meat can be overcome by drawing from the prana accumulated by such things as intense meditation. This is obviously not the most efficient use of our pranic build-up. One of the points of spiritual nutrition is that through eating high prana foods, eating lightly, and fasting periodically we become better superconductors and therefore we enhance the efficient use of energy in the system for our transcendence. This approach guides us more clearly to begin thinking about the body as an entity of energy.

Any mental and emotional tension in the system decreases the energy coming into the system by thickening and misaligning the subtle bodies. Because the chakras are not getting the normal energy they need to function from direct external sources, they pull more from the central Kundalini vortex. This too results in a blockage of the transcendence process by depleting the energy of the Kundalini vortex.

Kundalini Vortex

In this Kundalini transcendence process, the SOEFs become more and more organized as the energy is drawn up. Our body tends to become more etheric. The increasingly energized Kundalini vortex draws up and transmutes more matter and more energy from the more dense subtle energy systems until the subtle energy of the whole organism is drawn into one energy vortex. This is the point at which the two Kundalini energies merge. We literally become one and experience ourselves as whole and complete. An experiential reminder of this is the almost continual awareness of myself as a single vortical transcendent energy field resonating with and being drawn back up into the cosmic energy vibration. This vortical resonating and merging experience, particularly during periods of silent meditation, seems to penetrate to the very atomic level of my being.

At the time of the two Kundalini energies merging, the chakras and the subtle bodies become absorbed into the more purified powerful energy of the Kundalini vortex. Enough of the chakra energy is left to maintain us on the physical plane, but the chakras lose their predominant role and significance. What is left is the continual experience of the pulsation of the pure prana flowing in the Kundalini vortex. This becomes the central energy source of the physical system. The crown chakra changes at Kundalini awakening from a minor portal of energy entry to that of the most important source of energy in the system. The whole system has reached a higher level of SOEF organization and provides a model that explains the process of resurrection. It may also explain the passage in John 20:17 in which Jesus said to Mary Magdalene, "Stop clinging to me. For I have not yet ascended to the father," and in John 20:19 and John 20:26 in which John passed through the locked doors of his disciples' dwellings to bless them with peace. What may be happening is that Jesus's SOEF was so highly organized and his physical structure was so nearly transmuted into the etheric level, that he was able to go the next step and make his body totally etheric by the use of his mind. This would allow him to pass through locked doors. By projecting his mind down into the vortex, he could draw up the materials needed into the SOEF to repattern and recreate his own body as needed to serve the will of God. This is a theoretical extension of our total vortex and SOEF aspects of our new nutritional paradigm.

Transcendence After the Merging
Of Kundalini into the One

Ever since the 40-day fast, I feel as if I am wearing a pulsating skullcap all the time and the top of my crown chakra has been cut off like the bottom of the skullcap, and the divine energy is intensely pouring in through it. It feels. Muktananda, I believe, would refer to this continual pranic crown chakra pulsation when he occasionally mentioned in public lectures that he breathed through the sushumna. Da Love Ananda (Da Free John), I believe, refers to his transcendent shift to a central vortex energy predominance and the absorption of the basic chakra energy into this central vortex, when he describes an experience in which he felt that the topmost part of his crown chakra was severed and the life current, another name for Kundalini, was no longer bound to the chakras as a necessary structure.[3] This experience of crown chakra severing and subtle cosmic pranic pulsation is a direct inner and outer total transcendent harmonic connection with the pure cosmic vibration. It is but another reminder of our true formless reality. It is the ultimate food for transcendence. It is the delicacy of spiritual nutrition. It is food from God and the energy of God as God. The unitary Kundalini vortex is so energized by the cosmic prana that we are transformed into shining vortexual bodies of light. It is a basis for understanding the subtle meaning of Exodus 34:28 and 29, "And he was there with the Lord 40 days and 40 nights; he did neither eat bread, nor drink water... And it came to pass, when Moses came down from Mount Sinai with the two tables of the testimony in Moses' hand, when he came down from the mount, that Moses knew not that the skin of his face sent forth beams while He talked with him."

Transcendence is the evolutionary process by which the vortexual energy of the Kundalini progressively transmutes us from the gross matter of our bodies to a more refined and highly organized and energized SOEF. It is the physical parallel to the transmutation of our consciousness to the Love of unity awareness. Eventually it takes us into complete absorption of our form into the formless ground of being of God. From the time the Kundalini is awakened, we gradually become more etheric, but even after the total merging of the Kundalini energies, enough of our physical body and chakra system is left so we can function in the world. My lack of direct experience beyond this point does not allow me to go much further in our discussion. It is the process of transcendence which explains the physical transcendence of Tukaram, Elijah, Enoch, and Jesus. Our spiritual potentials are awesome. This physical transcendence is not necessarily the goal of spiritual life as much as it represents a total freedom to follow God's will. In any case, whatever happens, it is enough just to... Be.

Summary Chapter 23

1. Transcendence is the extension of regeneration. It is the evolutionary process in which the SOEF organization of the body reaches a more organized and higher level of energy in which the physical matter of the body is transmuted, or is in the process of being transmuted, to its etheric level. It is the physical parallel to the transmutation of our consciousness.
2. The process of transcendence begins with the awakening of the Kundalini.
3. There is a central Kundalini vortex of energy which is the central mechanism for drawing up energies from more dense states to less dense states. It has enough energy to initiate this function after the awakening of the Kundalini.
4. If we eat high-energy, light, biogenic foods the Kundalini vortex is more energized and thus more active in transmuting us from matter to energy.
5. The closer we move to pure prana in our foods, the less dense our physical system becomes. This facilitates the process of transcendence.
6. Heavier foods and meats slow the vortex energy and slow the transcendence process.
7. Mental and emotional stress also slows the process.
8. At the time when the two Kundalini energies completely fuse into one central energy, the Kundalini vortex becomes the body's main energy center . It draws energy from the chakras into its higher vortexual transcendence.
9. After this time, there is only enough energy and form left in the chakras to maintain the physical body.
10. Once this Kundalini vortex becomes the predominant energy system for the organism, the pure prana entering through the crown chakra becomes a most important source for energizing the system. In some, it may be the only source. These people are dining on the direct nectar of God. This is the ultimate spiritual nutrition.

24

A Time of Integration:
An Individualized Approach to an
Evolutionary Diet

Purpose of Diet

To design a diet for ourselves requires a clarity of purpose. Just as an architect does not design a building without the purpose of the building in mind, to transcend the unconscious gobbling of our food we also need a perspective of what we want from our diet. Six purposes have been developed in this book:

1. To develop a diet as an aid to our spiritual unfolding in the context of right life, right association, meditation, and love.

2. To increase our ability to assimilate, store, conduct, and transmit the cosmic, heightened, evolutionary energies now being generated on our planet and the intensified energy released by our own spiritual development so that these energies either activate and increase our energy potential for the Kundalini awakening or further support the already awakened Kundalini which acts as a spiritualizing force in our body-mind-spirit complex.

3. To maintain, purify, and honor the body as the physical aspect of the spirit and as the temple for the spirit in a way that keeps our minds clear and our bodies physically able to cope with the demands of the spiritual process of full body enlightenment.

4. To develop a diet that regularly balances our individual chakras, balances the chakras as a whole system, and directly aids our meditation process.

5. To use the process of developing a diet for spiritual life, which we call the art of spiritual nutrition, as a spiritual practice in itself.

6. To develop a diet that regularly honors and enhances our food as a main interface between ourselves and nature, that brings us into harmony with nature and its universal laws, and that establishes us in harmony with the ecological issues of food and peace on our planet.

Individualizing the Diet

There are many factors affecting our development of an individualized diet: our dosha constitution, the principle of biochemical individuality, the seasons, the political and social climate, our age, the amount we meditate per day, our degree of physical activity, the unpredictability of our daily needs, our state of digestion and general health, our present stage of detoxification, and our present type of diet. This is why computer diets have limited value. There is a computer system, however, that is effective, one that gives us the answers in terms of our appetite, tastes, food desires and aversions, instincts, impulses, and intuition. It is the computer of our own inner sensitivity. As with any computer, we have to learn how to work with it consciously. In this computer the data of our own direct experience as to what, when, how, and how much we eat is the most important. There is no one diet for everyone. Books such as this one can only be guidelines for where to start in our personal exploration. To do this effectively we must become our own laboratory with ourselves as the researcher as well as the subject being researched.

As in any experiment, we have to limit the variables to obtain clear data. Four basic variables are the time we eat, the environment in which we eat, how much we eat, and what we eat.

Regular timing of meals is important. Regularity helps the body adjust its physiology to those times. Some people recommend no breakfast, a big lunch, and medium dinner. Others, such as certain groups of Buddhists, do not eat after 4 p.m. I once met a French healer who discovered an ancient system that said we could eat a large meal in the morning, and another large meal for lunch, and we would have excellent health as long as we did not eat or drink anything after 2 p.m. He had hundreds of case histories to support his point. Most systems agree that between 12 noon and 2 p.m. is the time to have the main meal or even the only meal, of the day. It is the time when the pitta or digestive forces are the strongest. For myself, if I eat more than a minimal supper or eat too late (one hour before sunset), it is harder to get up early in the morning for stretching, breathing exercises, and meditation. But three or four hours later, when I am finished meditating, my body is hungry for some fruit or occasionally some fruit and soaked nuts or seeds. This may not be what is recommended for kapha types, but it works for me. The key to timing is not to listen to the experts but learn to eat when we are hungry and drink when we are thirsty. The corollary to this is to refrain from eating when not hungry or thirsty. We have to discover for ourselves when and how much to eat at a particular time of day. The general recommendations for the timing and amounts can serve as a starting place for our experiments in self-observation. A stable mental and emotional environment is also important for obtaining clear information. By not eating when emotionally upset, by daily meditating before meals, and eating in a calm, quiet environment, we help the emotional factors influencing digestion to become consistent.

How much we eat, another important nutritional factor, is part of the art of spiritual nutrition that requires particular attention. No matter what we eat, if it is excessive, we will not get clear information about that particular food we have eaten. It is good to allow time for complete digestion between meals so we can observe the whole digestive process of the food. Unless we have hypoglycemia, it is good to allow at least four to five hours between meals. How good a food is goes beyond the immediate taste. It needs to be good for us in the whole process of digestion, assimilation, energization, and excretion. It must be good for us all day. Some diet changes are deceptive in that they initially make us feel good, but after a few months they turn out to be toxic to us. For example, many people do well initially on the traditionally recommended high protein hypoglycemia diet, but they often call me two months later asking for help in finding some other diet because they feel so toxic. A meat diet, although detrimental in the long run, can also sometimes make us feel good initially because the excess protein reverses the uncomfortable detoxification process that we may be experiencing, and the uric acid in meat which is close to caffeine in its structure can act as a temporary stimulant. It is said that Gandhi, in order to observe the long term effects of each change in diet, would only change his diet every four months.

The immediate sensory effects which give us feedback as to whether we are eating the wrong food or amount are such basics as a full stomach, gas and bloating from putrification and fermentation, increased mucous production, sluggish mind, and a feeling of enervation. The data on this level are not subtle if we are willing to pay attention. At the level of the more refined sensitivity of our spiritual unfolding there are some additional criteria that are of value. It is useful to eat what increases our experience of our love communion with God. If the energy in our body is unimpeded by our diet pattern so that we can focus on the communion, then we are on the right track. If we are eating too much or the wrong foods, too much energy is involved in digesting and assimilating the foods. This draws energy away from our focus on the communion. If our love communion is blocked before, during, or after the meal this is feedback that we are not on the right track. If our ability to sustain meditation is enhanced, then the diet is appropriate for us. If, while preparing and eating our food, we experience a greater harmony with the forces of nature, this is a sign of right diet. If we experience ourselves as becoming better and better superconductors of the cosmic energy, this is positive feedback. If our experience of the movement of Kundalini in the body is blocked, this is feedback that we need to reconsider our program. In general, if our diet obstructs the pranic flow of energy in the body, whether or not the Kundalini is awakened, so that our mind and body feel sluggish and unclear in a way that we are not able to focus our attention on the Divine, the diet is not appropriate.

Self Awareness and the Individualized Diet

As our awareness expands, the physical needs of our body change. It is important to be able to sense when to make a dietary shift to maintain harmony with our spiritual evolution. Intuition, guided by subtle changes in taste, response to textures, quantities, and appetite for different types of foods is key for this. It requires that we be free enough to distinguish between immediate needs and responses secondary to habitual eating patterns, ego needs, and peer pressure. These decisions to eat less or differently are not meant to deprive us but to teach us to eat in harmony with our evolutionary unfolding. This is the art of spiritual nutrition.

The art of spiritual nutrition is the process of self-study applied in the exploration of the basic guidelines discussed in this book and in the context of a full spiritual life. It is the creation of right diet which is the letting go of nonfunctional patterns of relating to food. For many of us food is associated with psychological cues. For example, as a kid, I used to love my mother's cherry pie. Over the years, this food transference, psychological attachment or aversion to a particular food based on a previous psychologically associated experience, has led me to order several organically baked cherry pies which, according to my empirical post-eating response, were not appropriate for me to be eating. Because of the negative feedback of the post-eating experiences and my awareness of the transference, my desire for cherry pie has stopped. In loftier terms, I have transcended my desire for cherry pie and am no longer controlled by it. Through this process of self-study, we are able to sort out the signals that have a non-nutritional basis. In this process we become more aware of our subtle inputs, food transferences, and post-eating results. This constant attunement to our overall food and energy needs allow us to shift our diet to be in harmony with our evolving process. It allows us to be free to reorganize it at each stage of spiritual evolution to enhance greater states of health and awareness.

Some of this shifting of diet seems to happen spontaneously as our consciousness evolves. This was suggested by a 1986 survey I made in conjunction with MSH Associates, who have developed a program called *Synchronicity, the Recognitions Experience* which involves accelerating the expansion of consciousness by the use of holographically programmed audiotapes. The survey was filled out by a group of 110 people who had been in the program from three to eighteen months. The main finding was that 63 percent were conscious of making some degree of shift toward a healthier diet. The majority of these shifts seemed to be away from junk foods and other foods of the bioacidic category, toward healthier foods within their established diet pattern. Eight percent of the group distinctly described a major shift toward eating less food and seven percent became vegetarians. Before they started on the recognitions program, 47 percent were using alcohol, coffee, or tobacco. In this survey, 35 percent had decreased their use of these toxins. Within the Recognitions program, there was no formal teaching about diet. These people were not told in advance that a study would be done. It is my feeling that the higher evolutionary forces naturally draw us in the direction of health. The art of spiritual nutrition is the conscious act of cooperating with this natural transition.

An approach to right diet that involves self-study and cultivation of an artful self-awareness becomes a spiritual practice on its own. It is part of the skill of self-awareness required to develop a right life in harmony with all our worldly functions such as work, play, family, and world social responsibility.

Transitional Detoxification Phenomenon

As we shift to healthier diets, the stored toxins in the system begin to be excreted. This is called detoxification. As part of our nutritional and environmental background, it can be safely said that all of us have some degree of toxicity. In a simplistic but accurate way, the process of detoxification can be understood via the analogy of diffusion. In the process of diffusion elements move from areas of higher concentration to areas of lower concentration. Nutrients and toxins flow into the blood and lymph systems from the intestinal tract. If they are in higher concentrations than the toxins in the cells, they "diffuse" their way into the cells and even precipitate as crystals or bind to intracellular protein complexes, which is how the cell tries to keep them out of circulation. When we decrease our toxicity level by a cleansing diet or fasting, the diffusion concentrations shift and there are fewer toxins in the bloodstream than inside the cells. The result is that toxins are drawn out of the cells into the bloodstream and lymph systems. This essentially corresponds to the process described by the Wendt Doctrine in which the protein-clogged basement membranes begin to clear when the protein in the diet is decreased. The toxins which come out of the cells are excreted from the body via the eliminative organs such as the kidneys, lungs, skin, and bowels.

In the process of this toxin elimination, so much toxic substance is in the blood and lymph that we may not feel or smell good. Many people, if they detoxify too quickly, have a healing crisis in which they appear to get sick. Disease, as defined by J. H. Tilden, M.D., is simply a toxemia crisis.[1] The crisis usually occurs when the vitality of the body reaches a point where there is enough energy to throw off the toxins. The crisis may last for a three day cycle or it may go on for weeks. My clinical experience is if a person slowly detoxifies over the years rather than trying to do it in a few months, the discomfort of a major healing crisis is minimized. The recovery from the healing crisis is accelerated by daily enemas, plenty of rest, alkalinizing fluids such as vegetable juices, and maintaining a positive attitude. After the healing crisis passes, we level off at a feeling of well-being for the diet level at which we are eating. At each new stage of purity we experience more flow of energy, love, and light in our system, and more energy is available for the focus on the transcendental awareness that is so important for our spiritual evolvement.

Although we are focusing on diet, the key to toxemia is more than diet. Dr. Tilden points out that any habit of body or mind which decreases our nerve energy (enervation) results in the build-up of toxins. This is because enervation slows or stops the natural body process of detoxifying, and therefore results in the accumulation of toxins in the system.[2] Poor diet is one of the major stresses on the system, but to really detoxify and create harmonious health, we need to develop a right life that keeps us totally in communion with the Divine. A good detoxification program involves a change of lifestyle that gives us time for meditation, exercise, rest, sunshine, fresh air, and joy in our lives. All these factors, plus an appropriate diet, increase the SOEFs of the body. This increases the nerve energy that Dr. Tilden mentions, and therefore the body becomes better organized so it can function appropriately and detoxify itself naturally.

It is important to understand that toxin production is a normal part of metabolism. For example, exercise produces lactic acid and protein metabolism produces sulphuric and phosphoric acid. As long as the body and mind have full vitality, these normal poisons are readily eliminated without a build-up in toxins. The idea is not to compulsively spend our time avoiding toxins, but to reach an appropriate body balance in which they are eliminated as they come into the system. Sometimes we get ahead of our system and become too pure. For example, if the basement membranes become porous like those of a baby, and all foreign proteins such as those in polluted air pass into our system readily and cause sensitization reactions our diet is not correct, no matter how pure it is. If we are not able to function adequately in our worldly roles, or are too reactive to the pollution for us to experience the love communion with the Divine, then it is important to let go of our purity concepts and make the necessary dietary adjustments. The key guideline is to find the diet that best supports the flow of spiritual energy in our system, the love energy of communion, and at the same time supports our function in the world. In the art of spiritual nutrition, our concern is not with the ideal of the purest diet, but with the most appropriate diet for our living situation.

Transition Diets

The Rainbow Diet way of organizing our food intake applies to any level of diet. Learning to eat the right amount to energize the system, to maintain whatever flow of cosmic energy we have into our system, and to maintain our present level of love communion with the Divine is also a basic which applies to any level of diet. The place to start our diet transition is with our immediate diet pattern. Unless we have hypoglycemia, it is an aid to the digestive system to cut down to three meals a day with only juices or an occasional piece of fruit between meals. Chewing our food well and creating a peaceful, joyful atmosphere in which to eat and to digest our food for ten to fifteen minutes after the meal immediately improves digestion. There are several major stages of transition diets. Each stage may take as little as one season in the yearly cycle, or it may take years. It is the responsibility of each of us to choose our own rate of transition. I use the word transition because we are all in transition on every level of our body-mind-spirit function. The word transition creates the possibility of continual and conscious change in our life. It keeps the doors open to evolution.

Diet Stage I

This transition is from all bioacidic foods. It means letting go of processed, irradiated, adulterated, fast, and junk foods such as white sugar, white bread, candy, T.V. dinners, Hostess Twinkies, soft drinks, any sort of meats that have been treated with nitrites and nitrates, pasteurized milk and cheeses, baked goods containing refined oils, foods containing additives, and alcohol. It includes organically raised red meats, fowl, fish, vegetables, fruits, grains, legumes, nuts, seeds, eggs, and unpasteurized dairy products. It is a basic shift away from a tamasic diet to whole, natural, organically grown foods. It is a time to begin our awareness of food combining and acid/alkaline balance. This stage takes time. It requires discovering and thinking about what has been put in the foods. It requires learning where to shop to get healthy foods. In this stage we may want to fast from all flesh foods for one week two times per year.

Diet Stage II

In this stage we eliminate all red meats and begin to add more fruits and vegetables into our diet. These are important because their alkaline-forming minerals help the system begin to rebalance and detoxify from the acid production of red meats. In this stage we may want to fast on fruits and vegetables and their juices for a seven-day spring and fall cleansing. This stage could be part of a one-season transition after stage I, or it could take years to make the transition. In considering this transition, remember that flesh foods are used as a treatment for slowing down the spiritualizing action of the Kundalini in the body.

Diet Stage III

This is a stage in which we completely stop eating all red meat, fowl, fish, and any other sort of seafood, animal life, or eggs. Although eggs are a lighter protein than flesh foods, they still have an animal vibration. They are part of the transition step between stage II and III. In stage III we become lactovegetarian or vegetarian. It includes raw dairy products, grains, nuts, seeds, legumes, vegetables, fruits, seaweeds, soaked and sprouted grains, legumes, nuts, and seeds. The two best-known diets that approximate the early part of this stage are the macrobiotic diet and Paavo Airola's lactovegetarian diet, which is the basic diet eaten by cultures around the world who are known for their health and longevity. Airola's diet recommends eating lots of grains, nuts and seeds, vegetables, and fruits. As a condiment he suggests, for those who are milk tolerant, raw dairy products from healthy, organically grown cows in the form of cultured yogurts, kefirs, and other soured milks. He suggests one to two tablespoons of cold pressed oils, some supplemental foods such as kelp, yeast, a little uncooked honey, and some low potency organic minerals and supplements. His book *How to Get Well* outlines his diet nicely.[3]

Supplements can be used to help correct deficiencies, to prevent deficiencies, and to act as an antioxidant protection against pollution. In high potencies they can act as a drug to stimulate healing of the system. In high potencies they may also act as stimulants to the system to compensate for stress in our daily lives. In stages I and II, people often use high potency multivitamins as stimulants to compensate for their enervating diets and life styles. We may use some supplements in stage III, but in this stage we start to tune into the subtleties of organic versus synthetic vitamins and our own internal harmony. Almost all vitamins are synthetics. One way to recognize the few natural vitamins and minerals on the market is by their low potencies. For example, natural B vitamins usually do not exceed ten milligrams of B_1, B_2, and B_6. From the theoretical view point of the SOEFs, synthetic vitamins have crystalline structures as do the natural vitamins, but they have weak SOEFs and bond less well to the appropriate places. To bond and act effectively in the body they take energy from our own SOEFs. Initially, because of their higher concentrations, we get a stimulating effect. For some, this stimulating effect may last a few months or even a year. Eventually, if the high synthetic potencies are taken for a long time, our SOEFs become depleted and the system is thrown into imbalance. As we get healthier, we also need fewer and fewer supplements. For these reasons, at stage III I recommend, with the exception of one to two grams of vitamin C, the use of concentrated food supplements such as yeast for B vitamins and minerals like chromium, and kelp or dulse for minerals. Dulse, because it is much higher than kelp in potassium and lower in sodium and is purple, makes a good addition to the evening meal. It is generally good to soak the dulse to get off the sea salt. If we take yeast, it is useful to take 250 milligrams of calcium to counterbalance the high phosphorus. Lecithin and vitamin E are well supplied by germinated nuts, seeds, and beans so they are not needed as supplements. As we move into stage IV, the increased ability of our body to absorb nutrients from food and the higher quality of the foods allows us to decrease the concentrated food supplements to a minimum. There may be some vitamin or mineral that our body, because of its own individualized biochemistry, is not adequately absorbing from food. For example, I have found that I need some calcium supplementation. We need to observe closely if any mineral or vitamin deficiencies occur in the dietary shifts and with fasting.

One deficiency scare for vegetarians is that of vitamin B_{12}. There is a myth that only meat contains B_{12}. There is B_{12} in milk, eggs, aged cheese, brewer's yeast, sunflower seeds, comfrey leaves, kelp, banana, peanuts, concord grapes, raw wheat germ, pollen, and fermented foods.[4,5] The healthy bacteria in our intestines provide an additional source of B_{12}. Cooking foods destroys 89 percent of vitamin B_{12}. The main cause that I have observed clinically for vitamin B_{12} deficiency is poor absorption.

There is another level of supplementation that I recommend using even in stage IV. It includes three supplements that work more on the energy level than the physical nutrient level. One class is the cell salts. They increase our ability to absorb the basic minerals into the system. I recommend taking one different cell salt one day per month in a monthly sequence as discussed in Chapter 11. The cell salts can be used for longer periods of time to remedy a particular mineral deficiency. This is how I am changing my need for calcium supplementation. Another class of supplements are the gem elixirs and flower essences. These directly supply energy to the SOEFs which may be imbalanced or depleted. They can work on physical levels to help with absorption problems or other physical imbalances. They help remove emotional or mental blocks or toxins to the system so we can become fully energized. On the more subtle spiritual planes, they can open us up to increasing the cosmic pranic energy entering into the system and help balance the chakras. The third supplement I have found to be effective is a blue-green algae, technically known as Aphanae-Klamathomenon flos-aquae, with the brand name of Blue-Green Manna. It is grown in pure and highly structured water in Lake Klammath which comes from underground streams. This particular brand is the only one, of which I am aware, that is not heated to kill bacteria because of the purity of where it is harvested. It has an extremely high SOEF field that regenerates mind, general body, and immune forces. In about 70 to 80 percent of the people who use it, it seems to particularly activate mind-brain function. Blue-Green Manna has been a boon to some people who do much mental work and want renewed energy for meditation. I have recently published a preliminary paper in the *Journal of the Orthomolecular Medical Society* reporting that it partially reversed one case of Alzheimer's disease and halted the progression of another.[6] This, I believe, is because of its specific enhancement of brain-mind SOEFs. These three classes of supplements can be of use in the adjustment phases of stage IV.

The standard macrobiotic diet recommended by Michio Kushi suggests that cooked grains be 50 percent of the volume of every meal; soup, preferably miso, 5 percent of the diet; vegetables at each meal, with two thirds of them cooked, 20 to 30 percent; and cooked beans and seaweed 10 to 15 percent.[7] The macrobiotic diet emphasizes the 50/50 balancing of the yin/yang energies of food. This diet is complex and requires some training in order to master the system and to cook the foods properly. The major difference in these two diets is that Airola recommends eating approximately 80 percent raw foods and more raw nuts and seeds. He also suggests only one grain meal per day and some raw dairy.

In stage III the yin/yang balance, acid/alkaline balance, awareness of food combining, low protein diets, how to prepare vegetarian foods, and the proper timing and amounts of foods become more refined. It is the beginning stage of awareness of sprouting skills and the meaning of rejuvenating foods. The refined stage III is primarily a shift to 60 to 80 percent bioactive (raw) and biogenic (life-generating) foods and 20 to 40 percent biostatic (cooked) foods. The cooked foods are usually potatoes, grains, and hard vegetables such as broccoli and cauliflower. The biogenic foods such as soaked and sprouted nuts, seeds, and legumes make up 20 to 30 percent of the diet. It is a stage of much exploration as to what works and what doesn't work. At this level one could begin to fast on juices for seven days twice a year. For many people this phase lasts a long time or is the diet chosen as the maintenance diet. Shifted to its purest and most refined form of 80% raw and biogenic food and 20 percent biostatic food, it will provide a gradual detoxification over the years, so that our bodies will slowly increase their ability to act as superconductors for the cosmic energy and will support and nurture the purifying action of the Kundalini. It is a diet that is fully adequate for and supportive of spiritual life.

Diet Stage IV

This stage marks the difference between a diet that nurtures and aids spiritual development and a diet which accelerates our readiness for the Kundalini to awaken, increases the spiritualizing power of the Kundalini when it is awakened, and is an intense form of spiritual practice on its own. The difference between stages III and IV is like the difference between hiking, jogging, and other forms of aerobic exercises, which quite adequately tone and maintain the cardiovascular system, and training intensively for intercollegiate athletics. The latter part of stage IV is more like training for the Olympics versus intercollegiate athletics. We are spiritual athletes training for and participating in the event of the planetary transformation of consciousness. Stage IV begins with a complete vegan diet of grains and bioactive foods such as raw seeds, nuts, vegetables, and fruits. Added to the diet is an increasing amount of life-generating foods such as all forms of soaked or sprouted grains including sprouted wheat, seeds, nuts, legumes, and grasses such as wheatgrass. As we detoxify and the yin expansion of consciousness continues, there is a progressive decrease in yang acid-forming cooked grains until there are none in the diet. There is a progressive increase in the percentage of bioactive and biogenic foods. Because the nutrients are able to move more easily into the cells, the total amount of food we eat will spontaneously decrease. The diet progresses to approximately 40 to 45 percent biogenic, 55 to 60 percent raw, and 5 percent undercooked hard vegetables. These are averages. There may be times when it is 100 percent raw and 66 percent fruit, such as during the summer. Each of us must find our own optimal percentages. I am not able to detect a significant difference between a 100 percent raw food diet and one that is 95 percent in terms of day-to-day energy and love communion. There may be a difference in terms of ultimate physical longevity, but this is not our primary focus. The 5 percent gives us a certain amount of social flexibility and helps us not have to be constricted by the conceptual purity of 100 percent.

Within this dietary progression there is an increasing amount of fruit. It increases to about 35 to 40 percent of the diet. Fruit is important because it contains 70 to 90 percent structured water which helps to dissolve toxins and increase the transport of nutrients into the cells. Fruit and the biogenic foods are the most oxygenated foods, and thus improve health. We are able to eat them without killing our plant friends. The juicier the diet is with fruits, the less liquid we have to drink. I am not suggesting that we become fruitarian because our basement membranes would become too porous for us to live in our toxic environment. The increase in biogenic greens such as wheatgrass, buckwheat, and sunflower greens is important because they may contain the most rejuvenating energy on the planet.

This is the "intercollegiate" diet. It is highly energizing and restorative to our SOEFs. It will create steady excellent health, increased vitality, and it will allow experience of the Divine love communion to be maintained easily. It enhances the total body-mind-spirit experience of the bliss of light and love. By increasing the flow of the prana into and through the system, this diet significantly increases the potential for the critical energy level to be reached for awakening the Kundalini. This diet also accelerates the purifying and spiritualizing action of the Kundalini once it is awakened.

Contrary to other diets, it is very simple to follow. I have arrived at this diet for myself and spend little time thinking about or preparing it, except to work with my indoor sprout, wheatgrass, buckwheat and sunflower greens garden a few minutes each day and to harvest from our outdoor garden. This garden attention is a constant reminder of my connection with the cycles of nature. I have done it for several years, and it has transformed my body into enough of a superconductor so that there is minimal blockage to the full flow of the cosmic prana entering and any prana moving through my system. This seems to be the case for other people I have observed on this diet. Although thinner than my football playing days, my weight has stabilized within the norm established by the life insurance height and weight averages. Part of the reason for this is that this diet supplies more than sufficient nutrients as compared to the RDA values established by the United States Department of Agriculture. Ann Wigmore's Hippocrates Diet, which is a similar to the one I am recommending, but with fancier food preparation and more emphasis on green and other fresh juices and fermented food preparations, compared the nutrients in her diet to the RDA values. She found that her almost 100 percent raw diet had six times the vitamin C, two times the B-complex vitamins, ten times more vitamin A, seven times more iron, two times the calcium, and an amount of B_{12} equal to that of the RDA.[8] Taken to its heavier side, she found that it could supply almost twice the protein but with half the fat. It is important to remember that in the process of our transmutation, less and less physical food is needed to maintain the physical body adequately, so too much focus on RDA values misses the point of the art of spiritual nutrition. I mention her data to leave no doubts about the adequacy of this type of diet for those still thinking in terms of the material concept of nutrition.

Ann Wigmore's book *The Hippocrates Diet and Health Program* and Victoras Kulvinskas's book, *Survival into the 21st Century* both give a detailed and clear discussion of how to prepare and grow many of the biogenic foods to which I have been referring. I support the use of green and fresh juices, but in many of our lives it is one step extra than what most of us are regularly willing to do. Although good for health it is not clear that daily green juices are necessary for our primary spiritual focus. I do recommend the fermented seed preparations as an additional way to have a source of easily assimilated and tasty protein. By increasing the protein and fat with biogenic seed cheeses, soaked nuts and seeds, avocados, and bananas we can increase our weight. Learning to adjust these nutrients to maintain optimal physical function and strength for our worldly work is part of the art of spiritual nutrition. In the food appendix, a more detailed discussion of food preparation will be given.

The Olympic part of stage IV is fasting. It is fasting one day per week, or three days in a row per month, and four ten-day fasts per year, usually at the change of seasons. It may also include at least one 40-day fast at some point in our evolution. As discussed in the spiritual fasting chapter, these are times of increased meditation and fasting from worldly activities. This is a powerful spiritual practice that enhances the transformational process. This practice, with increased meditation, most effectively turns our system into a superconductor for the Kundalini. After we reach a certain point of purification on this fasting program, the fasting program is no longer done for purification. By following the 40 percent biogenic, 95 percent raw diet, our body is able to purify at a rate equal to the internal metabolic toxin production and the environmental pollution exposure. One can then either chose to decrease or stop the fasting or use it to further enhance the superconductive Kundalini flow and transcendent transformation.

Final Perspective

"For the Kingdom of God is not food and drink, but righteousness, and peace, and joy in the holy spirit" (Romans 15:17)

No diet, without the full context of right life, love, right association, and meditation will bear spiritual fruit. Although our understanding is esoteric, we are dealing with a most basic and practical life process called eating food. Diet is not religion or searching for the truth, it is simply a part of right life. On this level the art of spiritual nutrition in developing a right diet is simply appropriate. It is one in a context of life practices that opens the door to our focus which is harmony and love communion with God. Optimal health is not the goal but a byproduct of this goal. For some of us spiritual nutrition is also a practice of self-awareness that deepens our understanding of right life. For others of us it is also a powerful spiritual practice of diet, fasting, and meditation that accelerates our spiritual unfolding by increasing the cosmic prana entering all the subtle bodies and the physical body. As this universal prana increases within us, the awareness of our own enlightenment is increased. Spiritual nutrition is a whole-person enlightenment approach which includes the spiritualization of the body as well as the mind and spirit.

Right diet is an expression of our natural attunement with the laws of nature as manifested by the oneness of God. When we are attuned with these laws, our health and spiritual life are supported. A spiritually appropriate diet is both the cause and the result of our state of being.

Because proper diet is the expression of our being and state of harmony, it manifests less appropriately if it is subjected to external formulas for diet or even recipes. The only formula that we need to follow is the thoughtful and intelligent application of the art of spiritual nutrition. The main guideline to developing our diet is our inner experience of the Kundalini or simply that, while eating or after eating, our body-mind complex should feel energized and good throughout the day. Diet approached in this way is a commonsense personal harmony. This is why I have maintained some vagueness about the details of the diet and focused on the principles.

The direct transcendental awareness of our true nature as that who is light, love, and the non-dualistic truth of God supercedes any dietary practice, purity consciousness, or dietary awareness. Throughout the Old Testament, food was an offering to God. It was an ancient symbol of God communion. "Whatever, therefore, ye eat or drink, do all things for God's glory" (Corinthians 10:32). Therefore, in the aware state we live as a love offering to God, and we live on that love as the primary food in our lives. In this way we become that Love.

Summary Chapter 24

1. Six purposes for developing an individualized diet for spiritual life are reviewed.
2. There are so many factors important to our process of developing an individualized diet that the only computer which can correlate them is that of our inner sensitivity. To use it effectively we need to become our own laboratory.
3. By stabilizing the patterns of the time we eat, the physical and emotional environment in which we eat, how much we eat, and what we eat, we can consciously begin the process of self-awareness and diet.
4. Our "feedback" system on the gross physical level is feeling good all day after eating or experiencing the ill effects of gas, bloating, and nausea from a diet that is inappropriate for us.
5. On a more subtle level, if the love communion with the Divine is blocked before, during, or after the meal, this is "feedback" that we are not on the right diet.
6. Diet is not static. It needs to evolve in a way that supports and maintains harmony with our spiritual evolution.
7. The art of spiritual nutrition is the process of self-study applied to the basic guidelines of spiritual nutrition in the context of a full spiritual life. It is the creation of right diet which involves letting go of nonfunctional patterns of relating to food such as food transferences.
8. Some of this shifting of diet happens spontaneously as our spiritual life evolves.
9. An approach to right diet that involves self-study and cultivation of an artful self-awareness becomes a spiritual practice on its own.
10. In the process of dietary purification we may go through a detoxification process which may be either mild or severe depending on how rapidly we

proceed.

11. The Rainbow Diet way of organizing our food intake applies to any stage of diet, as does learning to eat the right amount of food to be in harmony with all levels of our nutritional and spiritual needs.

12. There are four main stages of transitional diet.

13. Stage I is the removal of all bioacidic foods from the diet. It incorporates the use of flesh foods that are organically grown.

14. Stage II is the removal of all red meats from the diet.

15. Stage III is a vegetarian diet which means no fish, fowl, seafood, or eggs. It may be lactovegetarian or macrobiotic initially. By the end of stage III, we have evolved to a diet equal to 80 percent raw and 20 percent cooked foods, with 20 to 30 percent of the diet made of biogenic foods. This diet is fully supportive of and adequate for spiritual life.

16. Stage IV is a diet level that both accelerates spiritual development and is a spiritual practice on its own. It is a 95 percent raw food diet that is approximately 40 to 45 percent biogenic, 55 to 60 percent fruits and vegetables, and up to 5 percent cooked vegetables. It involves one day per week fasting or three days per month, and four ten-day seasonal fasts per year.

17. No diet without the full context of right life, right fellowship, love, and meditation will bear spiritual fruit.

18. Diet is an expression of our natural attunement with the laws of nature, as manifested from the oneness of God. By attuning to these laws, we support health and spiritual life.

19. Diet is both the cause and result of our state of being.

Epilogue

In the process of writing this book I realized that I was not writing about spiritual nutrition, the Rainbow Diet, or the awakening and evolution of Kundalini. I realized that this book is emerging as part of the rising spiral of planetary consciousness preparing itself to take a quantum leap into mass world enlightenment. We are transforming from a dysfunctional, self-centered awareness to a new global awareness centered in Divine love communion with God and in the unity awareness that everyone on this planet is of one body in the Self of All. We are almost ready to give up our individual and planetary dysfunctional patterns of wasting food and of world hunger, of hoarding resources and world poverty, of individual violence and world terrorism, and of individual alienation and nations fighting nations. The historical phase that emphasized personal salvation and enlightenment is merging into a new historical period of mass salvation and enlightenment in which we have the potential to realize as a unified planetary group our individual and collective God nature (which we have been all along).

Spiritual Nutrition and The Rainbow Diet is a blueprint of some of the conscious technology and evolutionary processes that we may use or experience in our individualized yet collective way. The transforming process of right diet, right life, right association, meditation, and fasting in the joy of God communion is a way of deliberately and consciously choosing to cooperate with the patterns of individual and collective evolution. It is a way of choosing to be synchronous with the will of God in the process of evolution. These patterns are not new. They have always been available to the masses, but few have taken advantage of them. God's grace has always been on this planet. These patterns, or teachings, are universal in their application and ageless in their wisdom. They were practiced by the Essenes several centuries before the time of Jesus and by the ancient Egyptians. They are practiced in the Zend Avesta of Zarathustra, in the teachings of Buddha, Mohammed, Lao Tzu, Yoga, Hinduism, the Pythagoreans; they are taught by the Tibetan Wheel of Life and in the Law of Moses. God's universal laws and patterns of evolution remain unchanged and are as applicable now as before. In the secluded communities of the Essenes three great figures -- Jesus, John the Baptist, and John of Revelations -- were trained to share and prepare the world for this evolutionary leap in consciousness. These teachings were given to accelerate the opening of the doors to the higher states of God consciousness. The only difference between now and then is that these teachings and the transformational processes are now beginning to be used by the public on a mass basis. This book is a small sharing of some of that eternal and simple wisdom. I chose to share some of my transformational experiences as part of a more personal and detailed expression of the teachings. These teachings help us develop ourselves as small holographic units of God awareness capable of resonating with cosmic consciousness on a mass scale to uplift the planet.

At each stage of evolution there is a more progressive synergy. Initially, atom was attracted to atom, then cell to cell. Then human Kundalini merged into the oneness of the crown chakra with the synchronization of right and left brain and male and female awareness. This creates a nondualistic world experience in which there is no separation between humans. It is an awareness that allows human to be attracted to human and social system synchronized to social system as members of the same Divine Body of God. We are about to make a quantum leap via a social synergy centered in the Love of unitary awareness. This is our destiny. This book is an invitation for all of us to enjoy the party.

Resource References
For further information on:

1. Ayurveda: *Ayurveda, The Science of Self-Healing,* by Vasant Lad. Lotus Press, P.O. Box 6265, Sante Fe,   N.M. 87502-6265.

2. Blue-Green Manna: for current information contact (707)-778-6501, Gabriel Cousens, M.D., 200 Spring Hill Road, Petaluma, Calif. 94952.

3. Flower Essences and Gem Elixirs: (303)-442-0139, Pegasus Products, Inc., P.O. Box 228, Boulder, Colo. 80306.

4. Food Irradiation: National Coalition to Stop Food Irradiation(415)- 566-CSFI, P.O. Box 590488, San Francisco, Calif. 94159

5. Germanium: (415)-639-4572; Germanium Revolution, P.O. Box 489, San Leandro, Calif. 94577.

6. Hubbard, Barbara Marx: *Manual For Co-Creators of the Quantum Leap* and other of her resource materials from New Visions,(904)-378-3661, P.O. Box 5102, 3051 SE 35 St., Gainesville, Fl. 32602.

7. Living Food Resources:
   (1) Brother Viktoras Kulkvinskas, M.S., Survival Foundation Inc. P.O. Box 255, Weathersfield, CT. 06109
   (2) Ann Wigmore, (617)- 267-9525, Hippocrates Health Institute, 23 Exeter St. Boston, MA. 02116

8. Muktananda's teachings of Siddha Yoga: (914)- 434-2000, SYDA Foundation, P.O. Box 605, South Fallsburg, N.Y.,12779.

9. Spiritual Nutrition programs and seminars: (707)-778-6501, Gabriel Cousens, M.D., 200 Spring Hill Road, Petaluma, Calif. 94952.

10. Synchronicity™, The Recognitions Experience: (804)-361-2323, MSH Association, Rt. 1 Box 192-B, Faber, Virginia 22938.

Appendix I: Biogenic Food Preparation

Why We Soak and Sprout Seeds

When we are not sprouting the seeds, we are soaking them. Seeds and nuts are soaked because the water activates the seeds to begin their germination process. The water also washes out the enzyme inhibitors, phytates (which block zinc and other mineral absorption), oxalates (which block calcium absorption and can cause stiffening of the joints), and other metabolic inhibitors in the seed designed to keep the seed from germinating until the appointed time. The water also activates the germination enzymes which begin the pre-digestion germination to break down proteins into free amino acids, fats into fatty acids, and starchs into simple carbohydrates.

Soaking Instructions

Sesame, pumpkin, sunflower, alfalfa, chia, flax, and oats need a minimum of six hours of soaking. Almonds, other nuts, legumes, beans, wheat, rice, millet, and rye soak for a minimum of 12 hours. The easiest seeds to use in these recepies are sunflower, pumpkin, sesame, and almond.

Seed sprouting

The easiest seed to sprout is alfalfa. To a quart sized wide-mouthed canning jar add three heaping teaspoons of alfalfa seeds. Fill the jar four inches above the seeds with water. Soak overnight or 8 hours. To remove hulls, scoop them off when they float to the top. Pour off the water through a screen lid or wire mesh held over the top of the jar. Rinse 3 times with fresh water or until the poured off liquid is clear. After draining, store in a dark place for 24 hours until the seeds begin to sprout. Then expose them to daylight as they grow. A tilted rack, such as a dish rack, provides a good drainage system for the sprouting jars. For the first 3 to 5 days of the sprouting process, rinse the sprouts 1 to 2 times per day. They can be ready to eat by the second day of sprouting and they reach their best by 5 to 7 days. They can be stored in the refrigerator. People often enjoy sprouting a combination of sprouts in the same jar for the variety of tastes. Mung, lentil, fenugreek, radish, and clover are commonly enjoyed together.

Seed and Nut Milk Preparation Instructions

After the seeds or nuts are soaked, blend them immediately at a ratio of one cup of seeds to one cup of water. Grind in the blender, slowly adding 1 cup of water. We can also let them sprout for 8 hours before blending. This additional sprouting may enhance their potency, but is not critical to insure digestibility and biogenic quality as a food. Once the basic seed or nut milk is made, add the secondary ingredients that add to the culinary quality and are for our specific body balance needs. For breakfast, bananas, soaked figs, or other fruit may be added to the blend. This mixture can then be directly eaten or be poured over fruit. These soaked and sprouted seeds become alkaline in their reaction with the body and combine well with all categories of fruit. For salad dressings and vegetable sauces, add vegetables, herbs, or spices. Ginger and cayenne help heat up and cleanse. Cucumber and dill cool down on a hot day. A cucumber-dill-pumpkin seed sauce is one of my favorites for lunch salad sauce. A variety of vegetables such a zucchini or beets, or even sprouts, add taste and texture. Avocado makes a great combination. Explore and have fun with it.

For sesame seeds, it is best to use those that are whole (unhulled) because the seeds stay fresh. Soak overnight, drain, and blend for two minutes. The blender breaks the hulls off. Separate out the hulls with a fine cheese cloth or a plastic sprouting bag; the remaining liquid is the seed milk. It is ready to be combined with other components or drunk by itself.

Preparation of Seed Cheeses

A seed cheese is made by letting the seed sauce ferment for 8 to 10 hours at room temperature to 110 degrees Farenheit. I enjoy making a tastier cheese by adding herbs and spices such as curry and dill. Airborn lactobacilus enter the seed sauce to create the fermentation; to enhance the process some seed cheese from the last batch can be added. Either way seems to work. The fermentation continues to predigest the protein and leaves us with a very high residue of Vit B_{12} and other B complex factors. As the seed cheese ripens, the whey will separate to the bottom and the cheese will remain on top. A lemonish smell indicates the process is ripe. Pour off the whey by pushing a hole in the seed cheese near the edge of the glass jar and gently pour the contents through a sprouting bag and squeeze the bag to force out the excess whey. If you squeeze too hard the bag may burst and the cheese will get "awhey!" If this happens, be comforted to know you were not the first. Squeeze the seed cheese as dry as possible for a few minutes and then hang to dry for 2 to 6 hours. Store in the refrigerator where it stays good for around three days. It can be served with salad or sweet or subacid fruit.

A seed yogurt is made in a similar "whey", but harvest it when the fermentation process is 4 to 6 hours in progress, before the whey separates.

Growing Wheatgrass

Wheatgrass instructions apply to growing other greens such as buckwheat and sunflower. Soak organic winter wheatberries 12 hours and sprout for 12 hours. Prepare one inch of compost rich soil, sprinkle wheatberries in a thin layer, and cover them with a thin layer of soil. One cup of wheatberries will fill a 10 by 14 by 1-inch tray. Grow at room temperature in indirect sunlight, and keep the soil moist. When the sprouts reach seven to ten inches they are ready for harvest. To harvest, cut as close to the soil as possible because the nutrients are the most concentrated near the soil. Sprinkle the greens on salads or juice them. Grass can be stored for one week, but juice begins to spoil after one half hour.

Preparation of Salads and Soups

A variety of salad dressing and soups can be made from raw foods with a blender. With avocado as a base, add a single additional ingredient such as carrot juice, cucumber, tomatoes, lemon juice, a variety of vegetables, or even sprouts. Add herbs and spices such as ginger, garlic, dill, corriander, and basil.

A unique soup for the Rainbow Diet evening meal is one cup of sliced raw beets blended with one avocado. Add some dulse and water to the right consistency. The avocado balances the taste of the beet.

For those people with digestive difficulties, it has worked very well to blend up whole salads into soups. These are more easily digested and allow us to enjoy the advantage of biologically active enzymes.

Food preparation in this way is creative, healthy, quick, and most important of all, simple. There are no complicated recipes to follow except that of our own inner sensitivity. It is for the playful, creative noncooks.

For further details see: *The Hippocrates Diet* by Ann Wigmore or *Survival Into the 21st Century* by Victoras Kulvinskas.

"A King that cannot rule him in his dyet,
Will hardly rule his realm in peace and quiet."
Anonymous, Regimen Sanitatis Salernitanum 11th Century

Appendix II: Meditation

Meaning of Meditation

Meditation is a regular part of our life. When we concentrate on driving a car, playing a sport, listening to a lecturer we are meditating. Meditation is the process of focusing on an object. When we focus inward on the light of God, on the Self, rather than on outer object this is what is formally known as meditation. When we become directed in our concentration, thought stops, time stops, and the the light of the God Self within shines through into our awake state as a perfect moment. Many of us have experienced these "perfect" moments in our lives in such simple acts as watching a beautiful sunset or listening to beautiful music. The only difference between these sporadic moments of meditation and formal meditation is that the Self is not transitory and the practice of daily meditation strengthens our ability to concentrate on the Self. The idea is to lengthen the time we are in touch with the Divine. The more we are in touch with the Self, we begin to think about ourselves differently. We become aware that we and all of creation are one with God. When we understand this, we begin to understand everything as it is. This is the knowledge gained in meditation. This experience of this Truth is opposite of what we are often taught, which is that we are sinners, we are no good, we are evil. To some, this knowledge is profoundly transformative; others may be afraid to give up their old patterns. We meditate not to attain God, but to become aware of the God within us. Psalms 46:11 says "Be still and know that I am God." This is love communion with God.

A Technique of Meditation

The main issue in meditation is learning how to relate to the mind. It is the mind that distracts us from the communion. So we must learn not to focus on or fight our thoughts. It is best to try to witness them as part of the play of the mind rather than to identify them as real or as who we are. It is like watching a movie and remembering that it is only a movie. Our true Self is the white screen of awareness on which the movie is played. It is important not to give them any energy by fighting or judging them. Many unusual experiences come up in meditation and it is best to let them pass through and let our system be cleansed of them.

Another powerful technique for working with the mind is to use a mantra. The word mantra means that which protects us, especially from our mind. There are many mantras, but I can share with you the ones that I have learned. The first one is "Om Namah Shivaya" which roughly means that I bow to the God within myself. It is one of the many names of God. Its meaning is important because our mind becomes permeated by what we are thinking. By repeating this mantra we are calling to God within us. It is prayer in the sense that it is letting God know that we want to make contact. Meditation is listening to God's response in the stillness of our heart. In meditation we mentally repeat this mantra at any rate we choose or even harmonize it with the breath. The best mantra to repeat with the our breath is the universal "So Ham" (I Am That I Am) because it is the natural sound and rhythm of the breath. We think Ham on the in breath and So on the out breath. The still space between the innerward breath of Ham and before the beginning of the outward breath of So, where the mind is still, is the space of the Self. As we meditate, this silent space may become more extended. For example, in Exodus 3:14 it was the "I Am That I Am" which Moses was given as the name of God. When we reach a point in which the mind is still, it is time to let go of the mantra and simply Be in the awareness of God.

For meditation it is important to find a comfortable position so we can sit still for the duration of the meditation. Sitting on the ground in a cross legged position or on a bench or pillow is what most people associate with meditation, but sitting upright in a chair with both feet on the ground is fine. Any position in which the mind can be at rest is fine. The best time to meditate is early morning before we have eaten, when the world is still quiet. However, any time we find conducive for meditation is the right time. The more regularly we meditate, the easier it becomes. People often start with twenty minutes and work up to an hour. Ultimately, when we become one with the knowledge of meditation, every moment of our life becomes a meditation, a love communion with God.

References

Author's Introduction

1. Callahan,Philip. *Tuning into Nature.* Old Greenich Conn.: Devin-Adair Press,1975.
2. Dosset, Larry, *Space, Time, and Medicine.* Boulder: Shambhala Publications Inc.,. 1982.
3. *The Teachings of Bhagavan Sri Ramana Maharshi in His Own Words.* edited by Arthur Osborne; Madras, India: published by T. N. Venkataraman, 4th ed. 1977.

Chapter 1

1. Kervan C. L. and Abehsera, M. *Biological Transmutations.* New York: Swan House Publishing Co.,1972.
2. Ibid
3. ibid
4. ibid
5. ibid
6. Ibid
7. Szent-Gyorgyi. *Introduction to Submolecular Biology.* London: Acad.Press,1960.
8. Kervan C. L. and Abehsera, M. *Biological Transmutations.* New York: Swan House Publishing Co.,1972.
9. Williams, Roger. *Biochemical Individuality.* Austin: U. of Texas Press, 1956.
10. Kervan C. L. and Abehsera,M. *Biological Transmutations.* New York: Swan House Publishing Co.,1972.
11. Brewer, Richard and Hahn, Erwin. *Scientific American.* Dec. 84 vol. 251 pp 50-57.
12. Kervan C. L. and Abehsera, M. *Biological Transmutations.* New York: Swan House Publishing Co.,1972.

Chapter 2

1. Personal communication, Marcel Vogel.
2. Beardon. T. E. *The New Tesla Electrommagnetics and the Secrets of Electrical Free Energy.*
3. Personal communication, Adam Trombley, 1986.
4. Dept. of Defense Program Solici-tation for F/Y, 1986 AF 86-77.
5. Callahan,Philip. *Tuning into Nature.* Old Greenich Conn.: Devin-Adair Press,1975.
6. Bearden,T. E. *Toward a New Electromagnetics, Part III: Clarifying the Vector Concept.* Millbrae, Calif.: Tesla Book Co., 1983.
7. Sheldrake, Rupert. *A New Science of Life.* Los Angeles: J. P. Tarcher, Inc., 1981.
8. Toben, Robert. *Space, Time, and Beyond.* New York: E.P. Dutton and Co., Inc., 1975.
9. Friedman, H.L., Krishman, C.V. and Jolicoeur, C., *Ionic Interactions in Water.* Ann. N. Y. Acad. of Science 204: 77-99.
10. Clegg, James. "Metabolism and the Intracellular Environment: "The Vicinal Water Network Model", in *Cell Associated Water*, (Drost-Hansen, W. and James Clegg; Eds.) New York: Academic Press, 1979.
11. Cope, Freeman," Structured Water and Comlexed Na^+ and K^+ in Biological Systems Water Structure at the Water-Polymer Interface." Proceedings of American Chemical Society Symposium, edited by H.H. Jellinek, New York: Plenum Press, 1972.
12. Ling, Gilbert, "Water Structure at the Water-Polymer Interface." Proceedings of American Chemical Society Symposium, ed. by H.H. Jellinek, New York: Plenum Press, 1972.
13. Hansen, J. Yellin, "W. NMR and Infra Spectroscopic Studies of Stratum Corneum Hydration", Proceedings of American Chemical Society Symposium, ed. by H.H. Jellinek, New York: Plenum Press, 1972.
14. Clegg, James. "Metabolism and the Intracellular Environment: The Vicinal Water Network Model", in *Cell Associated Water*, (Drost-Hansen, W. and James Clegg; Eds.) New York: Academic Press, 1979.
15. Ibid.
16. Ibid.
17. Hazelwood, Carlton," A View of the Significance and Understanding of the Physical Properties of Cell Associated Water". in *Cell Associated Water*, (Drost-Hansen, W. and James Clegg; Eds.) New York: Academic Press, 1979.

18. Mikesell, Norm, " Cellular Regeneration", San Jose: Published by Psychic Research Newsletter, 1985.

19. Ibid.

20. Bachechi, Orie.,*When light Touches Many Changes Take Place*, Kiva, Inc. Albuquerque, N.M.,1984.

21. Ibid.

Chapter 3

1. Nisargadatta, Maharaj, *I Am That.* Bombay: Sudhakar S. Dikshit, 1976.

2. Hotema, Hilton, *Higher Consciousness.* Mokelumne Hill, CA: Health Research, 1962.

3. Yogananda, Paramahansa, *Autobiography of a Yogi.* Los Angeles, Ca: Self-Realization Fellowship, 1972 .

4. Chia, Mantak and Winn, Michael, *Taoist Secrets of Love.* N.Y.: Aurora Press, 1984.

5. Ibid.

6. Airola, Paavo, *Worldwide Secrets for Staying Young.* Phoenix, AZ: Health Plus, 1982.

7. Ibid.

8.Hotema, Hilton, *Higher Consciousness.* Mokelumne Hill, CA: Health Research, 1962.

9. Murty, T.S. Anantha, *Maharaj.* San Rafael,Ca.: The Dawn Horse Press,1972.

10. Zevin, Rabbi S. Y., *A Treasury of Chassidic Tales* . N.Y.: Mesorah, 1981.

11. Ibid.

12. Yogananda, Paramahansa, *Autobiography of a Yogi.* Los Angeles, Ca: Self-Realization Fellowship, 1972.

13. Ibid.

14. Ibid.

15. Ibid.

16. Ibid.

17. Ibid.

18. Burkus, J. ,*Terese Neumanaite.* Chicago: Suduvos Press, 1953.

19. Chia, Mantak and Winn, Michael, *Taoist Secrets of Love.* New York: Aurora Press, 1984.

20. Yogananda, Paramahansa, *Autobiography of a Yogi.* Los Angeles, CA: Self-Realization Fellowship, 1972.

21. Lo'ez, MeAm, *The Torah Anthology.* N.Y./Jerusalem: Maznaim, 1977.

22. Ibid.

23 Ibid.

24. Szekely, Edmond Bordeaux, *The Essenes by Josephus and his Contemporaries.* U.S.: International Biogenic Society, 1981.

25. Murthy, T. S. Anantha, *Maharaj.* San Rafael, CA: The Dawn Horse Press, 1972.

26. Ibid.

27. Airola, Paavo, *Worldwide Secrets for Staying Young.* Phoenix, AZ: Health Plus, 1982.

28. Ibid.

29. Wallace, R.K., "Reversal of Aging in Subjects Practicing the TM and TM Sidhi Program", Annual Meeting of American Geriactics Society, Washington, D.C.: 1979.

30. Little, W.A. , "Superconductivity at Room Temperture", *Scienticfic American,* 212, 21;1965.

31. " Melanin as Key Organizing Molecule", *Brain Mind Bulletin.* Los Angeles, CA: Interface Press, Aug., 1983.

32. McClare, C.W.F. , "Resonance in Bioenergetics", *Annals of the N.Y. Acad. Of Sciences.* 227: 74-91, 1974.

33. Yogananda, Paramahansa, *Autobiography of a Yogi.* Los Angeles, CA: Self-Realization Fellowship, 1972.

34. Ibid.

35. *The Lost Books of the Bible and The Forgotten Books of Eden.* N.Y.: World, 1972.

36. Wilber, Ken, *Quantum Questions.* Boulder, CO: Shambhala, 1984.

Chapter 4

1. Steiner, Rudolf, *Agricultural.* London, N.W.J.: Bio-Dynamic Agricultural Association, 1977.

2. Vogel, Personal Communication, l986.

3. Schmidt, Gerhard, *The Dynamics of Nutrition.* RI: Bio-Dynamic Literature,1980.

4. Ibid.

5. Nisargadatta, Maharaj, *I Am That.* Bombay: Sudhakar S. Dikshit, 1976.

Chapter 5

l. Motoyama, Hiroshi, *Theories of the Chakras: Bridge to Higher Consciousnes..* Madras, India/ London,England: The Theosophical Publishing House, 1985.

2. Joy, W. Brugh, *Joy's Way.* Los Angeles: J.P. Tarcher, Inc., 1979.

3. Badgley, L, "New Method for Locating Acupuncture Points and Body Field Distortions", *American Journal of*

Acupunture. Vol. 12 no. 3 July-
September 1984.
4. Neff, Dio, "The Great Chakra
Controversy", *Yoga Journal.* Berk-ely,
CA: California Yoga Teachers
Association, Nov/Dec, 1985.
5. Motoyama, Hiroshi, *Theories of the
Chakras: Bridge to Higher
Consciousness.* Madras, India/
London,England: The Theosophical
Publishing House, 1985.
6. Joy, W. Brugh, *Joy's Way.* Los
Angeles: J.P. Tarcher, Inc., 1979.
7. Motoyama, Hiroshi, *Theories of the
Chakras: Bridge to Higher
Consciousness.* Madras, India/
London,England: The Theosophical
Publishing House, 1985.
8. Joy, W. Brugh, *Joy's Way.* Los
Angeles: J.P. Tarcher, Inc., 1979.
9. Murphy, Michael and White, Rhea
A., *The Psychic Side of Sports.* Menlo
Park, CA/London/ Amsterdam/Don Mills,
Ontario/ Sydney: Addison-Wesley, 1978.
10. Colton, Ann Ree, *Kundalini West.*
Glendale, CA: Arc Publishing, 1978.

Chapter 6
1. Brother, Charles, MSH, Personal
Communication, 1986.

Chapter 7
1. Jung, Carl, and Hauer, J., *Kundalini
Yoga.* Unpublished manuscript, 1932.
2. Krishna, G., *Kundalini: The
Evolutionary Energy in Man.*
Shambhala, Berkeley: 1971.
3. Muktananda, *Kundalini: The Secrets
of Life.* N.Y.: SYDA Foundation, 1979.
4. Ibid.
5. Katz, R., "Education for
Transcendence: Lessons from the ! Kung
Zhu Twasi", *Journal of Transpersonal
Psychology.* Nov. 2, 1973.
6. Luk, C., *The Secrects of Chinese
Meditation.* N.Y.: Samuel Weiser, 1972.
7. Rohrbach, P., *The Search for St.
Therese.* N.Y.: Dell, 1963.
8. Sannella, Lee, *Kundalini-Psychosis
or Transcendence?* San Francisco, CA:
Sannella, 1976.
9. Ibid.
10. Ibid.
11. Ibid.
12. Muktananda, Swami, *Kundalini, The
Secret of Life.* N.Y.: SYDA Foundation,
1979.

13. Ibid.
Chapter 8
1. *The Lost Books of the Bible and The
Forgotten Books of Eden.* N.Y.: World,
1972.
2. Wurtman, Richard J., "The Effects of
Light on the Human Body", *Scientific
American.* San Francisco, CA: W.H.
Freeman and Company, Vol. 233, No. 1,
p. 68-77, July, 1975.
3. Brody, Jane E., "Surprising Health
Impact Discovered for Light", *Science
Times.* N.Y.: The New York Times,
Nov. 13, 1984.
4. Ibid.
5. Ibid.
6. National Institute of Mental Health,
*Biological Rhythms in Psychiatry and
Medicine.*
7. Ibid.
8. Downing, John , Personal
Communication, 1986.
9. Wurtman, Richard J., "The Effects of
Light on the Human Body", *Scientific
American.* San Francisco, CA: W.H.
Freeman and Company, Vol. 233, No. 1,
p. 68-77, July, 1975.
10. National Institute of Mental Health,
*Biological Rhythms in Psychiatry and
Medicine.*
11. " Melanin as Key Organizing
Molecule", *Brain Mind Bulletin.* Los
Angeles, CA: Vol. 8, No.12/13, July
11/Aug. 1, 1983.
12. Ibid.
13. Levine, Steve, "Oxygen,
Bioelectricity and Life", *American
Chiropractor.* July, 1986.
14. Levine, Steve, "Oxygen Immunity,
Cancer, and Candida", presented at
Society of Environmental Medicine.
Clearwater, Fl.: Oct. 1986.
15. Babior, B.M., ""The Role of Active
Oxygen in Microbial Killing by
Phagocytes. In: Pathology of Oxygen."
Edited by A.P. Antoe, N.Y.: Acad. Press,
1982.
16. Levine, Steve and Kidd, Paris,
*Antioxidant Adaption; Its Role in Free
Radical Pathology.* San Francisco, CA:
Biocurrents Press, 1985.

About Food. Molelimne Hill, Ca.:Health Research, 1968.

19.Kamen, Betty, "Vit. O: The Oxygen Nutrient", *Let's Live.* Vol. 54, No. 7, July, 1986.

20. Kazuhiko, Asai, Mircale Cure Organic *Germanium.* Japan: Japan Publications, Inc.,1980.

21. Ibid.

22. Leadbeater, C.W., *The Chakras.* Wheaton, Ill.,U.S.A./Madras, India/London, Eng.: The Theosophical Publishing House, 1980.

23. Chia, Mantak and Winn, Michael, *Taoist Secrets of Love.* N.Y.: Aurora Press, 1984.

24. Kornfield, Jack, "The Sex Lives of Gurus", *The Yoga Journal,* Vol. 63, July/Aug., 1985.

25. *The Teachings of Bhagavan Sri Ramana Maharshi in His Own Words.* Edited by Arthur Osborne, Madras, India: published by T. N. Venkataraman, 4th ed., 1977.

26. Dubrou, Aleksander, *The Geomagnetic Field and Life.* N.Y.: Plenum Press, 1978.

Chapter 9

1. Hunt, Roland, *The Seven Keys to Colour Healing.* Rochester, Kent.: C.W. Daniel Company Ltd., 1971.

Chapter 10

1. Vogel, Marcel, Personal Communication, 1986.

2. Rein, Glen, "Biological Crystals", presented at the First International Crystal Congress, San Francisco: June, 1986.

3. Basset, Andrew C., "Biophysical Principles Affecting Bone Structure", *The Biochemistry and Physiology of Bone.* N.Y.: Academic Press, p. 1-76, 1971.

4. Basset, Andrew, "Biological Significance of Piezoelectricity", *Calc. Tiss.* Res.1, 252-272, 1968.

5. Basset, Andrew C., "Biophysical Principles Affecting Bone Structure", *The Biochemistry and Physiology of Bone.* N.Y.: Academic Press, 1971.

6. Basset, Andrew, "Biological Significance of Piezoelectricity" *Calc. Tiss.* Res.1, 252-272, 1968.

7. Ibid.

8. Bassett, L.S., Tzitzikalakis, G., Pawluk, R.J. and Bassett, C.A.L., "Prevention of disuse osteoporosis in the rat by means of pulsing electromagnetic fields". *Electrical Properties of Bone and Cartilage; Experimental Effects and Clinica*

Applications. Edited by C.T. Brighton, J. Black and S.R. Pollack, N.Y.: Grune and Stratton, p. 605-630, 1979.

9. Bassett, C.A.L. et al, "Modification of Fracture Repair with Selected Pulsing Electromagnetic Fields", *The Journal of Bone and Joint Surgery.* Vol. 64-A, No. 6, p. 888-895, July, 1982.

10. Basset, Andrew C., "Biophysical Principles Affecting Bone Structure", *The Biochemistry and Physiology of Bone.* N.Y.: Academic Press, p. 1-76, 1971.

11. Bassett, C.A.L., " Pulsing Electromagnetic Fields: A New Approach for Surgical problems". *Metabolic Surgery.* Edited by Henry Buchward, M.D. and Richard L. Varcho, M.D. N.Y.: Grune and Stratton, p. 255-306, 1978.

12. McClare, C.W.F. , " Resonance in Bioenergetics", *Annals of the N.Y. Acac. of Sciences.* 227: 74-91, 1974.

13. *Liquid Crystals and Ordered Fluids.* Ed. by Johnson, J.F. and Porter, R.S., N.Y.: Plenum Press, 1970.

14. Miksell, "Structure water: its Healing Effects on the Diseased State", San Jose: PRI, 1985.

15. Rapp, P.R., "An Atlas of Cellular Oscillators", *Journal Exp. Biol.* 81, 281-306, 1979.

16. Gurudas, *Gem Elixirs and Vibrational Healing, Vol. 1.* Boulder, CO: Cassandra Press,1985.

Chapter 11

1. Rein, Blen, "Biological Crystals", presented at First International Crystal Conference, S.F.: 1986.

2. Ibid.

3. Vogel, Marcel, Personal Communication, 1986.

4. Gurudas, *Gem Elixirs and Vibrational Healing, Vol. 1.* Boulder, CO: Cassandra Press,1985.

5. Basset, Andrew C., "Biophysical Principles Affecting Bone Structure", *The Biochemistry and Physiology of Bone.* N.Y.: Academic Press, p. 1-76, 1971.

6. Basset, Andrew, "Biological Significance of Piezoelectricity", *Calc. Tiss.* Res.1, 252-272, 1968.

7. Basset, Andrew C., "Biophysical Principles Affecting Bone Structure", *The Biochemistry and Physiology of Bone.* N.Y.: Academic Press, p. 1-76, 1971.

8. Lipton, Bruce, "Liquid Crystal Consciousness, The Cellular Basis of Life", presented at First International Crystal Conference, S.F.: 1986.

Chapter 13

1. Howell, Edward, *Food Enzymes for Health and Longevity.* Woodstock Valley, CT: Omangod Press, 1946.
2. Wigmore, Ann, *The Hippocrates Diet.* Wayne, NJ: Avery Publishing Group Inc.,1984.
3. Howell, Edward, *Food Enzymes for Health and Longevity.* Woodstock Valley, CT: Omangod Press, 1946.
4. Ibid.
5. Ibid.
6. Schroeder, Henry A., *The Trace Elements and Man..* Old Greenwich, CT: 1975.
7. Howell, Edward, *Food Enzymes for Health and Longevity.* Woodstock Valley, CT: Omangod Press, 1946.
8. Ibid.
9. Ibid.
10. Ibid.
11. Pottenger, F.M., "The Effect of Processed Foods and Methabolized Vit. D Milk on the Dento-facial Structure of Exp. Animals", *American J. Orthodontics and Oral Surgery.* Aug.,1946.
12. Kouchakoff, Paul, "The Influence of Cooking Food on the Blood Formula of Man", Proceedings: First International Congress of Micro Biology, Paris: 1930.
13. Kulvinskas, Viktoras, *Survival into the 21st Century.* Woodstock Valley, Ct., Fairfield, Iowa: 21st Century Publications, 1975.
14. Ibid.
15. Airola, Paavo, *Are You Confused?* Phoenix, Az.: Health Plus, Publishers, 1974.
16. Szekely, Edmond Bordeaux, *The Essene Gospel of Peace, Book One.* U.S.: International Biogenic Society, 1981.
17. Howell, Edward, *Food Enzymes for Health and Longevity.* Woodstock Valley, CT: Omangod Press, 1946.
18. Kulvinskas, Viktoras, *Survival into the 21st Century.* Woodstock Valley, CT., Fairfield,Iowa: 21st Century Publications, 1975.
19. McCluskey, C., *The Lancet.* 12, 29, 1973.

20. Szekely, Edmond Bordeaux, *The Chemistry of Youth.* U.S.: In-ternational Biogenic Society, 1977.
21. Szekely, Edmond Bordeaux, *The Essenes by Josephus and his Contemporaries.* U.S.: Inter-national Biogenic Society, 1981.
22. Szekely, Edmond Bordeaux, *The Chemistry of Youth.* U.S.: In-ternational Biogenic Society, 1977.
23. Szekely, Edmond Bordeaus, *The Essene Way Biogenic Living.* U.S.: International Biogenic Society, 1978.
24. Howell, Edward, *Food Enzymes for Health and Longevity.* Woodstock Valley, CT: Omangod Press, 1946.
25. Ibid.
26. Wigmore, Ann, *The Hippocrates Diet.* Wayne, NJ: Avery Publishing Group Inc.,1984.
27. Szekely, Edmond Bordeaux, *The Chemistry of Youth.* U.S.: International Biogenic Society, 1977.
28. Ibid.
29. Ibid.
30. Ibid.
31. Airola, Paavo, *How to Get Well.* Phoenix, AZ: Health Plus, Publishers, 1974.
32. Kulvinskas, Viktoras, *Survival into the 21st Century.* Woodstock Valley, CT, Fairfield, Iowa: 21st Century Publications, 1975.

Chapter 14

1. Airola, Paavo, *Are You Confused?* Phoenix, AZ: Health Plus, Publishers, 1974.
2. Ibid.
3. Ibid.
4. Ibid.
5. Kulvinskas, Viktoras, *Survival into the 21st Century.* Woodstock Valley, CT, Fairfield, Iowa: 21st Century Publications, 1975.
6. Airola, Paavo, *How to Get Well.* Phoenix, AZ: Health Plus, Publishers, 1974.
7. Ibid.
8. Ibid.
9. Wendt, L., Wendt, Th., and Wendt, A., "Protein Transport and Protein Storage in Etiology and Pathogenesis of Arteriosclerosis", *Ernahrungswiss.* Dietrich Steinkopff Veriag, 1975.
10. Levine, Steve and Kidd, Paris,

Antioxidant Adaption; Its Role in Free Radical Pathology. San Francisco, CA: Biocurrents Press, 1985.
11. Airola, Paavo, *Are You Confused?* Phoenix, AZ: Health Plus, Publishers, 1974.
12. Airola, Paavo, *How to Get Well.* Phoenix, AZ: Health Plus, Publishers, 1974.
13. Kulvinskas, Viktoras, *Survival into the 21st Century.* Woodstock Valley, CT, Fairfield, Iowa: 21st Century Publications, 1975.
14. Airola, Paavo, *Are You Confused?* Phoenix, AZ: Health Plus, Publishers, 1974.

Chapter 15
1. Scharffenberg, John A., *Problems with Meat.* Santa Bar-bara, CA: Woodbridge Press, 1979.
2. Ibid.
3. Airola, Paavo, *Are You Confused?* Phoenix, AZ: Health Plus, Publishers, 1974.
4. Ibid.
5. Ibid.
6. Schmidt, Gerhard, *The Dynamics of Nutrition.* RI: Bio-Dynamic Literature,1980.
7. Swank, Roy , and Pullen, Mary-Helen, *The Multiple Sclerosis Diet Book.* N.Y.: Doubleday and Company, Inc., 1977.
8. Schmidt, Gerhard, *The Dynamics of Nutrition.* RI: Bio-Dynamic Literature,1980.
9. Ibid.
10. Ibid.
11. Shim, Kin, M.D. Ed., *A Cancer Journal for Clinicians.* 24, No.3, 189, 1974..
12. Ibid.
13.Kulvinskas, Viktoras, *Survival into the 21st Century.* Woodstock Valley, CT, Fairfield, Iowa: 21st Century Publications, 1975.
14. Cott, Allan, *Fasting: The Ultimate Diet.* Toronto, New York, London, Sydney: Bantam Books, 1981.

Chapter 16
1. Thakkur, Chandrashekhar G., *Introduction to Ayurveda.* India: Shri Gulabkunverba Ayurvedic Society, 1976.
2. Ibid.
3. Hass, Elson M., *Staying Heal-thy With The Seasons.* Millbrae, CA: Celestial Arts, 1981.
4. Lad, Vasant, *Ayurveda : The Science of Self-Healing.* Santa Fe, N.M.: Lotus Press,

1984.
5. Ballentine, Rudolph, *Diet and Nutrition.* Honesdale, PN: The Himalayan Intl. Institute, 1982.

Chapter 17
1. Airola, Paavo, *How to Get Well.* Phoenix, AZ: Health Plus, Publishers, 1974.
2. Morishita, Kellchii, *The Hidden Truth of Cancer.* Oroville: GOMF, 1976.
3. Ibid.
4. Kulvinskas, Viktoras, *Live Food Longevity Recipies.* Woodstock Valley, CT: 1986.
5. Airola, Paavo, *How to Get Well.* Phoenix, AZ: Health Plus, Publishers, 1974.
6. Ibid.
7. Aihara, Herman, *Acid and Alkaline.* Oroville, CA: George Ohsawa Macrobiotic Foundation, 1986.
8. Ibid.
9. Heritage, Ford, *Composition and Facts About Food.* Mokelumne Hill, CA: Health Research,1968.
10. Hass, Elson M., *Staying Healthy With The Seasons.* Millbrae, CA: Celestial Arts, 1981.
11. Airola, Paavo, *How to Get Well.* Phoenix, AZ: Health Plus, Publishers, 1974.
12. Heritage, Ford, *Composition and Facts About Food.* Mokelumne Hill, CA: Health Research,1968.
13. Ibid.
14. Aihara, Herman, *Acid and Alkaline.* Oroville, CA: George Ohsawa Macrobiotic Foundation, 1986.
15. Ibid.
16. Ibid.
17. Ibid.
18. Kushi, Michio, *Natural Healing through Macrobiotes.* Tokyo: Japan Publishers, 1978
19. Szekely, Edmond Bordeaux, *The Essene Gospel of Peace, Book One.* US: International Biogenic Society, 1981.

Chapter 18
1. Schmidt, Gerhard, *The Dynamics of Nutrition.* RI: Bio-Dynamic Literature,1980.
2. Ibid.
3. Joint Nutritional Monitoring Commitee, U.S. Congress, 1986.
4. Saraswati, Srimat Swami Shivananda,

Yoga Therapy. Calcutta: Sree Gopal Press, 1978.

5. Ibid.
6. Ibid.
7. Airola, Paavo, *How to Get Well.* Phoenix, AZ: Health Plus, Publishers, 1974.
8. Hawkins, David and Pauling, Linus, *Orthmolecular Psychiatry.* San Francisco: W. H. Freeman and Copany, 1973.
9. Ibid.
10. Pfeiffer, Carl C., *Mental and Elemental Nutrients.* New Canaan, CT: Keats Publishing, Inc., 1975.
11. Ibid.
12. *Diet Related to Killer Diseases, V.* Hearing Before the Selected committee on Nutrition and Human Needs of the United States Senate, U.S.: June 22, 1977.
13. Mandell, Marshall and Scanlon, Lynne Waller, *5-Day Allergy Relief System.* N.Y.: Pocket Books, 1979.
14. Ibid.
15. Airola, Paavo, *Hypoglycemia: A Better Approach.* Phoenix, AZ: Health Plus, 1977.
16. Buckley, Robert E., "Hypoglycemic Symptoms and the Hypoglycemic Experience", *Psychosomatics.* Vol. X , Jan./Feb., 1969.
17. Airola, Paavo, *Hypoglycemia: A Better Approach.* Phoenix, AZ: Health Plus, 1977.
18. Lesser, M., Proceedings World Congress of Biological Psychiatry, Buenos Aires: 1977.
19. Fariss, B., *Diabetes.* Vol. 23, 1974.
20. Airola, Paavo, *Hypoglycemia: A Better Approach.* Phoenix, AZ: Health Plus, 1977.
21. Ibid.
22. *Diet Related to Killer Diseases, V.* Hearing Before the Selected committee on Nutrition and Human Needs of the United States Senate, U.S.: June 22, 1977.
24. Schauss, Alexander, *Diet, Crime and Delinquency.* Berkeley: Parker House, 1980.
25. Yeryura, J.A. and Tobias, F.A., *Orthomelecular Psychiatry.* Vol. 4, No 3, 1975.
26. Szekely, Edmond Bordeaux, *The Essene Gospel of Peace, Book One .* U.S.: International Biogenic Society, 1981.

Chapter 19
1. Cott, Allan, *Fasting: The Ultimate Diet.* Toronto, New York, London, Sydney: Bantam Books, 1981.

2. Ibid.
3. *The Essenes by Josephus and his Contemporaries,* Translated by Szekely, Edmond Bordeaux, U.S.: International Biogenic Society, 1981.
4. *Essene Science of Fasting.* Channeled by Kevin Ryerson.
5. Szekely, Edmond Bordeaux, *The Essene Gospel of Peace, Book One.* U.S.: International Biogenic Society, 1981.
6. Kaplan, Aryeh, *Gems of Rabbi Nachman.* Jerusalem, Israel: Chaim Kramer, 1980.
7. *Mathew the Poor-The Communion of Love.* Foreward by Henri J. M. Nouwen, Crestwood, N.Y.: St. Vladimir's Seminary Press, 1984.
8. Airola, Paavo, *How to Keep Slim Healthy and Young with Juice Fasting.* Phoenix, AZ: Health Plus, 1974.
9. Ibid.
10. Ibid.
11. Ibid.
12. Gurudas, *Gem Elixirs and Vibrational Healing, Vol. 1.* Boulder, CO.: Cassandra Press, 1985.
13. Gurudas, *Gem Elixirs and Vibrational Healing, Vol. II.* Boulder, CO.: Cassandra Press, 1986.
14. Gurudas, *Flower Essences.* Albuquerque, N.M.: Brotherhood of Life, 1983.
15. *Essenes Science of Fasting.* Channeled by Kevin Ryerson.

Chapter 20
1. Hoffman, Edward, "The Father of Holistic Healing", *East West Journal.* April, 1986.
2. Airola, Paavo, *How to Get Well.* Phoenix, AZ: Health Plus, Publishers, 1974.
3. Szekely, Edmond Bordeaux, *The Essene Gospel of Peace, Book One.* U..S.: International Biogenic Society, 1981.
4. Kramer, Penny, "Health and Longevity: What Centenarians Can Teach Us", *Yoga Journal.* Berkeley, CA: Goodfellow Publishers', Sept./Oct., 1983.
5. McCay, C.M., "Life Span of Rats", *Arch. Biochem.* Vol. 2, 1943.
6. Kulvinskas, Viktoras, *Survival into the 21st Century.* Woodstock Valley, CT, Fairfield, Iowa: 21st Century Pubs, 1975.
7. Howell, Edward, *Food Enzymes for Health and Longevity.* Woodstock Valley, CT: Omangod Press, 1946.
8. Szekely, Edmond Bordeaux, *Essene*

Science of Fasting and The Art of Sobriety.
US: Il Biogenic Society, 1981. 9.
Cornaro, Luigi, *Discourses on the Sober Life.* Mokelumne Hill, CA: Health Research, 1942.
10. Szekely, Edmond Bordeaux, *Essene Science of Fasting and The Art of Sobriety.* US: Intl Biogenic Society, 81.

Chapter 21

1. Hawkins, David and Pauling, Linus, *Orthomolecular Psychiatry-Treatment of Schizophrenia.* San Francisco: W. H. Freeman and Company, 1973.
2. Levine, Steve and Kidd, Paris, *Antioxidant Adaption; Its Role in Free Radical Pathology.* San Francisco, CA: Biocurrents Press, 1985.
3. Ibid.
4. Ibid.
5. Ibid.
6. Ibid.
7. Ibid.
8. "Science, Consciousness and Aging", Proceedings of the International Con., West Germany: MERU, 1980.
9. Ibid.
10. Ibid.
11. Murthy, T. S. Anantha, *Maharaj.* San Rafael, CA: The Dawn Horse Press, 72.
12. Tsu, Lao, *Tao Te Ching.* Translation by Gia-Fu Feng and Jane English, N.Y.: Vintage Books, 1972.
13. Hubbard, Barbara Marx, *Manual for Co-Creators of the Quantum Leap.* 1984.
14. Szekely, Edmond bordeaux,*The Essenes by Josephus and his Contemporaries.* US: Intl Biog. Soc., 81.
15. Ibid.
16. Hertz, O. R., Joseph, H., *Pirke Aboth.* N.Y.: Benjamin House , Inc.
17. Kirschner, H.E., *Natures's Seven Doctors.* Riverside, CA: H.C. White Publications, 1972.
18. Ibid.
19. Ibid
20. Ibid.
21. Singh, Renu Lal, *Right Life: Teachings of the Shivapuri Baba.* England: Coombe Springs Press, 1984.

Chapter 22

1. Tirtha, Vishnu, Swami, *Devatma Shakti.* Darya Ganj, Delhi: Swami Shivom Tirth, 1974.
2. Muktananda, *Kundalini: The Secrets of Life.* N.Y.: SYDA Foundation, 1979.
3. Tirtha, Vishnu, Swami, *Devatma Shakti.* Darya Ganj, Delhi: Swami Shivom Tirth, 1974.
4. Singh, Renu Lal, *Right Life: Teachings of the Shivapuri Baba.* England: Coombe Springs Press, 1984. 5. Nisargadatta, Maharaj, *I Am That.* Bombay: Sudhakar S. Dikshit, 1976.
6. Tsu, Lao, *Tao Te Ching.* Translation by Gia-Fu Feng and Jane English, N.Y.: Vintage Books, 1972.
7. Murthy, T. S. Anantha, *Maharaj.* San Rafael, CA: The Dawn Horse Press, 72.
8. Kaplan, Aryeh, *Gems of Rabbi Nachman.* Jerusalem, Israel: Chaim Kramer, 1980.
9. Kapleau, Roshi, *The Three Pillars of Zen.* Garden City NY: Anchor Books, 80.
10. Newbrough, John Ballou, *Oahspe.* Montrose, CO: Essenes of Kosmon, 35.

Chapter 23

1. Newbrough, John Ballou, *Oahspe.* Montrose, CO: Essenes of Kosmon, 35.
2. Ibid.
3. Da Free John, *The Dawn Horse Testament.* San Rafael, CA: The Dawn Horse Press,1985.

Chapter 24

1. Tilden, J.H., *Toxemia Explained.* U.S.: Keats Publishing, Inc., 1981.
2. Ibid.
3. Airola, Paavo, *How to Get Well.* Phoenix, AZ: Health Plus, Pub., 1974.
4. Kulvinskas, Viktoras, *Survival into the 21st Century.* Woodstock Valley, CT, Fairfield, Iowa: 21st Century Pub., 1975.
5. Wigmore, Ann, *The Hippocrates Diet.* Wayne, NJ: Avery Pub Group Inc.,1984.
6. Cousen, Gabriel, "Treatment of Alzheimer's Disease", *Journal of Orthodedicine-Orthomolecular Medical Society.* Vol. VIII, No. 1 & 2, 1985.
7. Kushi, Michio, *Natural healing through Macrobiotics.* Tokyo: Japan Pub, 78.
8. Wigmore, Ann, *The Hippocrates Diet.* Wayne, NJ: Avery Pub Group Inc.,1984.